Critical Muslim 42

Liberty

Critical Muslim is published quarterly by C. Hurst & Co. (Publishers) Ltd. on behalf of and in conjunction with Critical Muslim Ltd. and the Muslim Institute, London.

All editorial correspondence to Muslim Institute, Canopi Borough, 7-14 Great Dover Street, London, SE1 4YR
E-mail: editorial@criticalmuslim.com

C. Hurst & Co (Publishers) Ltd., New Wing, Somerset House, Strand, London, WC2R 1LA

ISBN: 9781787387171 ISSN: 2048-8475

To subscribe or place an order by credit/debit card or cheque (pounds sterling only) please contact Kathleen May at the Hurst address above or e-mail kathleen@hurstpub.co.uk

Tel: 020 7255 2201

A one-year subscription, inclusive of postage (four issues), costs £50 (UK), £65 (Europe) and £75 (rest of the world), this includes full access to the *Critical Muslim* series and archive online. Digital only subscription is £3.30 per month.

A Cataloguing-in-Publication data record for this book is available from the British Library

Critical Muslim

Subscribe to Critical Muslim

Now in its eleventh year in print, *Critical Muslim* is also available online. Users can access the site for just £3.30 per month – or for those with a print subscription it is included as part of the package. In return, you'll get access to everything in the series (including our entire archive), and a clean, accessible reading experience for desktop computers and handheld devices — entirely free of advertising.

Full subscription

The print edition of *Critical Muslim* is published quarterly in January, April, July and October. As a subscriber to the print edition, you'll receive new issues directly to your door, as well as full access to our digital archive.

United Kingdom £50/year
Europe £65/year
Rest of the World £75/year

Digital Only

Immediate online access to *Critical Muslim*

Browse the full *Critical Muslim* archive

Cancel any time

£3.30 per month

www.criticalmuslim.io

CM42

SPRING 2022

CONTENTS

LIBERTY

A Syrian boy waits with his family members in a women-only queue at the Zaatari refugee camp in Jordan. Photograph by Iason Athanasiadis

LIBERTY

INTRODUCTION: RETAKING LIBERTIES

Shanon Shah

One of my favourite film scenes comes from *Monty Python's Life of Brian*. The film tells the story of Brian Cohen, a Jewish-Roman man who is born on the same day as – and next door to – Jesus, and is subsequently mistaken for the Messiah.

In this standout scene – which I love so much that I can quote it from memory – the crowds have thronged in front of the window of the house that Brian lives in with his mother, waiting to hear him speak. At his wits' end, Brian decides to address the crowd, hoping for a win-win – they'll get to hear from him and then perhaps leave him in peace.

'Please, please, listen to me! I've got one or two things I need to tell you…' he starts, somewhat agitatedly.

'Tell us both of them!' the crowd chants in unison, hanging onto his every word.

'Look, you've got it all wrong….You don't need to follow anybody! You don't need anybody to tell you what to do!'

The crowd waits with bated breath. Brian continues, 'You are all individuals!'

The crowd roars back, 'Yes! We are all individuals!'

Brian tries again, 'You are all different!'

The crowd replies, 'Yes! We are all different!'

Then one sullen bloke interrupts and says, 'I'm not.' The crowd, irritated, shushes him.

Before reflecting further on this gem of an ironic punchline, some context is necessary. When I first moved to London more than a decade ago, I quickly bonded with some English Anglican friends partly because of our shared love of this film. A small group of us even had a little home screening once on Holy Saturday, the eve of Easter. And these weren't just nominal Christians – they were and still are regular and faithful church-goers. That they can share in the joys of Monty Python with their Muslim friend from Malaysia tells you everything you need to know about their spirituality. Because to them – and me – the film is a hilarious yet incisive critique not of religion per se, but of the dangers of knee-jerk, unreflective, and po-faced expressions of religion.

It's an interesting case to think about, however, because notwithstanding the film's cute and zany legacy, there was actually a time when democratic states in the 'enlightened' West deemed it blasphemous enough to be banned. Promoted by adverts as 'so funny it was banned in Norway', the film was denounced by many Western countries, Christian churches, and even the Rabbinical Alliance of America for being 'foul, disgusting, blasphemous'. For me, it is particularly symbolic that the film was released in 1979, a year that witnessed the siege of the Great Mosque of Makkah by Juhayman al-Otaybi and his followers in protest against the Saudi monarchy and, of course, the Iranian Islamic Revolution. This period of Muslim revolutionary upheaval shook not only Washington and other Western liberal democracies but the Saudi establishment, too. As a consequence, when I was growing up in the 1980s, the Islamic education I received in school was shaped by much more overt Saudi-Wahhabi influence than that of my older siblings. The officially Sunni sharia bureaucracy also constantly warned Malaysian Muslims against anything that even smelt remotely like Shiism. Things flipped temporarily in 1989, when Ayatollah Khomeini pronounced his infamous fatwa against Salman Rushdie in response to the publication of *The Satanic Verses*. I remember a lot of baying for Rushdie's blood in support of the fatwa from my schoolteachers, classmates, and the government-controlled media – albeit without any formal recognition of Shias as 'proper' Muslims.

I was eleven when the Rushdie Affair kicked off. Reading the international coverage in the English language press, I was distressed by some of the naked anti-Muslim sentiments I could glean from the responses of 'the West'. I was even more traumatised by several of my Islamic Studies teachers telling me and my classmates that it was our Islamic duty to murder Rushdie if any of us were to come across him.

Quite a few of my classmates agreed – their parents were advising the same.

We were just kids. The boys' voices had scarcely broken and the girls had barely started menstruating.

It is against this backdrop that I went on to witness a greater extent of anti-Western, specifically anti-American, polemics when the first Gulf War broke out in 1991 – not just in school and in the muzzled Malaysian media, but in everyday life. America was the Great Satan. This was a war engineered by the West – the inveterate enemies of Islam, controlled by the Jews. In addition to this war, 'they' were out to destroy 'us' by exporting their degenerate culture and lifestyles and 'freedoms'. The West was out to subjugate Muslims with a potent cocktail of bombs, AIDS, homosexuality, and, as many of my Malay-speaking Muslim teachers would quip in English, 'free sex'.

But authoritarianism can often turn underground activity and transgressions into normal facts of existence. Hence, while many TV shows and films were banned or censored by the Malaysian authorities, my late older brother had no trouble procuring pirated VHS copies of almost anything we wanted to watch. As a teenager, I had access to uncut versions of *Goodfellas*, *The Silence of the Lambs*, *Pulp Fiction*, and countless other titles my *bhaijaan* could get his hands on. Though, because I'm squeamish, I stayed away from violence and gore. This is how I chose to watch *Life of Brian* as a teenager, and how it changed my life. And so many of its jokes landed. Sure, I laughed at the slapstick and rude bits, but I also laughed because of something deeper. I didn't need to understand the specific references to Christian theology or the Bible – I laughed because I saw, in this film, a criticism of the political and religious attitudes I was witnessing in my own context. I could re-enact or rewrite my favourite scenes within the comfort of my own imagination, maybe with one of my teachers saying, 'You are all offended by apostasy!'

'Yes! We are all offended by apostasy!' my classmates would roar back.

'You are all disgusted by homosexuality!'

'Yes! We are all disgusted by homosexuality!'

And then there'd be cheeky me piping up, 'I'm not'.

This revised scenario deviates somewhat from the original Monty Python scene, but that's why I love the film so much – I could and still can make it work on so many levels. And the older I grew, the more entrenched this escapism in my adolescent imagination became. Because by this point, the 'straight path' as a Muslim did not just mean adhering to the five pillars of Islam. It meant risking the ire of the state-appointed, sharia-based moral police if a Muslim did not fast in Ramadan, or attend Friday prayers in the mosque, or was found drinking alcohol. It also meant being accused of 'insulting Islam' – an offence which carried serious punishment and public fury – if these rulings were questioned. Later, when I discovered the works of George Orwell, I sometimes wondered if I was living in a sharia-compliant version of *1984* or *Animal Farm*.

If you are now wondering whether I was on my way to becoming a Richard Dawkins-like Islamophobe, you are not far off the mark. My discomfort with the toxic ways in which Islam was interpreted and administered in Malaysia would have made me ripe for any kind of anti-religious propaganda. But after secondary school, I was awarded a scholarship to go to Australia to study for my undergraduate degree. There, I experienced the other side of the coin – rampant xenophobia, racism, and Islamophobia in a purported liberal democracy that respected 'free speech'. Liberty, it seemed, was a double-edged sword. In Malaysia, it was denied to people who were not Muslim enough while in Australia, it was withheld from people who were perceived as too Muslim (and/or not white enough).

The essays in this issue unpack these and other paradoxes relating to the ideals and realities of 'liberty'. Our contributors explore the contradictions or in-built prejudices in dominant conceptions of liberty – amongst Muslims, Western liberal democracies, and the political left, and in other circumstances. But we are not merely interested in criticisms. What is interesting is the attempt to reclaim the ideals of liberty from a variety of perspectives, which many of our contributors do. They tackle these issues from different vantage points – there are overarching pieces that analyse the social construction of liberty as a political project, personal spiritual memoirs that engage with the nuances of liberty and freedom, pieces that introduce adjacent concepts such as justice and solidarity, and conceptual attempts to unpack the very meaning of 'liberty'.

For starters, I wish that Mustafa Akyol had written his eloquent piece when I was a teenager. Akyol challenges the dominant 'Islamic' responses to three contentious areas in contemporary Muslim societies – the policing of personal morality, apostasy, and blasphemy. True, I might have been discouraged to learn that the sharia-based moral police in Malaysia – 'anti-vice officers', as they are formally known – are indeed an institutional legacy of Islam. But it would have blown my mind to discover that the *hisbah* – the name given to the religious police in many Muslim countries – actually began as a way of monitoring trade and financial transactions in public markets. Whenever I heard my Islamic Studies teachers mouthing the Arabic phrase *amar maruf nahi munkar* – 'commanding the right and forbidding the wrong' – all they seemed to care about was non-marital sex, alcohol-drinking, and headscarves for women. Financial integrity was given short shrift – perhaps unsurprisingly, given the scale of corruption in Malaysia even back then. Akyol succinctly explores the transformation of the *muhtasib* – literally, one who does the *hisbah* – 'from market inspector to religion police' within a context of politicised and polemical interpretations of 'commanding the right and forbidding the wrong' in early Muslim societies.

Akyol's revisionist account of religious policing in Islam is complemented by Vinay Lal's masterful overview and history of the contradictory aspects of 'liberty' as a concept that developed in Western political thought. Dominant understandings of liberty today, according to Lal, have as their basis an unexamined Orientalism – the West's ideological construction of its opposite or 'shadow', the Orient, which then informs Western self-definitions. Different varieties of Orientalist dichotomies have found expression in different historical periods, but Lal argues that the Orientalist bias inherent in today's notions of liberty echoes the anti-Persian prejudices within ancient Greek political thought. He writes, 'As freedom is to the Greeks and slavery is to Persians in the ancient period, so Enlightenment and liberty are to Europe what despotism is to the Orient in the period of European colonization of the world'. In other words, 'we' the ancient Greeks/modern Europeans are free and enlightened, while 'they' the ancient Persians/modern Orientals are barbarians and despots. This explains why the modern genesis of the concept of liberty – born of the paradigmatic American and French revolutions of the late eighteenth centuries – could go hand-in-hand with the trans-Atlantic slave trade and Western colonialism. How else can we make sense of the violence of the British Raj which happened alongside the liberal parliamentary reforms in England, or the brutal suppression of the Haitian Revolution by France, the birthplace of *liberté, égalité,* and *fraternité?*

Anyone who thinks that former colonial powers have moved on needs only to read Jack Wager's personal essay to understand the enduring impacts of the Rushdie Affair on a young person in contemporary Britain. In Wager's own words: 'I was born nearly a decade later than the Salman Rushdie affair of 1989, and too young to remember the events of 9/11. But I have known nothing other than the aftermath, the ensuing demonisation of Islam and Othering of Muslims, and polarisation and reactionary patriotism.' It was the contradictory responses to the gruesome 2015 *Charlie Hebdo* murders that eventually drove Wager to engage deeply with *Distorted Imagination: Lessons from the Rushdie Affair* by Ziauddin Sardar and Merryl Wyn Davies.

What comes to be referred to in historical shorthand – the Rushdie Affair, in this case – can therefore have transnational, transcultural, and trans-generational repercussions. The pioneering work of Sardar and Davies, for example, continues to force individuals like Wager and I – who come from different generations and social contexts – to rethink the Rushdie Affair and the geopolitics of neo-colonialism and Islamophobia more broadly. It follows that people's conceptions and experiences of liberty – or the lack of it – are also contextual.

Consider the trajectory of second-wave feminism in post-war Europe and North America. Certainly, there was a need for vast numbers of women to object being treated as the 'weaker sex' and denied the same educational and employment opportunities as men. Sexual and reproductive rights were also justifiably fought for by this generation of Western feminists – at the time of writing, these hard-won rights appear once again to be under grave threat in the US. The point is that many of the household names from this generation of feminist activism were challenging a particular kind of sexism within a particular social stratum within the West. It was, rightfully, a feminism of white middle-class women seeking to undo the workings of patriarchal violence within white middle-class environments. This in itself is not a problem. The problem was when this white, middle-class, Western experience of feminism started to misunderstand and even distort the struggles and priorities of women in other contexts. Yet, as early as the mid-nineteenth century, the African American abolitionist and first-wave feminist Sojourner Truth (c.1797-1883) had already complicated the notion that sexism was monolithic or that there was a one-size-fits-all approach to feminism. It is worth quoting the most famous part of her speech to a women's rights convention in Ohio at length:

> That man over there says that women need to be helped into carriages, and lifted over ditches, and to have the best place everywhere. Nobody ever helps me into carriages, or over mud-puddles, or gives me any best place! And ain't I a woman? Look at me! Look at my arm! I have ploughed and planted, and gathered into barns, and no man could head me! And ain't I a woman? I could work as much and eat as much as a man – when I could get it – and bear the lash as well! And ain't I a woman? I have borne thirteen children, and seen most all sold off to slavery, and when I cried out with my mother's grief, none but Jesus heard me! And ain't I a woman? . . . Then that little man in black there, he says women can't have as much rights as men, 'cause Christ wasn't a woman! Where did your Christ come from? Where did your Christ come from? From God and a woman! Man had nothing to do with Him.

The rhetorical force and analytical clarity of this speech is undeniable. One could well imagine a young hijab-wearing woman of colour in France repurposing it today, in contradistinction to what an elite, secular white French feminist might say: 'Those folks over there say that women are free to wear what they want and enjoy whatever they want. Well, nobody tells me I'm free to wear my hijab and enjoy being a Muslim! And ain't I a woman?'

A cluster of our contributions therefore explore the idea of liberty through the lens of personal experience, specifically in relation to their encounters with different varieties of Islam. The first of these, by Sulaiman Haqpana, opens in a similar way to Wager's personal reflection on the Rushdie Affair – with a summary of political history and personal biography. Born into a middle-class family in Afghanistan in 1986 during the Soviet occupation, Haqpana's childhood years were scarred by the ensuing Afghan civil war of 1989 to 1992. His personal essay does not trivialise the horrors of later Taliban rule, but it does remind us that the dominant Western image of Afghanistan now – a rogue state ruined by

Islamic fundamentalism (or simply by Islam, depending who is spouting this stereotype) – is an Orientalist construct. Afghanistan has been impoverished by decades, if not centuries, of interference from its neighbours and distant imperialist regimes, including Pakistan, the Soviet Union, Britain, and the US. It is this historical context that makes Haqpana's personal memory of the Taliban takeover of Herat in 1995 particularly disturbing. In his own words:

> We were sitting outside our house when I first saw the Taliban, driving past us in their cars and tanks down the road. In front of our house, there was an old man who was repairing radios. He had his radio loudspeaker turned on, and instead of the everyday music programme we heard the songs of the Taliban with no music or instruments. The verses of the song that I still remember meant that 'the Taliban came to the country, and the people are now free.' As a curious child, I wondered where they had come from. Did they come to us from outside the country? And free from what? What were they liberating us from?

What follows is a harrowing story of luck, survival, and humility which also profoundly albeit indirectly foreshadows the Taliban's return to power in 2021. Now based in the UK, Haqpana is pursuing a PhD and combines his scholarship with music – he plays the *tabla* – so that he can 'bring communities together'. To him, 'freedom and liberty from extremism, ignorance and oppression, have to be gained by the individual rather than simply granted to them by others'. 'In gaining these freedoms,' he writes, 'we develop dignity that acknowledges the value of others, regardless of their class, religion, race, gender or abilities.'

Haqpana's personal journey is accompanied by two contributions from Europeans who embraced Islam – Ole Jørgen Anfindsen and Katharina Schmoll. Again, their sensitive essays remind us that personal context is crucial, lest we subsume their experiences within the stereotype of the 'Western convert' to Islam. After all, they come from different generations and political environments. Anfindsen was born in Oslo, Norway in 1958, and his formative years were shaped by the post-war Evangelical Christian revival of the 1970s and 1980s. In fact, he confesses, 'by the time I was seventeen years old, I was a full-fledged Bible fundamentalist'. But this eventually led to a crisis of faith in his early forties. For comfort and answers, Anfindsen started reading the works of the New Atheists – Richard Dawkins, Daniel Dennett, Sam Harris, and Christopher Hitchens. He even became an anti-Muslim immigration activist in Norway, setting up a blog, *HonestThinking*, and published a couple of books along these lines. What, then, led him towards and into Islam? No more spoilers, but his contribution is a must-read.

Schmoll, on the other hand, was born in 1989 in West Germany, barely nine months before the Berlin Wall fell. She is therefore a child of, in the words of Francis Fukuyama, 'the end of history', of the supposed triumph of liberal democracy. Yet Schmoll also became disenchanted with her default Christian heritage and started exploring other spiritual pathways. Her beautiful essay examines the tension between, in her words, the 'question of freedom and restraint' – 'something many Muslims grapple with at some point in their lives'. Schmoll juxtaposes the 'restraints' imposed by Islam, such as dressing modestly and fasting in Ramadan, with the restrictions of the coronavirus lockdowns of 2020 and 2021.

After all, did many people not say that, as shocking and disruptive as the first lockdown of 2020 was, it gave them the freedom to slow down, to breathe, and to appreciate the simple pleasures in life? But the pandemic is far from over, especially in the Global South. The virus has mutated and many governments have had to implement repeated lockdowns over the past couple of years. The simplicity and bliss of that first lockdown soon unleashed impatience and even fury at the supposedly draconian measures taken by liberal democracies regarding social distancing, mask-wearing, and vaccination. In the West, these same voices were often silent about the neo-liberal, capitalist destruction of public healthcare that left the door open for this pandemic to become a global crisis in the first place, but that's another story.

The point is that this fluctuation of our experiences and temperaments during the course of this pandemic is not very different from the fluctuations related to our spiritual life. Schmoll addresses these fluctuations eloquently and honestly. Trying to make sense of our individual rhythms and tendencies, she writes that 'navigating faith and freedom can be a daunting challenge', especially for Muslims in the West. 'We find freedom and comfort in restriction,' she writes, 'but often we also find ourselves confronted with having to justify our choices to the people around us.' Especially when the dominant image of Islam in the West is not that of the bubbly *Great British Bake Off* winner Nadiya Hussain making a souffle or the smouldering Oscar-winner Riz Ahmed rapping about refugee rights. Muslims in the West are far more likely to have to justify their choices to people whose idea of Islam is a mash-up of the Iranian Revolution, the Rushdie Affair, 9/11, *Charlie Hebdo*, and the Taliban. In other words, the political and cultural mainstream.

But is liberty purely about the individual or can it undergird struggles for structural and systemic change? Haqpana's theory – that the struggle for our own freedoms will lead us to respect the freedoms of others – is insightfully tested by two essays that examine the notion of solidarity from different ideological vantage points. Naomi Foyle critiques the responses of parts of the political left towards Russia's February 2022 invasion of Ukraine whilst Giles Goddard probes whether EM Forster truly believed in the universal ideals of liberty. From these different perspectives, Foyle and Goddard reflect on the ethical implications of taking the concept of liberty to its logical conclusion.

Foyle's main target is the whataboutism of parts of the left that dilutes or downright prevents their support of Ukraine's resistance to Vladimir Putin's military invasion. This is a very specific and focused critique – Foyle wastes no time in dismantling the Eurocentric, imperialist and frankly racist calls for solidarity with Ukraine from the Western political right. But she is even more vexed about how some leftist ideologues could 'argue strenuously that NATO expansion was to blame for the war' by somehow 'forcing Putin's hand'. Not that all 'whataboutery' is unjustifiable – Foyle reaffirms criticisms from Palestinian, Syrian, and other Global South activists about the hypocrisy of the West's 'solidarity' with Ukraine. These criticisms remind us that 'it is nevertheless surely the case that the West too has oceans of blood on its hands'. But Foyle's argument ultimately boils down to the simple logic that two wrongs don't make a right – the West's double standards cannot and must not stand in the way of solidarity with Ukraine, alongside other countries suffering from foreign invasions.

Foyle invokes the moral and spiritual authority of none other than Dr Martin Luther King Jr, who said that 'injustice anywhere is a threat to justice everywhere'. But what is the logical implication of this ideal, held by a peace activist and civil rights martyr who was in turn influenced by

Gandhi's non-violent activism? Would solidarity with Ukraine not entail military support for its resistance fighters? And, if this is the case, how could the defence of liberty for Ukrainians be congruent with peace activism? Foyle lays her cards on the table. 'I support Western military aid to Ukraine,' she writes. 'I also support foreign fighters joining the Ukrainian army.' Anticipating counter-criticisms of inconsistency, Foyle admits that these are not positions she has arrived at easily but she remains steadfast. She maintains that her position – indeed the very act of writing her essay – is a demonstration of solidarity with her Ukrainian colleagues, whom she also pays tribute to in this contribution.

In his essay about E.M. Forster, Goddard also detects this streak of internationalist solidarity in the famous novelist's body of work – albeit in a more muted manner. This is the same Forster whose novel *A Passage to India* (1924) – and its stage and film adaptations of 1960 and 1984 – have become paradigmatic examples of Orientalism, both the imperial British and Hollywood variety. The argument is that while Forster does criticise the hypocrisy and violence of the British Raj, he never really opposes the master-servant relationship between the British and the Indians. This leads to the charge of inconsistency in his ideas about liberty. But to dismiss Forster's thought and actions purely on this basis is to do a disservice to his overall legacy. True, Forster was no political activist, writes Goddard, yet in the decade after *A Passage to India* was published, he became the first president of the National Council for Civil Liberties (NCCL), founded in 1934 – known today simply as Liberty. His opening speech to the first International Congress of Writers in Paris in 1935 – 'Liberty in England' – was muddled and nervous, but it was clearly an expression of his distress at the rise of fascism in Europe. He would also go on to campaign for the legalisation of homosexuality in Britain.

This last point is worth reiterating. Gay activism in Forster's time was not what it is today, where calls for equality and full inclusion of queer, trans, and non-binary people can build upon a string of recent political advancements. Forster lived in constant fear of being outed as a homosexual, despite his privileged upbringing. In the 1930s, homosexuality was not only criminalised by the British state, it was subjected to intense blackmail, public shaming, and violence, both from the state and from vigilantes. Forster, in fact, wrote a gay love story,

Maurice, in 1914, but only allowed for it to be published after his death. He was convinced that he had to keep the manuscript hidden while he was alive, just because it had a happy ending.

In Goddard's assessment, Forster's larger body of work – his novels, his BBC broadcasts, and his work with Liberty – show us a man who cared deeply about the liberty of his fellow human beings, within Britain and beyond. Perhaps he did not go far enough for some of us today – or even by the standards of some of his contemporaries – but he tried more than most. In his writings and other passions, we see someone who did try to oppose Nazism, British colonial rule, homophobia, censorship, and the British class system. His own insecurities and fears might not have made him the boldest political thinker, but his worldview is perhaps best captured by his plea in *Howards End* – 'only connect'. 'Liberty, for Forster,' Goddard writes, 'meant freedom to connect.' And true connection – with the Other, with the inner self, with the sacred – is perhaps what enables us to maintain, as Dr King did, that injustice anywhere is a threat to justice everywhere. For another relevant illustration of nexus between liberty, solidarity, and the imperative to connect, read Maha Sardar's review of *How I Survived a Chinese 'Re-education' Camp: A Uyghur Woman's Story*.

Yet solidarity, too, is a double-edged sword. After university, I returned to Malaysia and started getting involved in the arts and social justice scene. One of my proudest moments was becoming the first-ever male Associate Member of Sisters in Islam, alongside my other volunteering work with Amnesty International, the Malaysian AIDS Council and the Centre for Independent Journalism. It was in this capacity that I was invited to present a paper at a conference on Islam and democracy organised by the Australian National University.

This was shortly after 9/11, and I was getting used to additional security checks at airports. So, it did not take me completely by surprise when I was stopped and searched – 'randomly', I was told – by the airport security staff in Canberra. I was wearing a plain t-shirt and jeans, but my rucksack was adorned with a collection of social justice badges, including one from Sisters in Islam. 'Oh, what's this?' asked the blond, female border control officer. 'It's an Islamic feminist organisation in Malaysia,' I answered, proudly. 'Oh, really? Well, I'm a feminist, too. What's your understanding of feminism?' I wondered if this was a trick question, but decided to give the most succinct answer I could manage: 'It's the radical idea that men and women are equal.' A tad binary, but the best I could come up with on the spot. She did not seem impressed, but decided to let me go. 'Wait a minute,' I wanted to say. 'You think I'm just a Malaysian, a mixed-race man who doesn't have the most sophisticated wardrobe, and that all these badges on my cheap rucksack are pretentious. But I have read amina wadud, Ziba Mir-Hosseini and Fatima Mernissi, and I have campaigned for the rights of Muslim women in the areas of domestic violence, polygamy, divorce, and child custody. And ain't I a feminist?'

The irony is that some of the Indonesian conference delegates from fundamentalist Islamist parties sailed through security – perhaps because they were all wearing expensive tailored suits. When I got to the conference venue, the Indonesian progressives – in simple t-shirts and jeans like me – were all complaining about getting stopped and searched, too. 'That's it!' one of them joked. 'I'm turning fundamentalist.'

This experience came at a crucial point in my spiritual and activist journey. It made me ask, what *is* feminism? What *is* social justice? What *is* Islam? Sure, these were concepts and ideals that meant a lot to me, but could they or would they ever mean the same thing to other people? I've struggled to define them and I abhor the effort, but I still make the endeavour to this day. Because although defining such abstract notions comprehensively is difficult and near-impossible, the attempts to do so are still useful if we are to apply them or pursue them as political goals.

This brings us to two contributions by Jeremy Henzell-Thomas and C Scott Jordan, that go to the heart of what 'liberty' and its concomitant concept of 'freedom' mean. As Henzell-Thomas points out, the two words are often used interchangeably but they have different repercussions depending on the context. To distinguish the two terms conceptually, he quotes the scholar of English literature, Bert Hornback's conclusion:

> that the essential difference between them is that 'freedom is a social word; liberty a selfish, anti-social word. Freedom requires of us responsibility; liberty is the assertion of our refusal of responsibility.' In other words, if freedom is a term rooted in relationship, liberty is tainted by egoism and solipsism.

Jordan, on the other hand, speculates differently, suggesting that 'based on its use in English, I would offer that freedom is the broader term for "uninhibited" while liberty is the legal ability or authority to exercise said freedoms'. 'In that case,' he continues, 'rights and liberties are essentially synonymous.'

There is no need to adjudicate on the semantic and philosophical merits of either writer's position. The more interesting point is that, despite their different approaches, Henzell-Thomas and Jordan highlight a recurring motif in our other essays – the importance of relationship and relationality in shaping our conceptions of liberty. Both of them therefore invite us to unthink and rethink entrenched understandings of liberty. And this rethinking must, in many ways, entail looking afresh at what it means to be an individual person. As they both suggest, 'liberty' and 'freedom' are often seen as the properties of a self-sufficient, self-contained, rights-bearing individual. It is *my* liberty (or freedom, if you prefer) to wear what *I* want. To have sexual relations with whomever *I* want. To bear arms to protect *myself*.

Yet we learnt very early on in the coronavirus pandemic that the most effective ways to protect our wellbeing and the people we loved were counter-intuitive. In order to ensure we were all safe, we had to *not* be around each other physically – we were not even allowed to touch each other. We had to wear masks not to protect ourselves, but to protect the people around us who were more vulnerable or immunocompromised. In many liberal democracies, however, the fact that we were compelled to do these things as rights-bearing individuals became anathema to many a libertarian who insisted on exercising their own freedoms and liberties. But such libertarian ideas of individual liberty and freedom can only make sense amid a shallow appreciation of our interconnectedness. I am reminded of the African philosophy of ubuntu, which literally means 'humanity' but can be translated as 'I am because you are' or 'I am because we are'. In other words, one's individuality is only possible because of the vast web of relationships and connections that one's existence is embedded in. So, of course we are all special and deserve to enjoy freedom and liberty but, as the saying goes, 'until all of us are free, none of us are free'.

This certainly changes the Monty Python sketch I opened with beyond recognition. What would the punchline be? 'You are all individuals!' 'Yes, we are all individuals! I am because we are!'

The critical insight these turns of phrase can provoke are made poignant by several injustices that have sprung out of one global crisis after another. Some of these – such as the crises of climate change and the rising cost of living – were not completely unexpected. But, as Petro Sukhorolskyi observes, 'in numerous forecasts for 2022, both Russia and Ukraine were conspicuous by their absence'. This, Sukhorolskyi argues, is but one of the many aspects that justify a postnormal analysis of the current crisis in Ukraine. His summary and analysis of Ukrainian history and politics introduces yet another conceptual companion to this issue's exploration of liberty – 'independence'.

Sukhorolskyi juxtaposes this idea alongside a postnormal analysis of Ukraine not just in relation to its present crisis, but from its history as one of the Soviet socialist republics and its independence in 1991. Ukraine provides a captivating case study in the fluctuations of the building and rebuilding of state and nation. Through this analytical prism, Sukhorolskyi suggests that 'freedom' and 'liberty' are not only works in progress – their evolution as concepts and ideals is embedded within postnormal conditions that we can no longer afford to ignore. Yet, even Sukhorolskyi holds fast to this issue's recurring theme of relationality and connection as a bedrock:

> Freedom in postnormal times is clearly not just freedom from outside interference or freedom of empty existence in an automated world. It has to be based on values, the real core ones, critically considered and developed in the changing context of our world. How do we see others; how do we live and let live.

Amid the many upheavals and unrest scarring the planet, Sukhorolskyi argues, the struggle in Ukraine shows us that 'self-organised resistance, based on common values, trust, and equality' can be a force for positive social change.

It might seem depressing to end an introduction on reclaiming liberty by meditating on a country that is being pulverised by war. But perhaps this is the best way to remind ourselves of what is truly at stake when we consider liberty and its paradoxes. Sukhorolskyi's essay makes me think of the legacy of Harriet Tubman (1820-1913), the African-American slave-turned-abolitionist who, after securing her freedom, risked her life to save others as a conductor on the Underground Railroad. A famous account of Tubman's leadership has always sent chills down my spine, and is a fitting conclusion here. Apparently, Tubman always carried a loaded pistol which she would point at the slaves she was helping who got disheartened and considered running back to the familiarity of slavery. 'You'll be free,' she would tell them, 'Or you will die.'

ISLAM AND FREEDOM

Mustafa Akyol

What is freedom? What does it mean?

If you ask this question to a conservative Muslim scholar or an Islamist intellectual, it is probable that you may get an answer like this:

> We must first define *real freedom*, as taught by Islam. It is not the freedom of the materialist West where it means license to follow your selfish ambitions and carnal desires. This false freedom makes people slaves to money, sex, fame, and other human beings. No, real freedom is being saved from the yoke of all these created things, and to seek refuge in only the Creator. Real freedom, therefore, is slavery to Allah.

The last verdict, 'Real freedom is slavery to Allah', is in fact a motto one comes across often in the Muslim universe. In Turkey, it was the topic of a 2017 sermon given in all mosques in the nation. It is endlessly repeated on the internet and social media.

There is certainly some truth to this view, because 'slavery to Allah', in the sense of voluntary submission to God, can really save a human being from the weight of worldly fears and anxieties. Relying on God, or *tawakkul*, gives a sense of relief against the ups and downs of life, while belief in the afterlife makes death less frightening. Religious practice also helps self-discipline, guarding one against obsessions and addictions. Therefore, true believers in Islam really may achieve a sense of 'real freedom'.

It is not just Islam, though. Other religious traditions offer a similar bliss to their believers. Christians, especially those who have a 'personal relationship with Christ', also feel liberated, as their faith offers 'freedom from sin, from law, from corruption and death'. No wonder Roger Olson, a devout Christian author, defines 'real freedom' as 'being a servant to Jesus Christ'. Meanwhile, Buddhism also preaches its own 'real freedom', which is defined as 'freedom from thinking, freedom from all attachments'. Buddhist monks pursue that peculiar freedom by living a life of absolute poverty.

Now, imagine a devout Muslim, devout Christian and devout Buddhist living happily in a neighbourhood, all enjoying their 'real freedoms'. Also imagine, though, that the neighbourhood is targeted by an authoritarian government, which is paranoid about sedition, and arrests these three people based on their political remarks on social media. While rotting in jail, these believers may still retain their subjective 'real freedoms' in their hearts and minds. But they will have certainly lost a more tangible freedom: the right to move around freely, to speak their minds without persecution.

What this example illustrates is that there are two kinds of freedoms— 'inner' and 'outer'. The religious believers who claim to have found 'real freedom' in their worship are in fact referring to inner freedom. That is of course a very important ideal, but it is a matter of spirituality, and it is also very subjective as it depends on what one believes in.

Meanwhile outer freedom—the freedom from external constraints—is not only a very important ideal as well, but it is also an objective value on which we can build principles and rules. In other words, in the story above, we can't make laws to bring more inner freedom to the Muslim, the Christian, and the Buddhist— that is their own spiritual struggle—but we can make free speech laws to keep them out of prison.

That is why, as a universal value, what really matters is outer freedom. It is the kind of freedom, as philosopher Friedrich A. Hayek put it, which 'refers solely to a relation of men to other men, and the only infringement on it is coercion by men'.

So, by this measure, how does the Islamic tradition fare?

On the one hand, it fares well—according to the standards of its own time. This was acknowledged by a critic of Islam no less sceptical than the British American historian Bernard Lewis, who noted, 'the medieval Islamic world...offered vastly more freedom than any of its predecessors, its contemporaries and most of its successors'. This was mainly thanks to the Sharia, which established a rule of law, protecting the lives and properties of individuals. Thanks to the Sharia, for example, Muslims could devote their wealth in charitable foundations that rulers could not dare to confiscate. This allowed the rise of a robust civil society, with schools, hospitals and charities operated by merchants, guilds and Sufi orders. The Sharia also often acted as a constraint on the rulers, because as the law of God, it was above everyone, including the mightiest sultans and caliphs.

On the other hand, though, the Sharia itself had imposed serious limitations on freedom, which became painfully obvious in the modern era and its new sense of individual liberty. This is the very problem Islamists and conservatives are trying to evade when they present inner freedom as the only 'real freedom' we should aspire for. They insist that Islam requires 'freedom *from* the self, as opposed to freedom *of* the self', because there are serious issues with the latter.

These issues are reflected in the coercive measures of the Sharia, all aiming to serve these three broad objectives: Keeping Muslims observant—by banning sin; keeping Muslims within the religion and its orthodoxy—by banning apostasy and heresy; and making non-Muslims respect the religion—by banning blasphemy.

So, what are the origins of these coercive measures, and how can they be reformed without compromising the immutable tenets of Islam?

Hisbah

In the mid 2010s, the terrorist army that called itself the 'Islamic State' (IS) took control of large parts of Iraq and Syria. While shocking the world with its monstrous violence against non-Muslims, Shiites, and even fellow Sunnis who merely dissented, it also established a totalitarian regime under its self-declared 'caliphate'. A key function of this regime was the imposition of the practice of Islam according to the IS's extremely strict definitions. Ordinary people would find themselves in jail, and even face torture, for failing to perform their daily prayers or keeping the fast of Ramadan. Consuming alcohol or smoking tobacco would lead to public floggings. Militants would patrol the streets in vans, and shout out to people: 'It's prayer time! Go to mosque! Hurry up! Shut your business. You, woman, cover your face!'

The IS department which carried out all this zealous religious policing had a name: *al-Hisbah*. But this Arabic term, which roughly means 'accountability', is a concept that goes beyond IS. Other Islamic states—such as Saudi Arabia, Iran, Sudan, Afghanistan under the Taliban, the Aceh province of Indonesia, or the Kano state in Nigeria—also have police forces devoted to *hisbah*. Compared to IS, they are often milder, but they follow the same idea: Muslims should be prevented from committing sin, at least publicly.

Unfortunately, all this religious policing goes back to authoritative texts from classical Islam. One of them is *The Ordinances of Government* penned by the eleventh century Ash'ari scholar Al-Mawardi. 'The task of *hisbah* is one of the fundamental matters of the *deen*', or religion, he wrote in a long chapter devoted to the duty. He also listed the crimes that must be gone after, which include 'not performing the obligatory prayer until after its time'. He then explained the views on punishment:

> If the person abandons [the prayer], claiming that it is not an obligation, then he is a nonbeliever; and the same ruling as that governing the renegade applies—that is, he is killed for his denial, unless he turns for forgiveness. If he has not done it because he claims it is too difficult to do, but while acknowledging its obligation, then the *fuqaha* [jurists] differ as to the ruling: Abu Hanifah considers that he should be beaten at the time of every prayer, but that he is not killed; Ahmad ibn Hanbal and a group of his later followers say that he becomes a kafir by his abandoning it, and is killed for this denial... Al-Shafi considers... he is not put to death until he has been asked to turn in *tawbah* [repentance]... If he refuses to make *tawbah*, and does not accept to do the prayer; then he is killed for abandoning it—immediately, according to some, after three days, according to others. He is killed in cold blood by the sword, although Abu' Abbas ibn Surayj says that he is beaten with a wooden stick until he dies.

Soon after al-Mawardi, al-Ghazali, the eleventh century theologian and jurist, also wrote a long chapter about *hisbah* in his landmark book, *Revival of Religious Sciences*. He explained it as a duty of every Muslim to prevent sins with 'direct acts', such as 'breaking the musical instruments, spilling over the wine and snatching the silk garment from him who is wearing it'. (Music was banned because it 'incites to the drinking of wine', and it would bring together all the 'dissolute people'. Silk was banned, for men, as it seemed indulgent.) Hanbalis would expand the list of banned items with chess and backgammon.

The only space that offered freedom from this strict social control was the home, whose privacy was guarded by a Qur'anic directive: 'Do not enter houses other than your own, until you have asked permission.' However, al-Ghazali explained, even household privacy had its limits:

> If the voices rise and become too high to hear from outside the house, the hearer has the right to enter it and break the musical instruments. Similarly, if

the voices of the drunk rise and become audible to those walking in the street, *hisbah* becomes obligatory. The same is true of the smell.

Not just al-Mawardi or al-Ghazali, but countless other classical jurists defined such religious policing as a part of Islam. They only disagreed on whether *hisbah* was a duty for all ordinary Muslims, or only appointed officials—the *muhtasib*, which literally means 'the one that does *hisbah*'. They seem to have taken for granted that the duty was established by both the Qur'an and the Prophet. However, both sources are in fact much more ambiguous, leaving us room to reinterpret what *hisbah* should mean today.

Let's begin with the Prophet. One of his important qualities, which is rare among the founders of religions in world history, was that he was a longtime merchant, which gave him a good sense of commerce. Hence, soon after he established himself in Medina, he founded a new marketplace in the city. 'This is your market', he said reportedly 'let it not be narrowed, and let no tax be taken on it'. He also began frequenting it. On one visit, a narration tells us, he found out that a vendor had watered his grain to make it weigh heavier. In return, the Prophet appointed someone to oversee the market and to prevent any possible fraud. Interestingly enough, at least one source tells us that this official was a woman named Samra bint Nuhayk al-Asadiyya. Then Caliph Umar and other rulers continued the practice.

In this first century of Islam, these inspectors were called *amil al-suq*, or 'overseer of the market'. In Muslim Spain, they would be called *sahib al-suq*, or 'the master of the market'. The functions of the latter were described by the Cordoban scholar Yahya bin Umar (d. 901) who only wrote about 'the orderly running of the market place, particularly with regard to weights, measures and scales'. Remarkably, his treatise had 'no religious connotations nor concern[ed] itself with censure of public morals'. Other reports, too, define the job of market overseers as checking the quality of the products, the accuracy of weights and measurements, the genuineness of coins, in addition to the safety of buildings, cleanness of the streets and the water supply.

However, as time went by, the functions of the Muslim market inspector began to grow, assuming a 'wider duty' of the 'ordering of social life'. These new functions included what al-Mawardi or al-Ghazali speak about: enforcing prayer or fasting, pouring out wine and silencing music, banning free mixing of the sexes in streets. In the meantime, the term *amil al-suq* was conspicuously replaced by *muhtasib*—the one that does *hisbah*. That is why, in the words of Tunisian historian Yassine Essid,

> In reading the different treatises devoted to the *hisbah* we discover two categories of responsibilities, or rather, we find ourselves looking at two different figures: the censor of morals who breaks musical instruments, pours out wine, beats the libertine and tears off his silken clothing, and the modest market provost, a man who controls weights and measures, inspects the quality of the foods on sale, ensures that the markets are well supplied, and occasionally sets the prices of goods.

As time went by, moral policing became the primal duty of the *muhtasib*, whereas market supervising turned trivial. This was unmistakable in *Nisab al-Ihtisab*, a book where fourteenth-century Indian jurist Umar bin Muhammad al-Sunami described *hisbah* mainly as correcting 'moral and religious behavior which is contradictory to the correct teaching of Islam', while addressing market supervision 'only on some occasions'.

In short, what eventually turned into religious policing seems to have begun under the Prophet Muhammad merely as market inspection—something that every society would need and appreciate.

Besides market inspection, did the Prophet go strictly after sinners? One answer is that he didn't need to, because all his companions were fervent believers who followed all Qur'anic injunctions willingly—an exceptional experience that cannot be replicated in any modern society. Yet still, there are a few reports of punishing personal sin, most particularly wine. After the Qur'an banned wine, we read in the hadith literature, the Prophet ordered forty lashes to a man who was caught drunk—an incident which became a precedent for all the later punishments for alcohol consumption. However, there are reasons to think that the goal here was not mere piety but social order. 'There were things that happened [in Medina] due to the consumption of intoxicants, before they were made unlawful', as we read in the literature on the occasions of revelation. In one case, a group of drunken Muslims had a fight, where one them had his nose broken. In another case, the Prophet's own uncle, the legendary Hamza ibn Abdul-Muttalib, got drunk and slaughtered and mutilated someone else's camels. No wonder the verse that soon banned wine also noted that with it, along with gambling, 'the Satan seeks only to incite enmity and hatred among you'. This may give an idea about the rationale behind both the religious ban on wine and its public enforcement—a rationale which still outlaws 'public intoxication' in many secular democracies, including the United States.

The duty of *hisbah* is based not merely on the hadiths, though. It is also based on a Qur'anic concept: 'commanding the right and forbidding the wrong'. Several verses define this duty as incumbent on both the prophets and ordinary Muslims. One of these verses even calls for a specific group to carry out the duty: 'Let there arise out of you a band of people inviting to all that is good, enjoining what is right, and forbidding what is wrong: they are the ones to attain felicity' (3:104). This is why the religion police in Saudi Arabia calls itself 'Committee for the Promotion of Virtue and the Prevention of Vice'. The one operated by the Taliban has a similar name.

However, what the Qur'an means by 'commanding the right and forbidding the wrong' is much less clear than what these religion police forces believe. We can see this in the writings of the earliest commentators of the Qur'an. One of them was Abu al-Aliya (d. 712), who was among the *tabiun*, or the first generation after the Prophet, who described the duty as 'calling people from polytheism to Islam and... forbidding the worship of idols and devils'. A little later, Muqatil ibn Sulayman (d. 767), whose three-volume book is considered the oldest commentary on the Qur'an, also defined the duty in minimal terms. For him, 'commanding the right' meant 'enjoining belief in the unity of God,' whereas forbidding wrong meant 'forbidding polytheism'.

Meanwhile, a political interpretation of 'commanding the right and forbidding the wrong' also emerged in the first century of Islam. Accordingly, the duty primarily implied standing up to tyrants—by either moderate or radical ways. The moderate way was what we today call 'speaking truth to power'. It was supported by a hadith that defined the highest form of jihad as 'speaking out in the presence of an unjust ruler', 'and being killed for it', as some versions added. The radical way was armed rebellion against an unjust ruler. While the Kharajites took this license to the extreme, the Zaydis and Mu'tazilites defined it more sensibly.

However, what ultimately defined the meaning of 'commanding the right and forbidding the wrong' is the Sunni mainstream, which equated 'right and wrong' with all the commandments of the Sharia. The third century Qur'anic exegete al-Tabari was stressing this point when he wrote 'commanding right' refers to *all* that God and His Prophet have commanded, and 'forbidding wrong' to *all* that they have forbidden.' So, since God commanded daily prayers and forbade wine, all Muslims had to command prayer and forbid wine to each other. The transformation of the *muhtasib* from market inspector to religion police seems to have been underpinned by this totalistic approach to 'commanding the right and forbidding the wrong.'

What if people disagreed on what 'right' and 'wrong' means? Al-Ghazali addressed this question and answered it by granting some legal pluralism. 'The Hanifites have no right to disapprove Shafiites for eating mastigure, (large spiny-tailed lizards)', he wrote, 'nor do the Shafiites have the right to disapprove the Hanifites for drinking the *nabidh* (an alcoholic drink made out of dates or barley, which early Hanafis, considering it different from wine, allowed in non-intoxicating amounts—an interesting fact unknown to many Hanafis today)'. But al-Ghazali limited this nice pluralism to the four Sunni schools, whereas he condemned all other interpretations of Islam as heretical 'innovations'. The latter could not define *hisbah*. Quite the contrary, *hisbah* was needed against them—a *hisbah* 'more important than against all the other evildoings'.

But who could guarantee that al-Ghazali's own interpretation of Islam was not an 'innovation'? What if someone tried to purge this interpretation with a counter *hisbah*—as it happened indeed under the *mihna*, or 'trial', of Caliph al-Ma'mun? This was the first blind spot in the classical *hisbah* theory.

The second blind spot was that neither al-Ghazali nor al-Mawardi nor others saw a contradiction between coercion and another value they believed in: sincerity of intentions behind religious acts. Al-Ghazali has a whole chapter devoted to this matter, where he warns Muslims not to pray, fast or give charity with ungodly intentions such as showing off to people, 'to be recognised for it', or even just to feel good about themselves. 'Sincerity,' he keeps insisting, is to worship God 'in such a way that there is no motive other than it'. Yet he never considers that coercing someone to pray or fast, or abstain from sin, would also generate a motive other than worship.

Now, if we fast forward from the time of al-Ghazali to today, and look at contemporary examples of *hisbah*, we will see that the two blind spots in the tradition devolved into big black holes.

One is the imposition of one interpretation of Islam on all other Muslims. In Saudi Arabia, this interpretation is Wahhabism, and hence Shiites can be 'savagely beaten' for holding Shiite-style prayers. In Iran, it is the opposite: Shiite Islam is the official religion, and Sunnis can be banned from holding Eid prayers. Even al-Ghazali's limited legal pluralism can't work anymore, for all modern states are centralised entities with a standard law of the land. Meanwhile, Muslim-majority societies have become only more diverse, with new 'modernist' interpretations of Islam, along with non-practising Muslims. Any attempt at religious policing is nothing other than the imposition of the Islam of whomever has power in any given territory. What is imposed is not 'God's law', in other words, but the law of Wahhabi clerics, Shiite ayatollahs, or Shafi jurists.

The other, and even darker, black hole is the unintended consequences of religious policing: hypocrisy and resentment. Both are quite visible in Iran, where forty years of religious policing by the Islamic Republic made Iranian society not more pious, but only less so. The policy of *gozinesh*, or 'choosing', which means promoting state employees according to their religious observance rather than professional competence, only made people 'pretend to be religious'. In wider society, the ban on alcohol only boosted home-made production, which led to many incidents of death. Meanwhile, the oppression by the 'Islamic' regime made many dissidents despise not just the regime but also Islam. As a result, many Iranians left the religion, converting to Christianity or atheism.

Some Iranians have seen the disastrous impact of all these dictates. Among them was the exceptionally liberal Ayatollah Montazeri who warned in 2008 that 'mandating the performance of the Sharia' only causes 'the evasion of religion and hostility towards religiosity'. Yet still, as I was writing these lines, Iranian authorities were chasing women on the streets to make them cover their heads, and punish thousands who defied their rule.

Is there a way out of this blind insistence on religious policing?

Yes, there is, and that is to revisit what 'commanding the right and forbidding the wrong' means. And for that, a much-bypassed nuance should be highlighted: what we keep translating as 'right' in 'commanding the right' actually reads *ma'ruf*, which literally means 'known'. It is not *ma'ruf bi-l-shar*, or 'known by the Sharia', but just 'known'. This can well be, in the words of Shiite scholar Tabatabai (d. 1981), what 'people know by insight as earned by experience in social life' or what they grasp 'intuitively'. In other words, it can be a wisdom not specific to Islam and Muslims, but accessed by all human beings.

And this distinction can allow us, Muslims, to reinterpret the duty of 'commanding the right and forbidding the wrong'. First we can separate between what is known merely by religion and what is known by reason. The latter is something on which we can build laws, as all people may agree, through 'public reason', that murder or theft should be 'forbidden', or stopping at a red light should be 'commanded'. But truths known exclusively by religion—all the rituals, commandments and prohibitions of any religion—are subjective. So, their implementation should be left to individuals and communities who have agreed to live by them.

But, wait, can individuals really choose to live by religion—or not? Can they leave it, if they chose to do so?

That question requires a discussion on another key matter in the intersection of Islam and freedom, which is apostasy.

Apostasy

In a TV interview in 2006, Yusuf al-Qaradawi, one of the most prominent Sunni scholars in the Arab world, said something which proved more viral than he had probably expected. 'If they left apostasy alone [free], there wouldn't have been any Islam,' he said. 'Islam would have been finished right after the death of the Prophet.' To his Muslim audience, he was trying to explain why apostasy—the abandonment of Islam—is indeed a grave crime that should be punished. To some others, however, he was only confessing that Islam has survived to date thanks to violent coercion.

This matter, the punishment of apostasy, is the zenith of the coercive tradition within Islamic law. Accordingly, if a Muslim openly renounces his faith, to adopt another religion or no religion, he must be seized and asked to recant. If he doesn't recant, he must be executed. All the four Sunni schools of jurisprudence, along with their Shiite counterparts, unanimously agree on this grim verdict. They only differ in minor details. Hanafis and Shafis think that the apostate must be given three days to recant before execution. Malikis allow up to ten days. For Hanbalis, no waiting period is necessary. Hanafis and Shiites also accept a minor leniency for female apostates: instead of being executed, they must be imprisoned, and beaten in regular intervals so maybe they can see the light and come back to Islam.

For worse, these verdicts do not remain buried in classical books of jurisprudence, but make the laws of more than a dozen contemporary Muslim states. As of 2022, these included Saudi Arabia, Iran, Sudan, Afghanistan, Brunei, Mauritania, Maldives, parts of Nigeria, Somalia, Qatar, United Arab Emirates, and Yemen, all of which criminalised apostasy as a capital offence. In milder cases such as Malaysia, Jordan, Kuwait, and Oman, there were not direct laws in the penal code, but still Islamic courts could decree prison sentences, enforce 'rehabilitation', or annulment of marriages—as apostates don't have the right be married to Muslims. Meanwhile, even in countries where apostasy isn't banned by law, there can be vigilante violence against apostates—real or purported. Grim cases of such violence have occurred in Egypt, Pakistan, and Bangladesh.

The harsh verdict on apostasy is also one of the key justifications of terrorism in the name of Islam. Because terror groups like IS and Al Qaeda kill fellow Muslims by declaring them as apostates first. Luckily, mainstream scholars condemn these terrorists as 'extremists', saying that the latter have no right to declare other Muslims as apostates. But they rarely question whether *any apostate* really deserves to be targeted.

In short, the *umma*, the global Muslim community, has a big problem here. Killing somebody for their lack of belief in Islam—or even a specific interpretation of Islam—is not only a gross violation of human freedom, but it is also absurd. For by threatening, 'believe in Islam again, as I define it, or I will kill you', what can you really achieve other than hypocrisy and resentment?

This would have been quite obvious to all Muslims, if they all followed the Qur'an, and nothing else, for religious instruction. For the Qur'an, which discusses apostasy in no less than twenty-one separate verses, decrees no earthly punishment for it. It does have several verses that threaten apostates with God's wrath in the afterlife, but that is the afterlife, not this life. Moreover, the Qur'an has verses that one can use against the punishment on apostasy—such as the famous phrase, 'there is no compulsion in religion' (2:256).

But the mainstream Islamic tradition 'abrogated' or limited such verses more than a millennium ago. That is why some modern translators of the

Qur'an insert a few words into the no-compulsion phrase that dramatically reduce its scope: 'There shall be no compulsion in religion (*in becoming a Muslim*).' You are free to become a Muslim, that means, but you are not free to become an ex-Muslim.

Like almost all other coercive elements in Islamic law, the punishment for apostasy comes from not the Qur'an, but the hadiths. While many Muslims take these narrations as binding, there are good reasons to be cautious of them. First of all, they were canonised about two centuries after the Prophet, before spreading as oral traditions and mixing with many myths and forgeries. The scholars who collected and classified them—Ahmad bin Hanbal, Bukhari, Muslim and others—claimed to have figured out all the 'authentic' ones. Yet while we should respect their pious efforts, we cannot rule out their shortcomings—including their focus on establishing the chain of narrators, while refraining from evaluating the content of the narrations in the light of the Qur'an, reason, and moral intuition. Hence there is legitimate room, and dire need, to question the traditional hadith collections, as argued by various contemporary Muslim scholars, such as the Pakistani theologian Israr Ahmad Khan, author of *Authentication of Hadith: Redefining the Criteria*.

With that general caveat in mind, let's have a look at the two hadiths on which the apostasy ban is based. Both are in the all-authoritative *Sahih Bukhari*. The first one plainly reads: 'Whoever changes his religion, then kill him'. The second repeats the same verdict while listing three reasons for the death penalty: 'The blood of a Muslim... is not lawful to shed unless he be one of three: a married adulterer, someone killed in retaliation for killing another, or someone who abandons his religion and the Muslim community.'

Now, while all hadiths may be questioned, there are some specific reasons to suspect the authenticity of these two. First of all, even by their collectors, they were classified as *ahad*, which means they have a single source, in comparison to *mutawatir*, which means coming from multiple sources and being much more reliable. Also, the narrator of the first one, Ikrima bin Abu Jahl (598-634), is a controversial figure even by the standards of classical hadith collectors.

Secondly, both hadiths are suspiciously devoid of any context. We hear the Prophet ordering the killing of apostates, but there is no detail on where and when he said this, and what really happened after that. Other narrations do not present us any story that can match these verdicts. Quite the contrary, they tell us about instances that the Prophet in fact did *not* go after apostates. One is a Bedouin who came to Medina, asked the Prophet, 'Cancel my pledge', meaning religious allegiance, and left the scene without anyone following him. Another instance, reported in the Qur'an, is a group 'from the People of the Book' who said to each other, 'at the beginning of the day, believe in what has been revealed to these believers [Muslims] then at the end of the day reject it'. This seems to be not even mere apostasy, but apostasy with the clear intention of confusing Muslims. Yet still the Qur'an only ordered a mild verbal response—to say, 'True guidance is the guidance of God'—and we have no narration that the Prophet did anything different.

Third, there is something more bizarre about the apostasy hadiths: We don't hear them being quoted in some of the key disputes in early Islam in which apostasy was the burning issue. The first of these was the major incident during the rule of the first caliph Abu Bakr—*ridda*, or the refusal of some Arab tribes to pay tribute to the Muslim state in Medina. The incident provoked controversy in Medina, where the caliph favoured a hawkish response, whereas others pleaded for leniency. The curious point is that the caliph is on the record for asserting his own opinion, but not for quoting any hadith. That is strange, because he would have most likely referred to the apostasy hadiths if they were really known at that point.

Another incident from early Islam is one of the most outrageous exploitations of the verdict on apostasy: the execution of Ghaylan al-Dimashqi (d. 723). The pious Syrian theologian was not an apostate at all, but merely a defender of the doctrine of freewill, which refuted the contradictory doctrine of predestination that the Umayyad dynasty promoted to justify its despotism. His brutal execution took place after a show trial, which included a fatwa by Abd al-Rahman al-Awzai (d. 774), who was a Sunni jurist, a zealous enemy of freewill, and a minion of the throne. Al-Awzai's justification of political murder was no big surprise, but it is remarkable that his fatwa doesn't include any of the apostasy hadiths.

These all suggest that the hadiths about the execution of apostates may not have been around until the late second century after the Prophet Muhammad, when hadith collections such as *Sahih al-Bukhari* were not yet written. That is probably why, writing at this time, early jurists such as al-Nakha'i (d.713) and al-Thawri (d.772) could write that the apostate 'should forever be asked to recant'—not asked for a few days before being killed, as later *ijma*, or 'consensus', decreed.

All this makes it quite possible that the grim verdict on apostasy didn't come from the Prophet, but rather was projected back on to him by Muslims who found the verdict necessary.

But why would early Muslims find it necessary to punish apostasy? There are two answers, one being somewhat innocent, the other less so.

The more innocent answer is that 'apostasy' had a more alarming meaning in the pre-modern world, as the very concept of 'religion' was more comprehensive than what we think of today. It was not just a belief, but also communal belonging and political allegiance. The apostate would be renouncing all these loyalties, and also perhaps joining a deadly enemy. That is why, the Christian Byzantine Empire, too, had no sense of religious freedom. According to the Justinian Code of 534 AD, all citizens were forced to profess Christianity, while those who stayed true to Hellenic paganism—'the heathens'— were stripped of property, and at times killed and crucified. 'Not by their own free choice but under compulsion of the law', wrote Byzantine chronicler Procopius (d. 570), 'they had changed the beliefs of their fathers'. Islam was born into such a world, and Muslims seem to have adopted its norms.

The second and more cynical use of the apostasy ban was that it was a great tool to silence any Muslim dissident. The Umayyads' murder of the defenders of freewill—Ghaylan al-Dimashqi and Mabad al-Juhani—were the first stark examples. Then came al-Ghazali's grim verdict on 'the philosophers' such as al-Farabi and Ibn Sina. Then came the whole literature on 'the words of disbelief', or utterances which would make a Muslim immediately an apostate deserving death. In a long list of such lethal words, Hanafi scholar Shaykhzadeh (d. 1078) included things like 'to assert the createdness of the Qur'an' or 'to assert one's belief in transmigration or in the uncreatedness of the world'. These were unmistakable references to the views of the Mu'tazila and the philosophers. Words of disbelief even included 'to ridicule scholars' and 'to address scholars in a derisive manner', unabashedly serving the very scholars who came up with these verdicts.

Today, the Justinian Code is long gone, along with other dark chapters in Christian history in which faith was dictated by brute power. Yet the Muslim ban on apostasy is still present, both in theory and practice. This leads to gross human rights violations, as ex-Muslims can be threatened, jailed, tortured, and executed. The more cynical use of the verdict is also at play. Muslim scholars and intellectuals who merely have critical ideas can be condemned as 'apostates' and then be targeted. Consequently, Muslim societies can't even begin to discuss their burning problems.

Scholars who defend all this oppression have implausible arguments. Yusuf al-Qaradawi, for example, argues, 'every community in this world has basic foundations that are to be kept inviolable', and therefore 'no community accepts that a member thereof changes its identity'. That is clearly untrue, as people in the modern world in fact can freely change their religion or, if they can, their nationality. A Vietnamese Buddhist doesn't face the death penalty, or any penalty, when he turns himself into, say, a Canadian Protestant.

To be fair, al-Qaradawi at least makes a distinction between 'major' and 'minor' apostasy, which has become the typical 'moderate' position on the matter. Accordingly, minor apostasy is a mere loss of faith, which in itself doesn't constitute a crime. In major apostasy, though, the ex-Muslim also 'wages war on Islam and Muslims', and that is why he deserves death. But what is 'war on Islam and Muslims'? If that means bombing mosques and killing people, sure, that is a grave crime, irrespective of the attacker's beliefs. Yet by 'war on Islam and Muslims', what al-Qaradawi means is merely 'proclaiming' the apostasy and 'openly calling for it in speech or writing'. That, he says, justifies the death penalty. Others make the same argument—that apostates deserve to be killed once they 'start championing and spreading their spiritual and intellectual disorders to others'.

To see what is wrong here, we Muslims should consider a universal rule of ethics: the Golden Rule, which says, 'treat others as you would like others to treat you'. Many people from other faith traditions freely and openly convert to Islam, and some of these new Muslims criticise their old faiths as well. How would we feel if their former co-religionists condemned them for apostasy and set on killing them? If that would be outrageous, then our apostasy laws are outrageous, too. Asking for an exception for Islam because it is the 'true religion' would not work as well, because every religion is true to its believers, and none can claim universal rules favouring only itself.

A contemporary Muslim who has grasped and articulated the point here is Rached Ghannouchi, Tunisian scholar and politician. In his 1993 book, *Public Liberties in the Islamic State*, he said the following:

> And if it is the right, indeed the duty, of a Muslim to address his message (*dawa*) to his non-Muslim compatriot, then the latter also has the same right. And if there is any fear for the faith of the Muslims, then there is no other solution for them but to grow deeper in their faith... Antithetical viewpoints will reach Muslims by any means, and the only means of protection against any discussion is to offer another discussion, this one better, more intelligent, and more cogent.

So, Ghannouchi was making a case for not just freedom of religion but also freedom of speech: That Muslims could hear speech that goes against their faith, but all they should do was to offer a better speech.

But what if people 'insulted' Islam? What if they mocked God and His prophet? What should Muslims do to such blasphemers?

That requires the third major issue on the intersection of Islam and freedom: free speech and blasphemy.

Blasphemy

Asia Bibi is a poor Christian woman from Pakistan who has seen hell on this earth. Until June 2009, she used to work on a farm in Punjab. But on a fateful day, she had a quarrel with Muslim co-workers, one of whom went to the police and complained that she 'insulted the Prophet Muhammad.' Soon she was arrested, put on trial, and was sentenced to death by hanging. She spent the next eight years on death row and in solitary confinement, only to be released thanks to the Pakistani Supreme Court who found her innocent. Yet angry Islamist groups still wanted to see her dead, so she saved her life only by silently fleeing to Canada in May 2019.

While I watched this whole Asia Bibi incident with sorrow, I was also intrigued by some curious detail in it. The Pakistani press ran many articles on the case, but they never explicitly said what the blasphemy in question was. In its fifty-six-page long decision that saved Bibi, the Supreme Court, too, only referred to the alleged 'derogatory remarks against the Holy

Prophet Muhammad (Peace Be Upon Him)', but never quoted those remarks.

Apparently there was a reason for this silence, which Pakistani novelist Mohammed Hanif explained, with a hint of humor, in an article in the *New York Times*. 'We can never know what she may or may not have said,' Hanif wrote, referring to the incident that put Asia Bibi in jail. 'Because repeating blasphemy is also blasphemy, and writing it down may be even greater blasphemy. So let's not go there.'

When I read this, I paused for a second. 'Alas,' I said to myself, 'with this logic, the Pakistanis must ban the Qur'an as well.' Because, with this logic, the Qur'an is also full of blasphemy. In fact, outrageous blasphemy.

What I am referring to are the Qur'anic verses which reflect the polemics between the Prophet Muhammad and the pagans of Mecca with whom he was trying to share the message of the Qur'an, only to get hostile reactions. We hear them saying, for example: 'Receiver of this Qur'an! *You are definitely mad*. Why do you not bring us the angels, if you are telling the truth?' Another Qur'anic verse also quotes the pagans, whose offensive words go uncensored:

> When Our revelations are recited to them in all their clarity, the disbelievers say of the Truth that has reached them, '*This is clearly sorcery*,' or they say, '*He has invented it himself.*' (46:7)

The Qur'an also quotes a 'stubbornly hostile' man who condemns the Qur'an by saying, '*This is just old sorcery*, just the talk of a mortal.' A group of unbelievers who dismiss the Qur'an are also quoted in full: 'We have heard all this before, we could say something like this if we wanted, *this is nothing but ancient fables*' (8:31). Blasphemous depictions of God are also quoted in the Qur'an as the words of misguided: 'God is tight-fisted,' 'God has a child,' or 'God has begotten.' When the Qur'an quotes these statements, it often answers them with counter-arguments. To those who said, 'God is tight-fisted,' it responds: 'Truly, God's hands are open wide: He gives as He pleases' (5:64). Against polytheists, it argues: 'If there had been in the heavens or earth any gods but Him, both heavens and earth would be in ruins' (21:22). And to those who claim that the Prophet Muhammad himself made up the Qur'an, it presents an intellectual challenge: 'Then produce a sura [chapter] like it, and call on anyone you can beside God if you are telling the truth' (10:38).

In other words, when the Qur'an encounters blasphemy, it responds to it with sensible arguments. At most, it threatens blasphemers with God's wrath in the afterlife, but it decrees no punishment in this life. It certainly doesn't decree that blasphemers should be jailed and killed, or that their words should be censored.

What if the blasphemy in question is not something you can reason with, but sheer insult? In that case, too, the Qur'an doesn't order any violent or coercive response. 'When you come across people who speak with scorn about Our revelations,' reads a verse, 'turn away from them until they move on to another topic' (4:140). This is in the Meccan sura An'am, so, by those who are fond of abrogation, it may be explained away as a temporary restraint due to lack of power. But the Medinan sura of Nisa repeats the same commandment with a reference to the earlier one:

'As He has already revealed to you in the Scripture, if you hear people denying and ridiculing God's revelation, do not sit with them unless they start to talk of other things, or else you yourselves will become like them.' (4:140)

Another Medinan verse also tells Muslims that insult is a 'test,' which they should bear:

'You are sure to hear much that is hurtful from those who were given the Scripture before you and from those who associate others with God. If you are steadfast and mindful of God, that is the best course.' (3:186)

Commenting on this verse, Fakhr al-Din al-Razi, the great thirteenth century exegete, wrote that while some jurists consider it as 'abrogated', others including himself don't think so. He also supported it with other verses of the same spirit. One is the commandment, 'Tell the believers to forgive those who do not fear God's days.' The other is a description of the believers as, 'The servants of the Lord of Mercy... who walk humbly on the earth, and who, when the foolish address them, reply, "Peace".'

Despite this tolerant spirit in the Qur'an, Islamic jurisprudence developed a harsh verdict for blasphemy—in particular blasphemy against Prophet Muhammad, called sabb or shatm al-rasul. Hanafis conflated it with apostasy, which means they took it as capital offence, while leaving room for repentance. Shafis took a similar position, whereas Malikis allowed repentance for only women, and Hanbalis allowed it to no one. The latter's severity was embellished by Ibn Taymiyya in his treatise, *The Unsheathed Sword Against the One Who Insults the Messenger*, which has proven highly influential even among non-Hanbalis. Accordingly, anyone who insulted the Prophet would be killed, even if he repented and asked for mercy.

Today, this medieval jurisprudential tradition is still influential, as it underlies the blasphemy laws that are in practice in some thirty Muslim-majority countries. (Some of these laws, such as in Pakistan, are leftovers of European colonialism, but the passion to preserve and implement them is unmistakably religious.) For worse, at the hands of militants, blasphemy laws turn into vigilante violence against 'those who insult Islam', real or perceived, from author Salman Rushdie to Asia Bibi, to the French magazine *Charlie Hebdo*.

If the Qur'an doesn't support all this severity, though, where does it come from? Like in the case of apostasy, the source is certain narrations about the Prophet Muhammad. This time we don't have any clear hadiths ordering violence against acts of blasphemy. We rather have stories in the books of *Al-Sira al-Nabawiyya*, or Prophetic Biography, written down by Muslim chroniclers about a century or so after the Prophet. These stories tell us about the targeted killing of several individuals who wrote hostile poems against the Prophet and his message. These stories have inspired militant Muslims, and also led some anti-Islam polemicists to joke about 'Muhammad's Dead Poets Society'. Both sides, however, seem to miss an important nuance.

For that nuance, we should look at the most iconic figure among these 'dead poets': Ka'b ibn al-Ashraf. He was a leader of Banu Nadir, a Jewish tribe in Medina which signed the 'constitution' with the Prophet Muhammad soon after the latter's arrival to the city. The early Muslim chronicler Al-Waqidi tells us what happened afterwards. 'When the Messenger of God arrived in Medina he desired to establish peace for them and he reconciled with all of them,' he writes, referring to the 'polytheists and Jews'. Some of the latter 'hurt the Prophet and his companions grievously,' with their bitter words, 'but God most high commanded His prophet and the Muslims to be patient and forgiving'. Yet still, Ibn al-Ashraf proved growingly hostile. After the Battle of Badr, where Medinan Muslims defeated Meccan pagans, he not only protested the victory, but also vowed: 'I will go out to the Quraysh and incite them.' Then he really did go to Mecca, met with pagan leaders and wept with them for their dead. His anti-Muslim rhymes reached a wide circulation there, rousing the Meccans 'to grief and anger and the desire for revenge.' There are also reports that Ibn al-Ashraf tore up a tent the Prophet set up in the Medina market, and even plotted with a group of his kinsmen to kill the Prophet.

Only after all this, Ibn al-Ashraf was assassinated by a group of Muslims acting on the order of the Prophet. Was he an offensive poet? Yes. But apparently, he was also more than that.

Most of the other 'dead poets' seem to have combined their offensive words with their active enmity. One was Nadr ibn al-Harith, who was one of the two captives executed after the Battle of Badr, while others were unharmed. The reason, told to his face, was 'you said thus and thus about the Book of God,' and 'you tortured [the Prophet's] companions'. Another was Abu Rafi 'who used to hurt Allah's Messenger, and help his enemies against him'. Others were targeted after the Conquest of Mecca when the victorious Prophet announced general amnesty to his former prosecutors, but with the exception of ten individuals. One was Abdullah ibn Khaltal, who 'used to recite verses abusing the prophet' but who had also murdered an innocent slave. Another one was Huwayrith ibn Nafidh who had attacked the Prophet's daughters when they were fleeing Medina.

Here is a point that may explain the murkiness in these stories. In early seventh century Arabia, poetry wasn't just poetry. There was a specific genre called *hija*, or 'invective poetry', where 'the poet could lead his people into battle, hurling his verses as he would hurl a spear'. In other words, there were no clear lines between verbal denigration and physical aggression, and Muslims might have conflated the two.

On the other hand, there are also incidents in Prophet Muhamad's life where he did *not* punish blasphemous words when they were just words. According to a narration in *Sahih al-Bukhari*, a Jew in Medina used a play on words while greeting the prophet. Instead of *as-salamu alaika*, or 'peace be upon you,' he said, *as-samu alaika*, or 'death be upon you.' Hearing this, some companions lost their nerve and asked: 'O God's Apostle! Shall we kill him?' The Prophet, said, 'No' and told them to only respond by saying *wa alaikum*, or 'on you, too'. In other versions of the same story, the prophet also said: 'Be gentle and calm... as Allah likes gentleness in all affairs.'

In a similar incident, another Medinan named Finhas mocked a Qur'anic verse on alms, saying, 'Muhammad's Lord is in need'. The ever-fiery Umar unsheathed his sword, but he was stopped by not just the Prophet himself, but also a new verse from God: 'Tell the believers to forgive those who do not fear God's days.' Umar complied, promising the prophet: 'You will see no more anger on my face.'

What all this means is that the 'dead poets' cannot justify violence against blasphemy, as the prominent Hanafi scholar Badr al-Din al-Ayni (d. 1453) had also argued. '[They] were not killed merely for their insults [of the Prophet],' he wrote, 'but rather it was surely because they aided [the enemy] against him, and joined with those who fought wars against him, and supported them.' Seven centuries before him, the very founder of the Hanafi school, the ever-sensible Abu Hanifa, had made a similar point. Non-Muslims who insult the Prophet are not to be killed, he wrote, 'because their [overall] unbelief is worse,' but they are not targeted for unbelief.

It is also quite telling that the verdict on killing blasphemers appeared at quite a late stage in Islamic law—as late as the early tenth century, or three centuries after the death of the Prophet. Also notable is that it grew among Malikis, whose geographic positioning in Spain and North Africa put them in close contact, and conflict, with Christians. The first big application was the notorious incident of 'martyrs of Cordoba', where some forty-eight Christians were publicly decapitated between 850 and 859 for denigrating the Prophet Muhammad. This Christian defiance seems to have catalysed the crystallisation of the verdict on blasphemy, which used to be unclear.

Today, Muslims who are eager to punish or silence blasphemy should know that, jurisprudentially speaking, they are on shaky ground. Rationally speaking, they are out of their minds. By their threats and dictates, they are only confirming the common accusation against Islam—that it is an intolerant and violent religion. They are also provoking more blasphemy against Islam, because their zeal to silence critics only makes the latter more agitated. Meanwhile, they are enfeebling Muslim societies, which do not learn how to respond to criticism with reason and civility. That is why, like the case in Pakistan, they can't even bear to hear blasphemous words, unlike the Qur'an which quotes them and often reasons with them.

No Compulsion in Religion, Really

It is quite remarkable that with all its coercive measures, mainstream Islamic tradition has turned the Qur'anic maxim, 'no compulsion in religion', upside down. Because in this tradition, there are all sorts of compulsion *in* the religion, whereas 'no compulsion' can be found only *outside*. Because only if you are not a Muslim, you will not be forced to practise the religion or be loyal to it. And only if you are outside of the reach of Muslims, you will be able to freely speak against it.

In the face of this grim freedom deficit, it is no surprise that Muslims who value freedom often distance themselves from the faith. Some totally abandon it. While I was writing these lines, there was a trending hashtag on Twitter which read, #AwesomeWithoutAllah. It was a campaign by ex-Muslims who celebrated their life after Islam. While some had problems with the core theology of the faith, more seemed to be angry with the dictates in its name, such as compulsory hijab, female genital mutilation, oppression of minorities, and all kinds of violence and bigotry one can find in the Muslim world. In a global world where individuals are becoming more educated and questioning, this trend is likely to grow, making more and more people not just post-Islamic but also anti-Islamic.

The remedy we modern-day Muslims need—call it a great 'reform' or 'renewal'—is really having 'no compulsion in religion'. It is, in other words, *giving up coercive power in the name of Islam*. This means no more religious and moral policing, no threats to apostates and 'innovators', no blasphemy laws, no public flogging or stoning, and no beatings in the family. It means accepting, 'religion is advice', as one of the better hadiths in *Sahih al-Bukhari*, and advancing Islam only with advisory means, such as preaching, counselling, exemplifying, and educating. Quite a few Muslims are already doing that—as minorities in the West, or as majorities in secular states ranging from Bosnia to Indonesia—and their experience presents a much brighter story than those in coercive states such as Saudi Arabia or Iran.

We would not be the first major world religion to have this transformation—although we may be the last. Christians, in particular, used coercive power for centuries, but European Catholics now recall the Inquisition with embarrassment, in the same way American Protestants remember the witch-hunts in the Massachusetts Bay Colony. They outgrew those dark phases thanks to the rational realisation that coercion is absurd, and the scriptural realisation that it is unnecessary. We Muslims, too, have the rational and scriptural resources to take the same step, to embrace freedom. And we should embrace freedom not because we don't value our religion, but, quite the contrary, because we do.

LIBERTY AND FREEDOM

Jeremy Henzell-Thomas

In his entry for the word liberation in *Keywords*, his seminal inquiry into the changing meanings of 131 keywords in English, Raymond Williams notes the parallel development in English from words derived from Latin *liber* and Teutonic *freo* (the source of *freedom*). He explains that in both cases the meaning depended on an opposing term: in Latin, *servus*, 'slave', and in the Teutonic languages 'those outside the household', who were also in practice slaves. He goes on to say that 'the extended political senses have developed mainly around the Latin group' in producing words like *liberty, liberal, libertarian*, and *liberation*.

The word *freedom* comes from Teutonic *frei* originating in the Indo-European root *prai*, 'beloved', hence 'precious' and also 'at peace with'. Sanskrit *priya*, 'dear', comes from the same root. The name Godfrey means 'peace of God'. Norse Freya or Frija is the Goddess of love. Old English *freond* from the same root is more than 'friend', also 'lover'. The original meaning of *free* was a term of affection uniting the members of a family in a common bond, but explicitly excluding their servants, serfs, or slaves. Later, the meaning shifted from 'affection' to 'freedom'.

The word *liberty* comes through Latin *liber,* 'free', from the Indo-European root *leudh*, still intact in the ancient Greek word *eleutheros,* 'free', applied to free-born citizens and not slaves. The original sense was 'mount up, grow, rise', applied to the population, as still in German *Leute*, 'people', and *Lettish,* a native or citizen of Latvia. The semantic development from the sense of 'grow, rise' to 'freedom' is not altogether clear. To 'deliver' something is etymologically to 'set it free' (as in 'deliver us from evil') but its meaning shifted to 'give up, surrender' and finally 'hand over' or 'provide'.

Williams correctly identifies the shared sense of *freedom* and *liberty* as a state of freedom (or liberation) from slavery or servitude, but he does not explore how the underlying connotations of the two words *freedom* and *liberty* are rather different even though the two words are often used interchangeably in modern usage. As Bert Hornback has noted, 'English is often blessed by its dual linguistic heritage, rarely more so than in this instance.' He explains that although the root of the word *liberty* had the sense of 'not being a slave', it has developed the sense of 'doing whatever you want to do', or 'doing your own thing'. The same root has given us *libido* (defined by Jung as 'the totality of psychic energy, not limited to sexual desire' or 'a desire or impulse which is unchecked by any kind of authority, moral or otherwise'), *libidinous,* 'given to indulging one's urges', *liberate, deliver, libertarian* ('relating to or denoting a political philosophy that advocates only minimal state intervention in the free market and the private lives of citizens'), *libertine* ('a rake or debauchee'), and (from the Greek) *libation,* an 'outpouring'. To Hornback's analysis might be added John Stuart Mill's assertion that 'Liberty consists in doing what one desires', an idea dismissed by Hegel as one of 'utter immaturity'.

The word *liberal* clearly carries both positive and negative connotations according to one's political viewpoint. Williams notes its association with 'progressive or radical opinions', but it also carries a range of negative connotations not only amongst conservatives and traditionalists, but also (as Williams notes) for socialists. These connotations include licentiousness, lawlessness, and lack of restraint, discipline, and rigour. *Liberalism* shares this ambiguity. It can refer to the political philosophy concerned with protecting the autonomy and freedom of the individual in the face of state control, repression, and interference, but may also be equated with the selfish individualism which ignores the 'greater good' of community, wider society, or nation.

As a political philosophy rooted in the principle of free will, *Libertarianism* may go further than liberalism in its advocacy of 'natural' individual rights over institutional authority. In an article in the *Observer* in December 2021 entitled 'Strange beasts, these "libertarians" who love to curb the freedom of others', Kenan Malik asks the awkward question 'When is a libertarian not a libertarian?' and answers 'When, apparently, it is the wrong kind of people whose liberties are being curtailed.' He was referring to the rebellion by 'libertarian' Tory MPs against the government's Covid Plan B involving the necessity for vaccine certificates or negative tests to attend large venues, mandatory vaccinations for NHS staff, and the compulsory wearing of masks in certain spaces. Although they claim liberty as a motive, Kenan noted that 'authoritarian impulses are never far away'. Although Tory MP Marcus Fysh asserted that 'We're not a "papers please" society', and 'This is not Nazi Germany', the fact is, as Malik noted, that 'for many people, Britain is very much a "papers please" society. "Papers please" is what the "hostile environment" for immigrants is built on—the demand that people who might be immigrants must show their papers before they can receive hospital treatment, rent a flat, or find a job. It's what lies at the heart of the Windrush scandal.' He is surely right that 'right-wing libertarians often have a selective view of who should be able to avail themselves of liberty'. And let us add that such a rebuke applies as much to authoritarian libertarians of any political persuasion or none. I have been harangued on a number of occasions by libertarian anarchists in the town where I live for wearing a mask. The authoritarian spectre of 'cancel culture' is also rapidly proliferating, not only in academe where lecturers have to watch every word they say, but also amongst comedians who are increasingly reluctant to tell jokes which might be interpreted as harbouring bigoted views.

While the term *liberal democracy* still holds a generally positive connotation across a broad spectrum of political persuasions, there is also the disparaging or derogatory association of *liberal* with 'weak and sentimental generosity', the excessive soft-heartedness of the 'bleeding-heart liberal' or 'well-meaning do-gooder'. That generosity, however, was the chief virtue attached to the original sense of the word *liberal* in English, as in *liberality* (spending freely, being open to new ideas, and free from prejudice) and in the *liberal arts*, those cultural pursuits and branches of learning regarded in classical antiquity to be essential for a free person to know in order to be worthy of the social status conferred by freedom, and thereby qualified to take an active part in civic life, including participation in public debate. The sense of 'generous' developed from the notion that generosity was an attribute characteristic of a free person and is reflected in the extension of Latin *liberalis* to mean 'noble, gentlemanly'.

The different origin and semantic development of the words *freedom* and *liberty* lead Hornback to the conclusion that the essential difference between them is that 'freedom is a social word; liberty a selfish, anti-social word. Freedom requires of us responsibility; liberty is the assertion of our refusal of responsibility.' In other words, if freedom is a term rooted in relationship, liberty is tainted by egoism and solipsism.

Although we may want to avoid such a categorical distinction between the two terms, the semantic connection between freedom and social responsibility and the balance between them points the way to one of the most important principles in any discussion about issues around freedom and liberty in the contemporary context. It is not a matter of choosing one term above the other as the 'best' term to use to inform our discourse, but of imbuing our own understanding of the core concept with the best connotations of both terms, while always being mindful of the negative connotations which indicate imbalance. In the same way as the fundamentally positive connotations of *freedom* can be taken on board (bond of affection, social responsibility, peaceful co-existence), so also can the best of *liberty* be salvaged from both its selfish and sentimental connotations. Individuality can be respected and nurtured without recourse to the strident individualism which denies respect to others. We can value the generosity and open-mindedness of an educated liberal outlook without succumbing to a disorientated 'anything goes' mentality devoid of conceptual rigour or moral compass.

Likewise, we can honour the 'radical' tradition of reforming liberalism, intelligent social activism, and legitimate dissent which has historically guided the progressive evolution of free, just, and tolerant societies, and reject the derogatory use of the word 'radical' when applied to Muslim contexts only to refer to the 'radicalisation' which breeds violent extremism. After all, Quaker 'radicals' have played a significant role in movements promoting peace, the abolition of slavery, equal rights for women, the humane treatment of prisoners and the mentally ill, and other areas of institutional reform.

Just before the COP26 Global Summit in Glasgow in November 2021 the Pope called for leaders to take 'radical action' on climate change, but no one would assume that he was advocating the kind of disruptive mayhem caused by a 'radical' protest group like Insulate Britain (an offshoot of Extinction Rebellion) in blockading motorways. Thirty-eight protesters blockading the M25 in September 2021 were arrested for various offences, such as criminal damage, causing danger to road users, wilful obstruction of the highway, and causing a public nuisance. Soon after the Conservative victory in the General Election of 2015, George Osborne promised 'radical devolution' for English cities, something clearly marked on the plus side. The BBC Sunday programme referred to David Cameron's 'radical heart' and an article in *The Guardian* claimed that 'Cameron has run the most radical government of our time'. But the ambivalence is never far away. Whereas that article equated his radicalism with a strongly anti-socialist agenda (cutting the state, sweeping away support for the weak, denuding local government, selling the NHS to private firms, and tripling fees to make universities effectively private), *The Observer* ran a major article at around the same time reporting that the Conservatives frame their 'radical agenda' as becoming the 'party of social justice' and thus keeping Labour out for a generation. In 2014, Fox News reported that 'Cameron talks tough on radical Islam', and yet stated before the recent general election that he 'must be radical on immigration to win back votes'. So, take your pick: radicalism can apply to a wide spectrum of political persuasions and agendas, and can be framed as either benign or malign depending on where you stand.

The freedom to protest is rightfully regarded as a positive aspect of our society, and although some may disapprove of the behaviour of the more radical activists within Insulate Britain and applaud their arrest for various offences, we can see how the boundaries of what is tolerated have shifted significantly over the years. In 1884 James Bryce MP introduced the first Parliamentary bill for a right to roam and the bill was re-introduced every year until 1914 and failed each time. In 1932 six people were sent to jail for leading a mass trespass on Kinder Scout in the Peak District in Derbyshire, causing national outcry and bringing the case for a right to roam into the public eye. It was not until 2003, however, that the right to roam on uncultivated land was enshrined into law.

The same navigational principle in relation to radicalism applies to *freedom*. If the connotations seem more typically positive, with the social dimension of the word including that of friendship and social responsibility, the concept of a common bond of affection uniting a family or community also carries the potential for tribalism, repressive conformity, and exclusivism. Ibn Khaldun recognised the equivocal nature of social bonding in his use of the term *'asabiyyah* (tribal partisanship). It can be a source of solidarity and social cohesion, but in its negative form it is that crudely jingoistic and smugly ethnocentric mentality which endorses tribal prejudice and parochial self-interest. The cry of 'freedom' or 'liberty' is still raised to project a nationalistic sense of civilisational superiority and ownership of higher 'values' often in the context of the spread of 'freedom and democracy' to less 'civilised' or 'benighted' parts of the world. Awareness of the multidimensionality of words puts us on our guard against the dangers of turning particular connotations into slogans or absolutising what is only a partial reality.

The power historically invested in families, dynasties, and tribes has been gradually transferred to nation states and is hopefully shifting in an even more universal direction to a shared bond of humanity in our increasingly globalised and interconnected world. At present this may seem like a forlorn hope, given the recent rise in populist nationalism, unilateralism, and isolationism that prompted the World Policy Forum (Global Solutions) in the run-up to the G20 summit in Rome at the end of October 2021 to appeal for the revitalisation of multilateralism. Freedom of religion and freedom of speech are both regarded as incontestable rights in secular, liberal democracies. Freedom of religion is broadly protected by procedural secularism as an advanced political system that separates freedom of conscience and the assertion of religious beliefs from conduct that contravenes public law. An important aspect of the separation of powers is the fundamental principle of liberty of conscience, a principle ardently advocated by Martin Luther, the father of Protestantism. Insisting that God requires voluntary and sincere religious beliefs, Luther sets out the principle that forbids human authorities from compulsion or coercion in matters of faith, since any such compulsion would render faith insincere. The role of the civil government is simply to maintain peace and order in society. The principle of liberty of conscience is absolutely in accord with the injunction in the Qur'an (2:256) that 'there shall be no coercion (*ikrah*) in matters of faith'. While certain beliefs may be sincerely held, those beliefs do not confer any right to act upon them to harm, injure, cause distress, or violate the rights of others. Whatever might be proscribed as 'sins' as a matter of personal conviction cannot all be translated into legal rulings and enforced on others. This is not only a matter of conforming meticulously to the law of the land wherever it regulates such matters, but is also a matter of abiding by the fundamental principle of mercy in governing relationships and fostering kindness, harmony, and reconciliation within family, community, and wider society. To that end, there is also a pressing need for the reclamation and implementation of the proper Islamic ethics and etiquette (*adab al-ihktilaf*) for engaging in respectful debate and disagreement in a plural world and a plural Islam in which diverse opinions can be freely and legitimately expressed.

Freedom of speech (and the press) has become an especially contentious issue, most notably in the context of the furore over the Danish cartoons of the Prophet Muhammad in 2006, the *Charlie Hebdo* shooting in Paris in 2015, and the murder of Samuel Paty, a French middle-school teacher in 2020 in a suburb of Paris. Paty had, in a class on freedom of expression, allegedly shown his students *Charlie Hebdo*'s 2012 cartoons depicting the Prophet, for which he was killed and beheaded by an eighteen-year-old Chechen Muslim refugee. In view of former protests by Muslims about the cartoons, Paty had actually permitted his students to avert their eyes or leave the room while they were displayed. Most recently, in March 2021, one of the cartoons of the Prophet, believed to be one published by *Charlie Hebdo*, was shown to pupils in a religious studies lesson at Batley Grammar School in West Yorkshire. The ensuing demonstrations outside the school were condemned by the Department of Education as 'completely unacceptable', and several politicians publicly stated that teachers should not be threatened or intimidated. The teacher concerned was suspended by the school for using 'a totally inappropriate image' in the lesson.

Acres of newsprint and hours of air time have been expended in the wake of these events and they raise many complex issues. Is freedom of speech really a non-negotiable and absolute right in liberal democracies? What is the ideal balance between a 'sacrosanct' freedom of expression and sensitive regard for the equally sacrosanct beliefs of others? To what extent should we require influential people in civil society, whether in the state, a corporation, or a newspaper, to use language and deploy images more responsibly than simply observing the bare minimum the law demands? To what extent have these events been caused, at least to some extent, by those masquerading as brave defenders of a precious freedom but actually wishing to fan the flames of a wished-for Clash of Civilisations between Islam and the West? Is there a connection between such events and an underlying rage provoked by perceptions of injustice, double standards, and hypocrisy in the treatment of Muslims by Western governments? At the time of the controversy over the Danish Cartoons, some of these questions were succinctly answered by Tariq Ramadan in an interview for *New Perspectives Quarterly*, the organ of the Center for the Study of Democratic Institutions. He made it clear that 'Muslims have to understand there is free speech in Europe, and that is that.' On the other side, he claimed that while 'there are no legal limits to free speech, there are civic limits' and 'there needs to be an understanding that sensitive issues must be addressed with wisdom and prudence, not provocation'—all the more so in the 'hybrid, multicultural societies we see in the world today.' He asks: 'Do I go around insulting people just because I'm free to do it? No. It is a matter of civic responsibility and wisdom not a question of legality or rights.' Others have questioned whether the issue is really one of civic responsibility, arguing instead that it is more a matter of Muslim immaturity.

It is striking how the essential point here about the necessary balance between legal rights and civic responsibilities reflects the different underlying connotations of liberty and freedom brought to light in their etymology. But at the same time it is important to qualify the assumption that there are 'no legal limits to free speech' as much as it is necessary to contradict the widely-held belief that free speech is an 'absolute value' in the 'Western' world.

On 15 January 2015, shortly after the attack on *Charlie Hebdo*, the Insted Consultancy remarked that 'headline writers and politicians throughout the Western world have been in agreement—the attack on *Charlie Hebdo* was part of a war on freedom, a war on the foundations of Western democracy. Anyone who does not express total solidarity with the victims by, for example, holding up a "Je suis Charlie" slogan, and does not declare their unwavering commitment to freedom of speech, seems to be on the side of the terrorists. This has been the dominant narrative in virtually all the coverage so far in the mainstream media, and in the vast majority of speeches and statements by political leaders.' They note that 'only a handful of voices have so far queried this dominant narrative' by daring to stress that 'one can *not only* have profound sympathy for the victims and for their families, friends, colleagues, and close followers; and can *not only* deplore the cruelty and callousness of the murderers; and can *not only* care about freedom of expression; but can *also* deplore the simplistic, hypocritical, racist, Islamophobic, and deeply damaging us-and-them thinking that has been at the heart of the mainstream media coverage, and of most political speeches.'

At the same time, they published a list of twenty-eight fine articles that had appeared during the week following the attacks and which 'query and deplore the dominant narrative and indicate alternative approaches to understanding what is going on.' One of them, an article by Simon Dawes in *openDemocracy,* makes it clear that both freedom of speech and freedom of the press are not 'non-negotiable' values. They are both already restricted by laws against defamation, incitement, and confidentiality, as well as 'social norms, by conflicts with other values (such as privacy and national security), and so on.' 'We need,' he concludes, 'to discourage misguided and reactionary representations of these attacks as simply attacks on free speech, and acknowledge that free speech itself is not an absolute value. We must recognise the validity of debates over what limits to free speech are acceptable—whether or not we approve of the kind of images that *Charlie Hebdo* has published, or with their mass republication on numerous websites this week.'

The titles of the other articles listed on the Insted Consultancy website in the wake of the *Charlie Hebdo* attacks speak for themselves and include: 'The moral hysteria of Je suis Charlie'; 'Where monoculturalism leads'; 'Mourning the Parisian journalists, yet noticing the hypocrisy'; 'The danger of polarised debate'; 'We must not forget the responsibility that goes with free speech'; 'When blasphemy is bigotry'; 'Free speech does not mean freedom from criticism'; 'Fed up with the hypocrisy of the free speech fundamentalists'; 'Is the *Charlie Hebdo* attack really a struggle over European values?'; 'Us and them'.

To these can be added, amongst many others, Pankaj Mishra's eloquent plea that 'after the Paris attacks: It's time for a new Enlightenment' in that 'we may have to retrieve the Enlightenment, as much as religion, from its fundamentalists.' Referring to Kant's definition of the Enlightenment as 'man's emergence from his self-imposed immaturity', Mishra is surely right that this task and obligation is never fulfilled; 'it has to be continually renewed by every generation in ever-changing social and political conditions. The advocacy of more violence and wars in the face of recurrent failure meets the definition of fanaticism rather than reason. The task for those who cherish freedom is to reimagine it—through an ethos of criticism combined with compassion and ceaseless self-awareness—in our own irreversibly mixed and highly unequal societies and the larger interdependent world. Only then can we capably defend freedom from its true enemies.'

In relation to freedom of speech in the United States, the ways in which this is an 'alluring and deceptive' belief have been well documented, as in Rey Barry's 'United States Myths and their Realities: Americans have Free Speech.' This myth is rooted in the First Amendment to the US Constitution which states that 'Congress shall make no law abridging the freedom of speech, or of the press,' and the Fourteenth Amendment also makes that applicable to the states. 'Patriotism focuses on that and sees no further, missing all the glaring contradictions. Yet it's the contradictions that control our life.' Barry points out that the First Amendment does not confer any absolute right of free speech but simply places a limit on the power of one branch of government to control speech, the Legislative branch. There is nothing, however, in the Constitution to prevent the executive or judicial branches from limiting free speech, and they 'do it routinely when it serves their interest'. Free speech is limited in countless ways (and many will apply much more widely than the United States)—through laws against defamation, slander, and libel, as well as incitement, threats of violence, and 'reckless endangerment'; through arbitrary lines draw by Congress in the 'public interest'; through intellectual property laws, copyright and trademark laws, and rules and penalties by local government and educational institutions that enforce 'political correctness' in the use of words which might be perceived as insulting; through limits on speech set by employers on their employees who have no constitutional protection against being fired for breaching them; through secrecy requirements in the Grand Jury system and on employees in or under the executive branch.

As I write this, I have heard the shocking news that Julian Assange, the Wikileaks founder, now faces up to 175 years in prison after the High Court in London ruled that he can be extradited to the US. This highlights only too starkly the perilous risks taken by journalists in exposing what Matthias von Hein has described as 'the dirty secrets of powerful governments, including war crimes, corruption, and torture.' And as he points out, 'it isn't the war criminals and torturers who are punished, but the journalist who brought these crimes to light. His reputation is systematically destroyed, his freedom is taken away, he suffers psychological torture. All this happens not in a military dictatorship or a one-party state known for such behaviour, but in Western democracies that portray themselves as shining examples when it comes to human rights.' Professor Nils Melzer, Chair of the Geneva Academy of International Humanitarian Law and Human Rights, and UN Special Rapporteur on torture has also raised strong doubts about the strength of our justice system in the face of powerful interests that manipulate and abuse it. And American journalist Glenn Greenwald pointedly remarks that the real measure of the freedom of a society 'is not how its mainstream, well-behaved ruling class servants are treated, but the fate of its actual dissidents.' As he says, 'powerful officials in Washington can illegally leak the most sensitive government secrets and will suffer no punishment, or will get the lightest tap on the wrist, provided their aim is to advance mainstream narratives. But low-level leakers whose aim is to expose wrongdoing by the powerful or reveal their systemic lying will have the full weight of the criminal justice system and the intelligence community come crashing down on them, to destroy them with vengeance and also to put their heads on a pike to terrorize future dissidents out of similarly stepping forward.'

With that in mind, it is sad to note the low standing of many Muslim-majority countries in the provision of freedom. In the annual Human Freedom Index (HFI) for 2019 (the most recent year for covering all the relevant data), out of 165 countries the lowest ranked included Syria (165), Yemen (163), Sudan (162), Egypt (161), Iran (160), Somalia (159), Iraq (157), Libya (156), and Saudi Arabia (155). The countries that took the top ten places, in order, were Switzerland, New Zealand, Denmark, Estonia, Ireland, Canada, and Finland (tied at sixth), Australia, Sweden, and Luxembourg. The United Kingdom ranked fourteenth and Germany, Japan, and the United States tied at fifteenth. The HFI, co-published by the Cato Institute and the Fraser Institute, is currently the most comprehensive freedom index representing 98 percent of the world's population. It presents the state of human freedom in the world based on a broad measure that encompasses personal, civil, and economic freedom. The index for 2019 uses seventy-six distinct indicators encompassing areas which include the rule of law; security and safety; movement; religion; association, assembly, and civil society; expression and information; legal system and property rights; freedom to trade internationally; and regulation.

According to the Human Population Review for 2021, theocratic government is prevalent in several of the Muslim-majority countries ranked at the bottom of the Human Freedom Index, and I uphold this without in any way intending to excuse secular liberal democracies for their own abuses of freedom. The denial of freedoms and suppression of dissent are of course also evident to a varying degree in many other countries, whether Muslim or otherwise, as in China (ranked 150 in the HFI), Russia (126), Turkey (139) and Venezuela (164). It is also worrying that according to the latest Social Progress Index (SPI) the world is declining significantly on personal rights – 116 of the 168 countries covered by the index have seen individual rights rolled back since 2011. 'While not universal, this trend is apparent across all regions and levels of social and economic development,' it concluded. The consistently low ranking, however, of Muslim-majority countries inevitably prompts one to question the extent of the role of religion in bolstering authoritarian rule.

In answer to this, let us be very clear that religion has historically played a transformational role in the advancement of freedom in many societies. As I have already pointed out, Quaker 'radicals' played a significant role in movements promoting the abolition of slavery in Britain at the beginning of the nineteenth century, as well as many other areas of institutional reform. The example of the abolition of the slave trade is particularly instructive. William Wilberforce's famous four-hour long speech in the House of Commons in 1789 (described as one of the greatest speeches ever given in the House) advocating this momentous reform was delivered to a largely hostile audience entrenched in self-interest.

A compelling idea in his speech was the absolute clarity of his moral judgement, derived from his Christian faith, that the trade was so 'irremediable and wicked' that the consequences of its abolition had absolutely no bearing on the issue: in other words, the damage done to people's economic interests was irrelevant and the moral justice of the cause overrode all other considerations. We should not of course forget that Wilberforce himself was the parliamentary spokesman for a tireless campaign whose driving force had been another Christian, the Church of England pastor Thomas Clarkson, with strong support from the Quakers.

Clarkson dedicated his whole life to the cause, travelling over 35,000 miles on horseback to gather support around the country.

We should not imagine that the abolition of the slave trade was easily accomplished. Slavery was a virtually unquestioned part of life in the 1700s, supported by both Church and State, and regarded as an indispensable basis for Britain's wealth and economic prosperity. 'If you had proposed in the London of early 1787 to change all of this,' writes Adam Hochschild in *Bury the Chains*, 'nine out of ten people would have laughed you off as a crackpot. The tenth might have admitted that slavery was unpleasant but said that to end it would wreck the British Empire's economy.' There was little support within parliament for the abolitionists' campaign, and even in 1791 a bill had still not been pushed through. What turned the tide was an outcry of public outrage, 'a whole nation crying with one voice' in the words of the poet William Wordsworth—which was unprecedented in British history and the model for future citizens' movements and campaigning organizations. In 1792, following a mass public petition, the government of the day had no choice but to capitulate to public feeling. A bill abolishing the trade was finally passed in that year, though blocked by the House of Lords. It was another fifteen years before the trade was finally abolished in 1807, and another thirty years before slavery itself was ended in the British colonies.

What was truly remarkable about the popular campaign was its altruism. The fact is that the trade did not adversely affect the lives of British people at the time. The livelihoods of many people depended on it. They could have continued to turn a blind eye to it. And yet, the British people overwhelmingly took up a cause dedicated to an overriding principle of justice, and put the improvement of the lives of others above their own self-interest.

A true Muslim hero and model of chivalry who exemplified such universal humanity was Amir 'Abd al-Qadir, the leader of the struggle and insurgency in Algeria against the French colonial forces until his surrender in 1847 and eventual exile to Damascus in 1855. In 1860, when the Muslim and Druze militia of that city attacked the Christian quarter and killed over 3,000 persons, 'Abd al-Qadir and his personal guard rescued large numbers of Christians, bringing them to safety in his house and in the citadel.

The religious basis of the altruism and moral compass of such icons of humanitarian values as 'Abd al-Qadir and William Wilberforce cannot be denied, and reminds us only too urgently of the role religion can play as one of the principal drivers in advancing the cause of freedom. It is important to acknowledge this in the face of persistent distortion of fact, as for example in the oft-repeated fallacy that religion has been one of the chief causes of human conflict. The reality is that in the ten worst wars, massacres and genocides in human history, in which 248 million people have died, only 3 percent of those deaths can be accounted for by religious causes. Although the horrors of religious persecution cannot of course be swept under the carpet (and I am only too aware as a direct descendant of Huguenots that 70,000 of those French Protestants were massacred by Catholics in France on St Bartholomew's Eve in 1572), we need to affirm the way in which religious beliefs have inspired and served humanitarian values, including the cause of freedom.

A VERY SHORT HISTORY OF LIBERTY

Vinay Lal

1. The Greeks

'The idea of liberty is and has always been peculiar to the West', wrote the libertarian economist Ludwig von Mises, and 'what separates East and West is first of all the fact that the peoples of the East never conceived the idea of liberty. The imperishable glory of the ancient Greeks was that they were the first to grasp the meaning and significance of institutions warranting liberty.' Athens has long occupied a place in Western thought as the cradle of democracy and the love of liberty. This is in spite of the fact that the leading philosophers associated with this celebrated city-state were deeply suspicious of the ability of the *demos* (the people) to carry out the affairs of the polis with judiciousness. Plato's critique of democracy, his disdain for the hoi-polloi, and his adulation of the philosopher-king may not have been shared entirely by his mentor, Socrates, but the great itinerant philosopher who wandered about the agora was no enthusiast of democracy, or rule by the people. Aristotle was scarcely thrilled that in democracies, rather absurdly, 'the poor—they being in a majority, and the will of the majority being sovereign—are more sovereign than the rich', and he was prone, as a close reading of his *Politics* shows, to complain that in a democracy 'each man lives as he likes—or, as Euripides says, "For any end he chances to desire".' Each man was free to do as he pleased—an outlook that, as Plato put it in the *Republic*, could have no outcome other than one in which women and slaves were as free as citizens, an abomination that was to be feared as much as deplored. How, then, did Athens acquire a reputation as the home of democracy in the ancient world, as the very fount of those freedoms—of speech, expression, assembly—that the West holds dear?

Before there were the Greek philosophers, there was Herodotus—a master storyteller born most likely between 490 and 480 BCE, a slightly older contemporary of Socrates and nearly 100 years older than Aristotle. Cicero dubbed him 'the Father of History', the designation by which he has been known ever since, and from his long and colourful narrative of the Persian Wars that consumed, indeed ravaged, the Greek world from around 500–450 BCE we derive a keen sense of how the Greeks birthed the narrative of their love of liberty. Sometime around 470 BCE, the Persian king, Darius, had sent messengers to Greek cities seeking signs of their willingness to submit to his overlordship. In Athens, Herodotus tells us, the barbarians—the word by which the Greeks designated all foreigners, whose language was incomprehensible and seemed to be but little more than a series of incomprehensible sounds ('bar bar')—were thrown into a pit and in Sparta they were 'pushed into a well and told that if they wanted earth and water for the king, those were the places to get them'. It would appear that the Greeks, having violated the universal tradition which guaranteed messengers and diplomats immunity from harm, had shown themselves to be the true barbarians—but let that pass. Around ten years later, Darius' successor, Xerxes, similarly sent messengers, but this time without any 'request for submission'.

In the meantime, the Spartans had been unable 'to obtain favourable signs from their sacrifices', and some in Sparta thought that the city had gone through bad times as a punishment for the egregious offence committed against Darius' emissaries. Two Spartans, Sperchias, and Bulis, 'both men of good family and great wealth', decided to offer their lives 'to Xerxes in atonement for Darius' messengers who had been killed in Sparta'. On their way to Susa, they stopped at the court of the Persian general Hydarnes, the governor of Ionia. The young Spartans were treated royally, and during their conversation the relations between the Greeks and the Persians came up as a subject of discussion. Hydarnes advised his guests to seek Xerxes's friendship and offered himself as an example of a man who had gained immensely from his acceptance of subservience to the Persian king. 'Both of you, if you would only submit,' Hydarnes tells them, 'might find yourselves in authority over lands in Greece which he would give you.'

The well-meaning Hydarnes had doubtless not bargained for a lecture by way of an answer, but he got one: you have spoken out of turn, not fully aware of the situation, Sperchias and Bulis tell him, and you only know half of the story: 'You understand well enough what slavery is, but freedom you have never experienced, so you do not know if it tastes sweet or bitter. If you ever did come to experience it, you would advise us to fight for it not with spears only, but with axes too.' Herodotus does not record Hydarnes' response, but rather goes on to reinforce the message that he had so sharply delineated: the Greeks cherished their freedom and were not about to compromise or relinquish it for some other worldly gain and much less to appease an absolute ruler. When Sperchias and Bulis were brought into the presence of Xerxes, the king's bodyguards sought to compel the Spartans to prostrate themselves before the king. The men refused to do so, or even to 'push their heads down on to the floor': it was not the custom in Sparta, they averred, 'to worship a mere man like themselves', but they let it be known that they had been sent by Sparta to make amends 'for the murder of the Persian messengers in Sparta'. It was for Xerxes to do with them as he wished. The civilised Xerxes 'with truly noble generosity'—these are Herodotus's words— 'replied that he would not behave like the Spartans', and he spared their lives.

2. Oriental Despotism

Sperchias and Bulis returned home alive. Western commentators took home from this episode the lesson that, though the Persians were, as Aristotle was to say, 'ruled and enslaved', an Oriental king was a capricious character and could even be in a forgiving mood when least expected. Aristotle distinguishes, as nearly every other Greek did, the 'free' from the 'unfree' or 'enslaved'. Some scholars may not unreasonably argue that the cult of Harmodius and Aristogeiton in ancient Greece suggests that the love for freedom among all Greeks but especially Athenians was intrinsic to them, scarcely requiring the enslaved Persians as the deprived other to make them aware of their unique blessings. The two lovers, whose story is recounted by Herodotus, Plutarch, and many other ancient writers but most remarkably in Thucydides' *History of the Peloponnesian War*, were possibly the first martyrs to the Greek love of freedom: their assassination of Hipparchus, the younger son of Peisistratus—the tyrant of Athens in 547-46 BCE, 'tyrant' here signifying someone who ruled outside the framework of constitutional law—and unsuccessful murder attempt on Hippias, the older brother of Hipparchus and the reigning tyrant of Athens in 528 BCE, earned them the epithet of 'tyrannicides' and the undying gratitude of the Greeks. Nevertheless, it cannot be doubted that, once we move into the period of the flowering of Athenian democracy, the Persians become indispensable as the foil against which the Greek love of freedom shines in splendid isolation.

Though Thucydides did not place the Persian Wars at the centre of his narrative, focusing rather on war among the Greeks, it is remarkable that throughout his *History* he suggests, sometimes explicitly, that at least some of the Greeks were inclined to view the Athenians as the counterpart of the tyrannical Persians. The Spartans had fought the war, Thucydides tells us with evident sympathy, on the rallying cry of liberating the Greek world from the Athenians, and evidently some of the other Hellenes thought so too. The Thebans describe how, after the 'barbarians' (Persians) were pushed out and they recovered their constitution, 'the Athenians attacked the rest of Hellas and endeavoured to subjugate our country', but more forceful still is the scathing indictment offered by the Corinthians at the Spartan Congress of 432 BCE: an Athenian 'conquest', they say, can 'have no other end than slavery pure and simple'. Their appeal, as they attempt to cajole the other Greeks to join them in a common cause of waging war against Athens, unmistakably summons ghosts from the past, placing Athens squarely in the position of how Persia was placed just some decades ago: 'We must believe that the tyrant city that has been established in Hellas has been established against all alike, with a programme of universal empire, part fulfilled, part in contemplation; let us then attack and reduce it, and win future security for ourselves and freedom for the Hellenes who are now enslaved.'

The celebrated classicist, Moses Finley, proposed that the history of ancient Greece be studied not in terms of the slave-free antinomy, but rather as an effort to understand a society caught 'between slavery and freedom'. This seems like a considerable advance over the view that has only or largely glamourised Greece as the home of democracy, the fount of Western civilisation, and effectively the reason for the West's supposed incomparable superiority over the rest of the world, but the tendency to minimise the extent to which Greece was enveloped in slavery persists.

The Spartan slaves known as helots outnumbered free men and in consequence the Spartans periodically allowed them to be killed with impunity. The condition of slaves in Athens and among other Greeks may have been better but nevertheless slaves were property. Western commentators down to the present day delight in quoting a passage from the second century Indian text *Manusmriti*, where a passage states that a woman shall never be independent, being subject to the authority of her father when young, her husband when married, and her eldest son when a widow or in old age, to suggest the servitude under which Indian women laboured, but there is less evidence to support this view than the evidence which suggests that women in ancient Greece were always under the guardianship of their fathers or husbands and indeed lived their lives in virtual seclusion. Whatever the Greek conception of freedom, it was envisioned only for a tiny elite.

Still, even as these critiques of the storied idea of 'Greek freedom' are compelling, they obscure the more vital point that the Greek conception of freedom first birthed the idea of what in the period of European hegemony would be termed Oriental Despotism. The word despot is, not surprisingly, of Greek origin, and in Book III of *Politics*, Aristotle sought to distinguish despotism, the most debased form of monarchy, from tyranny. He saw despotism, which he associated with the Persians, not as unlawful because the people subjected to it did not object to it, viewing their relationship to the despot as analogous to the relationship of the slave to the master. The tyrant, on the other hand, usurps power, exercising it against the will of the people. Despotism, in Aristotle's view, was incompatible with the character of the Greeks, and their natural inclination to freedom moved them to revolt against tyranny at the slightest opportunity.

The answer to what exactly is 'despotism' came in the seventeenth century as Europe started to push towards Asia in search of markets and in its quest for world domination. Under despotism, neither the life nor the property of any person is secure—barring that of the despotic ruler himself; or, as Kant was to explain, despotism is 'the principle by which the state executes, on its own authority, laws that it has itself made. Under despotism, the public will is therefore treated by the monarch as his individual will'. Kant, however, was merely echoing what other European philosophers had argued. For most of them, Francois Bernier's *Travels in the Mogul Empire: AD 1656-1668* would have been the first sourcebook for their idea of the political history of the Orient, especially the Levant, Turkey, Persia, and the Indian subcontinent. Bernier introduces his principal idea early in the text, namely that 'the land throughout the whole empire is considered the property of the sovereign,' and thus there could not be the equivalent of 'earldoms, marquisates or duchies'. The Timurid Emperor, says Bernier, is the 'proprietor of every acre of land in the kingdom, excepting, perhaps, some houses and garden which he sometimes permits his subjects to buy, sell, and otherwise dispose of, among themselves'. In such a system, there could be 'little encouragement to engage in commercial pursuits', or to work the land and improve the crop, since the wealth thus accumulated could only have the effect of attracting the attention of the despot who had the power to deprive 'any man of the fruits of his industry'. But far more than the lack of private property was entailed by Oriental Despotism: as described by Bernier, 'the Kings of Asia are constantly living in the indulgence of monstrous vices'. The Oriental Despot was just as cruel, capricious, and (often) corpulent as he was lazy, lecherous, and libidinous.

The idea of Oriental Despotism became deeply embedded in European political theory, travelling almost effortlessly across the continental divide from French thinkers such as Montesquieu to eighteenth-century English writers such as Alexander Dow and Robert Orme who gave shape to the dominant strands of the colonial historiography of India. It is not possible to discuss the nuances of the staggeringly large literature that has developed around the subject, or to delineate the finer distinctions between absolutism and despotism as suggested by Montesquieu's writings: a European ruler, and Louis XIV comes to mind, could be an absolute ruler, but this did not preclude some in the kingdom from partaking in law and administration and of course from holding private property. Under despotism, there is but one individual, the despot; all others are slaves. John Logan was but one of thousands of the herd of Europeans who gave it as his opinion, at a lecture at Edinburgh University in 1780, that 'One form of government hath prevailed in Asia from the earliest records of history to the present time. A despot, under the name of Great King, or King of Kings, possesses supreme or unlimited power... Sovereign and slave compose the only distinction or rank in the East.' The annihilation of all other ranks of men, in order to 'exalt the monarch', was to the mind of his fellow Scotsman William Robertson the 'distinguishing and odious characteristic of the Eastern despotism'.

There is, to take another instantiation of the features of the discourse on Oriental Despotism as developed by the Enlightenment thinkers, an unswerving fealty to the idea of climatic determinism, the notion that despotism was the natural form of government for the tropics. The idea is elaborated upon in Montesquieu's *Persian Letters* (1721) and *Spirit of the Laws* (1748), but we can see its flowering in India where the East India Company found itself in possession of vast tracts of land in the east before its military expansion enabled it to bring most of India under its rule. Robert Orme, historiographer to the East India Company, drew attention to the 'effeminacy of the inhabitants of Indostan', doubting not that 'the general tendency' of Indians was to 'indolence' and a sedentary life, but if the real import of this might not be altogether clear to the less than discerning reader, Alexander Dow, author of the highly influential *The History of Hindostan* (1770), was there to explain how the inclement weather of the country had made the people effeminate, unmanly, and thus indisposed towards liberty. Hindustan, Dow wrote in his disquisition 'concerning the nature and origin of despotism', had been 'the seat of the greatest empires' and 'the nurse[ry] of the most abject slaves'. Hindus were 'mild, humane, obedient, and industrious, [and] they are of all nations on earth the most easily conquered and governed.' It was easy to be decisive in this matter: 'The languor occasioned by the hot climate of India, inclines the native to indolence and ease; and he thinks the evil of despotism less severe than the labour of being free.'

As freedom is to the Greeks and slavery is to Persians in the ancient period, so Enlightenment and liberty are to Europe what despotism is to the Orient in the period of European colonisation of the world. Writing on the Englishness of the English in the twentieth century, Orwell noted what is most distinctive about England, it being an eccentric nation of stamp-lovers, coupon-snippers, and dart-lovers, but what is most prominent is the air the Englishman breathes—an air that smells of freedom. 'The liberty of the individual', Orwell writes with abandon in the midst of World War II, 'is still believed in, almost as in the nineteenth century…It is the liberty to have a home of our own, to do what you like in your spare time, to choose your own amusements instead of having them chosen for you from above.' Just how closely Orwell hews to the reasoning found in generations of British scholar-administrator types who governed India and Burma, where Orwell himself was a member of the colonial police force, is amply demonstrated by the writings of John Malcolm, Thomas Munro, and others of the Scottish school. Munro, the Governor of Madras Presidency, in his long 1824 'Minute on the State of the Country, and Condition of the People' in Madras, opined that 'a law might be a very good one in England, and useless here. This arises from the different characters of the people. In England the people resist oppression, and it their spirit which gives efficacy to the law. In India the people rarely resist oppression,' and they only knew 'implicit submission' to the native princes. This was intended, in part, as a rebuke to James Mill, the father of John Stuart, who believed that good laws make a good government: a law is only as good, Munro is arguing, as the character of the people. Britain's success in India, wrote the Governor of Bombay John Malcolm, could be attributed to the contrast that the native population were able to draw between the security and prosperity they now enjoyed and the 'misrule and violence' to which they had been subjected in the past. It all came down, as senior administrators across British possessions in India agreed, to something called 'character'. But Malcolm was not without hope for the natives, considering the long period of 'tyrannical rule' through which they had survived: 'Many of the moral defects of the Natives of India are to be referred to that misrule and oppression from which they are now in a great degree emancipated.'

3. *The Haitian Revolution*

It is, putting the matter mildly, altogether questionable whether the emancipation of 'the coloured races' from oppression mattered at all to Europeans. If France and the English colonies on the eastern seaboard of what would become the United States were being swept by revolutionary fervour in the late eighteenth century, it is remarkable that the greatest expression of the aspiration for freedom should down to the present day remain largely unrecognised. On the night of 22–23 August 1791, thirteen years after Jefferson authored the American Declaration of Independence and two years after the onset of the French Revolution which introduced the dream embodied in the slogan, 'Liberty, Equality, Fraternity', a slave rebellion broke out in the parishes of Acul and Limbé in Saint-Domingue, a French colony in the Caribbean. The rebellion spread to the rest of the colony and paved the way for the creation of Haiti, the first free black republic in the world, in 1804. Unlike the much-celebrated American colonists, who were free men and women, and whom the French aided in their own quest for supremacy in North America, the black slaves were poor, hungry, poorly armed, and hunted men who not only had to face the might of French arms but British troops who arrived in 1793 in an ignominious, wretched, and characteristically opportunistic attempt to attach the Caribbean's wealthiest colony to their own empire.

By any measure, the accomplishment of the black slaves is incomparably greater than the achievement of the white American colonists who, having established a free republic for themselves, set about to entomb black slaves in a living death and continue their wholesale slaughter of the native Americans. Much ink has been squandered over the supposed ambivalence of the founding fathers and others of their ilk about the institution of slavery, and the difficulty of reconciling the great principles put forward by the Enlightenment about universal reason, the dignity of the individual, and the human aspiration for freedom to the bare and brutal fact of the ubiquity of slave-ownership among the colonists. But this attempt to project moral anguish on the part of the unrepentant should be summarily dismissed for the moral insincerity, intellectual dishonesty, and sleight of hand that it is. Yet, more than two hundred years after the Haitian Revolution and the death of its greatest figure, Toussaint Louverture, who died in a French prison in 1803 and did not live to see the proclamation of the sovereign state of Haiti by his deputy, Jean-Jacques Dessalines, on 1 January 1804, 'neither Toussaint's astounding career not the successful struggle for Haitian independence, figures very prominently in standard history textbooks'. Such is the assessment of a recent biographer of Toussaint, but if anything he underestimates the extent to which the Haitian Revolution has been eviscerated in the popular imagination of the West and diminished if not wilfully ignored by professional historians. Napoleon was determined to obliterate Toussaint from living memory, and his biographer states 'his body was interred in an unmarked grave': 'There was to be no martyrdom for Toussaint Louverture, and there would be no relics either.' The intellectuals and historians of the established schools have, let us say, taken their cue from Napoleon: thus, in *The Birth of the Modern World 1780-1914*, a sweeping and yet finely detailed foray into the long nineteenth century by the late C.A. Bayly, a work described by Niall Ferguson as 'a masterpiece', the Haitian Revolution gets a mere two sentences, just another factotum among thousands.

The inimitable C.L.R. James, the Trinidadian writer whose account of the Haitian Revolution is racier than most novels, tells us just exactly what has been at the heart of the Western refusal to recognise the singular importance of a world-historical transformation that, in the words of Haitian-born anthropologist Michel-Rolph Trouillot, belonged to the realm of the 'unthinkable'. 'The slaves had revolted', James wrote plainly in his 1938 classic, *The Black Jacobins*, 'because they wanted to be free. But no ruling class ever admits such things'. The notion that black people, much as white people, may aspire for freedom was an utter novelty, an idea as incomprehensible as any to people in the West—even to the great Enlightenment philosophers. At that time, Saint-Domingue produced three-quarters of the world's sugar, and it exported 60 per cent of all the coffee produced in Europe; moreover, it accounted for a third of the Atlantic slave trade. The treatment meted out to the slaves need not be recounted in detail, and the lamentation of one slave who excoriated the slave-owners will suffice: 'Have they not hung up men with heads downward, drowned them in sacks, crucified them on planks, buried them alive, crushed them in mortars? Have they not forced them to eat excrement? Have they not thrown them into boiling cauldrons of cane syrup? Have they not put men and women inside barrels studded with pikes and rolled them down mountainsides into the abyss?'

No wonder, then, that in 1790, only months before the slaves rose in revolt, one French colonist wrote to his wife in France that 'there is no movement among our Negroes.' Life was tranquil, the slaves were 'obedient', and it was bliss to be alive: 'We sleep with doors and windows wide open. Freedom for Negroes is a chimera.' As if to shatter this great delusion, James writes, 'the slaves destroyed tirelessly. Like the peasants in the Jacquerie or the Luddite wreckers, they were seeking their salvation in the most obvious way, the destruction of what they knew was the cause of their sufferings; and if they destroyed much it was because they had suffered much'—and this was long before the revolution would take a far more violent turn. In the United States, a black person counted as 3/5ths of a person, and in Paris the Count of Mirabeau, objecting to the fact that the colonists had counted their slaves as persons with the sole object of increasing their representation in the National Assembly, begged to remind them that 'we have taken into consideration neither the number of our horses nor that of our mules'. The ontological order of the 'modern' West had no place for the black as a man: as Trouillot writes, sparsely but unsparingly, '*in 1791, there is no public debate on the record, in France, in England, or in the United States on the right of black slaves to achieve self-determination, and the right to do so by way of armed resistance*' (italics in original).

4. John Stuart Mill

History, for all the sophisticated debates that are thought to have energised the discipline over the previous few decades, still revolves around the 'event'. That is all the more true of popular history. The Haitian Revolution was, in the historiography of the West, a non-event; or, in the language of Trouillot, who calls to mind the inability of the greatest minds to comprehend that the lowly slaves desired freedom as much as they did, 'The Haitian Revolution thus entered history with the peculiar characteristic of being unthinkable even as it happened'. The more enlightened among the European thinkers exulted in the French Revolution, at least before 'The Terror' crept in and wrought havoc, as the apotheosis of the idea of the individual as a rights-bearing citizen and the enshrinement of the faculty of reason, but it required the Haitian Revolution to extend the gains of the French Revolution. *The Declaration of the Rights of Man and Citizen* was just what it said: women were neither men nor citizens, indeed black men were not men either as they were incomplete as human beings. That was its most obvious limitation, and the Girondist, actress, and playwright Olympe de Gouges said as much in her Declaration of the Rights of Woman. Still, from the vantagepoint of today, one can be critical of this document for another monstrosity, namely its anthropocentric vision of the world and its conception of liberty gained at the expense of nature. 'There is no document of civilisation', Walter

Benjamin once opined, 'which is not at the same time a document of barbarism.'

The history of freedom in the West has been generally cast as a story of incremental progress, a story of the constant pushback against liberty and the heroic struggle to keep the torch of liberty burning amidst repression and tyranny. The democratic ideals of ancient Greece seemed to be reincarnated in the political aspirations and ideas of the Jacobins of post-revolutionary France—and C.L.R. James, cognisant of this history, cleverly styled the Haitian revolutionaries 'Black Jacobins'. However, the first French Republic was short-lived: following the Terror, Napoleon gained power and crowned himself Emperor. This betrayal is best conveyed in the story of Beethoven's *Eroica* ('Heroic') Symphony, which the great composer had initially intended to dedicate to Napoleon. But when it became known that Napoleon had declared himself Emperor of France, Beethoven struck his name from the title page which originally bore the inscription: '*Sinfonia grande intitolata Bonaparte del Sigr Louis van Beethoven*' ('Grand Symphony titled Bonaparte by Mr Ludwig van Beethoven'). 'So he too is nothing more than an ordinary man', Beethoven reportedly told a pupil, 'Now he will trample on all human rights and indulge only his own ambition. He will place himself above everyone and become a tyrant'. But when Waterloo did Napoleon in, the monarchists rather than democrats gained the upper hand. The Revolutions of 1848, not least of all in France, held out the promise of restoring republican ideals, but everywhere they were crushed and greatly disillusioned the liberals. The second French republic lasted but four years, 1848–52, as Louis-Napoleon engineered a coup and throned himself at the head of the Second French Empire.

The restoration of monarchy did not, however, entail the complete loss of democratic principles, and in France universal manhood suffrage was retained. It is around this time that, in Britain, John Stuart Mill published what is perhaps the most well-known exposition in Western political theory of the idea of liberty. However, even if it is conventional and altogether reasonable to read his essay, *On Liberty* (1859), as a carefully reasoned work on the unimpeachable claims of liberty and as a treatise on 'the nature and limits of the power which can be legitimately exercised by society over the individual', it can with equal plausibility be viewed as yet another chapter in what I have described as the constant tussle between the adherents of liberty and the substantially greater number of intellectuals and writers who championed various forms of illiberalism and autocratic rule. By the early nineteenth century if not earlier, the industrial revolution had in Britain created 'the poor' and an urban proletariat who were sometimes viewed as only marginally less savage than colonised people. Though Mill may have been gravely concerned by encroaching state power and the constraints it placed upon people's liberty, calls for state intervention to bring the hoi polloi and the rejects of society under the rubric of social order were common. It was well and good to speak of liberty, but in neighbouring Ireland the English landlords, having forced Irish peasants onto small plots of land and made them wholly dependent on the potato, could doubtless be held responsible for genocide when the 'Great Hunger' stuck. Between 1845–48, at least a million Irish died, the victims as well of the economic doctrine of *laissez-faire* and the view that the poor, a blight on society, were deserving of death. Before the English colonised and brutalised India and parts of Africa, they colonised the Irish—and their various other alleged inferiors, including the poor and women. We shall return to this matter later, but for the moment it suffices to register the truth, unpalatable as it must be to John Bull, that *English liberty was always parasitic on the misfortunes and oppression of others.* The race question was not simply to persist throughout the nineteenth century, but rather got amplified as the European powers engaged in the scramble for Africa and each outdid the other in brutality and tyranny in an attempt not merely to extract profits but supposedly to civilise those who had tasted nothing of 'freedom'. What is striking is that, whether one is speaking of the frightful encroachments upon the popish Irish or the Caliban Africans, it was not only the state but the force of society that allowed for a permissive oppression.

Where Mill differs from Enlightenment philosophers, as the preceding discussion may suggest, is that he recognised that the source of oppression is not only the state but the power of society. Most discussions of Mill swivel around the conception of 'negative freedom': the phrase is not his and is of course drawn from Isaiah Berlin's famous essay on 'two concepts of liberty'. The external restraint that weighed down most heavily on the exercise of liberty, to Mill's way of thinking, was the coercive force of moralism that was the most distinctive feature of Victorian society. He was equally critical of the pernicious force of custom as a hindrance to the exercise of liberty, and he attributed the subjection of women, against which he authored a critique with his wife Harriet Taylor, to custom and the force of intolerant public opinion. Neither society nor state was within its rights to censor public opinion or restrain individuals from the pursuit of their activities unless such activities were calculated to produce harm to certain persons or the public good. Given his views, then, which point to Mill as an enlightened figure with an admirably ecumenical conception of liberty, one might expect that he similarly envisioned an expansion of liberty for colonised people. On the other hand, if one keeps in mind the insights of recent scholarship which has to great effect demonstrated that liberalism could simultaneously entail the commitment to political rights and advocate for limited authority to the state as well as justify imperialism, it should come as no surprise that Mill's broad-minded outlook of empire should appear to shrivel when it came to the question of empire.

Mill's *Considerations of Representative Government* offers some insights into his thinking on whether, and to what extent, colonised subjects were fit for liberty. The title of Chapter 4, 'Under What Conditions Representative Government Is Inapplicable', alone indicates the tenor of his thought. The book is liberally sprinkled with what can only be described as specious claims and shibboleths about the 'Orient'. Some of his views may be put down to the temper of his times, among them his adherence to the openly racist idea of an evolutionary scale so that the state of a people, 'in point of culture and development,' can be witnessed as ranging 'downwards to a condition very little above the highest of the beasts'. Mill describes his aversion to slavery, describing it as 'repugnant' to the 'government of law' and says that he is unable to envision its adoption 'under any circumstances whatever in modern society' as that would be a relapse worse than barbarism, but also describes the circumstances under which despotism may be viewed as acceptable. Good despotism is distinguished from bad despotism, just as legal despotism is differentiated from illegal despotism. What is still more disturbing and barely recognised by most of his biographers, who have sidestepped his long (and only) professional career as an employee of the East India Company, where he toiled his entire adult life and rose to the rank of Examiner of Indian Correspondence in 1856 before writing a rather pathetic plea arguing against the abolition of the Company at the end of the Rebellion of 1857–58 which saw India being transferred to the Crown, is that Mill wrote one 'dispatch' after another justifying the annexation of native or princely states. Mill himself gave but one terse sentence in his autobiography to describe his life-long association with India: 'In May, 1823, my professional occupation and status for the next thirty-five years of my life, were decided by my father's obtaining for me an appointment from the East India Company…immediately under himself.' Evidently, the place which provided Mill his livelihood mattered not a jot. How could it? The celebrated architect of the idea of liberty was, as his 1700 policy opinions on Indian native states demonstrably establish, a firm believer in 'benevolent despotism' and perhaps the most subtle defender of the British empire.

5. *English Colonialism*

13 April 1919 was a warm day, the first day of the spring harvest festival in north India. In the late afternoon, Reginald Dyer, an acting Brigadier-General in the Indian Army born in Murree, in what is now Pakistan, ordered fifty Gurkha and Balochi riflemen to commence firing without warning upon an unarmed crowd of 15,000–20,000 Indians gathered at an enclosure called the Jallianwala Bagh in Amritsar, a stone's throw from the Golden Temple. Public meetings had been prohibited in the wake of public disturbances, but many in the crowd, quite likely a majority, would have come in from the neighbouring villages and would not have heard of the order that had been passed. This is not to say that Dyer was under any circumstances justified in instituting firing; that he came determined to kill people is demonstrated by the fact that he brought two armoured cars, which he was prevented from using only because the sole passage into the enclosure was too narrow to accommodate them. The firing ended only when the troops ran out of ammunition; most of the 1,650 rounds met their target, judging from the official tally of 379 dead and some 1,200 wounded. Some Indian estimates of how many people were killed ran to about 1,000. As the narrator Saleem in Salman Rushdie's novel *Midnight's Children* recalls, Dyer told his men: 'Good shooting.' The men had done their duty, order had apparently been restored: 'We have done a jolly good thing.'

British censorship prevented the news of the massacre from being reported in India at all until weeks later. Not unreasonably, many Indians were enraged; moreover, unlike in the nineteenth century, they could scarcely be ignored. The British government in London sought to quell the uproar with their characteristic weapon, 'the committee of inquiry', hoping that the investigation would confirm what they believed to be true of themselves, namely their fidelity to the idea of 'fair play' and 'the rule of law'. The English in India complained bitterly that the inquiry had been forced upon the British government in India and that the authority and knowledge of 'the man on the spot' had been impugned by arm-chair politicians in Whitehall. The story of all that transpired is too long to be told here, but the debate that took place in the House of Commons, where Indian affairs ordinarily excited no more than a yawn, is of exceptional interest. The Secretary of State for India, Edwin Montagu, while applauding Dyer for his long years of service to the Empire, argued that his desire to 'teach a moral lesson to the whole of the Punjab' had led him to embrace 'a doctrine of terrorism'. He then went on to charge Dyer for 'indulging in frightfulness'. The grave import of this accusation would not have been lost on his fellow Parliamentarians: 'frightfulness' was the English rendering of *schrecklichkeit*, the word first used to describe the terrorism inflicted upon Belgian civilians by the German army in World War I. That an English army officer should stand accused of pursuing the policies of militaristic Germans was an intolerable idea, and some English thought that Montagu, a Jew, had his own ulterior motives for daring to equate the freedom-loving English with the hated Huns. However, Winston Churchill then arose to speak, and the patriotism of this scion of the establishment could scarcely be questioned. The 'slaughter' in Amritsar, Churchill thundered, was 'without precedent or parallel in the modern history of the British Empire'. Dyer, Churchill argued, had intended to terrorise not just the whole crowd 'but the whole district or the whole country', and had in doing so shamed England. 'Frightfulness is not a remedy known to the British pharmacopoeia' and the British empire scarcely required the 'aid' of 'terrorism'. 'Such ideas' as Dyer had brought forward in committing mass slaughter were 'absolutely foreign to the British way of doing things'.

What had happened at Amritsar was 'an extraordinary event, a monstrous event, an event which stands in singular and sinister isolation'. But was it all that exceptional? It has been a nearly unquestioned canon of scholarship, even if more critical voices are being heard these days, to argue that British colonialism was a relatively benign affair, certainly in comparison with, say, the genocide and brutalities unleashed upon black people in Leopold's Congo or the wholesale atrocities against the Herero perpetrated by the Germans in present-day Namibia. Gandhi is thought to have succeeded against the British precisely because they were British, or, to put it rather more colloquially, jolly good fellows. One commentator after another in the West has argued, with a little more than smugness, that had Gandhi attempted mass non-violent resistance against the Nazis, he would have been effortlessly crushed and never heard from again. In the British public sphere, especially, the view most commonly encountered is the one espoused by former British Prime Minister David Cameron who on a visit to India in 2013 remarked, 'I think there is an enormous amount to be proud of in what the British Empire did and was responsible for'. He was only emulating one of his predecessors, Gordon Brown, who on a visit to East Africa in 2005 as Chancellor of the Exchequer candidly declared, 'I've talked to many people on my visit to Africa and the days of Britain having to apologise for its colonial history are over. We should celebrate much of our past rather than apologise for it'. These two gentlemen might be given a long leash since neither has any claim to being a scholar, but academics such as Niall Ferguson and other mighty stalwarts of the good old Empire are staunchly in the camp that believes that the British brought the 'rule of law' to their colonies. Such a view seems oblivious of the consideration that jurists, lawyers, and administrators have been known to acquiesce in, and then legitimise, the illegal and brutal seizure of power, as happened in Nazi Germany, and similarly it would be tiresome to list all the barbarities inflicted by the English upon the people they colonised across a wide swathe of Asia, Africa, and the Caribbean. To set an example to the country when a rebellion that threatened their rule in India broke out in 1857-58, the British tied captured rebels to canon and blew them into the sky, and the Mau Mau Rebellion in Kenya a century later was suppressed with mass killings and every strategy of torture that exists in the playbook.

It is to the credit of postcolonial theorists that they have shown how British barbarism was dressed up in the language of liberal reform and the supposedly principled struggle to enhance the sphere of freedom. It is also perhaps the case that the Anglophone empires have been far more diligent and successful in pressing the case that they have stood for 'liberty' and the 'rule of law' than other European colonial powers. Britain's critically important place in the Atlantic slave trade has been occluded in most histories, and a recent critical assessment of Britain's slave empire avers that 'Britons were taught—and many still believe—that slavery had never been a foundation of their country's commercial prosperity but was a millstone that needed to be removed so capitalism could truly flourish.' Political philosophers and liberal commentators point to inconsistencies in the life and work of John Locke, who opened his *Two Treatises of Civil Government* with the famous proclamation that 'slavery is so vile and miserable an estate of man' that it was inconceivable that 'an Englishman, much less a gentleman, should plead for it', but nevertheless played a principal role in authoring the constitutions of the Carolinas which guaranteed Englishmen 'absolute power and authority' over slaves in the colonies. Locke's deep involvement in slavery, one scholar has argued, offers 'an embarrassment of riches', but it would be almost banal to suggest that hypocrisy is just as natural to the English as the bite is to the mosquito. The problem ran much deeper. The British empire transported nearly 3.5 million slaves to America between 1660-1807, more than all other slave-trading nations put together. The commerce in enslaved Africans was immensely lucrative and the empire that they helped build, while a prison for them, was a gateway to religious and political dissenters, the mediocre, the wannabees, criminals, and numerous others who could build a life for themselves and then sing hosannas to 'British liberty'.

6. Mohandas Gandhi

The slave trade and likewise outright genocide apart, European colonial powers and particularly the British acted on the principle that people can be allowed to sink into a morass of poverty and depression and even die in many ways with little if any consequence for the colonisers. Before England colonised India and Africa, it colonised the Irish and brutalised its own working-class and women. It is now fashionable to speak of the 'weaponisation' of this or that thing, and the present unprovoked war launched by the Russians in Ukraine has brought forth many commentaries on the weaponisation of hunger by Putin as his army attempts to starve the recalcitrant Ukrainians into submission and the antecedents of this in the famine (the 'Holodomor') that Stalin brought upon Ukraine in 1932-33 which may have caused the death of as many as 3.5 million Ukrainians. But about the same proportion of people, and perhaps more as a percentage of the population, were killed in 'The Great Hunger' in Ireland when the potato crop failed in the mid-1840s over three successive years. Ireland lost at least a quarter of its population of 8 million: one million died and another million emigrated, largely to the United States. As the work of Amartya Sen and other scholars in his wake has decisively shown, famines are never caused entirely, and often not at all, by food shortages, and this was very much the case in Ireland. It is British policies that led to the macabre outcome: a succession of draconian Penal Laws forbid Irish Catholics from buying land, pushed them into increasingly smaller plots of land, and forced them to adopt the potato as the only crop that would give them sufficient calories and thereby permit their survival. When the crop failed, the dominant economic doctrine of *laissez-faire* was invoked to argue that there was no need to aid the millions who were afflicted. It is this sadism that doomed the Irish to annihilation. In India, it is not too much to say that British rule was bookended by mass starvation: after the initial conquest of Bengal, as many as ten million people are thought to have been killed in the famine that occurred in the midst of the anarchy introduced by the British, and the Bengal famine of 1943, which took a toll of around 2–3 million, was, it seems, their swan song as they prepared to exit India.

Though the anti-colonial critique would follow many trajectories, and many exemplary figures may be summoned as having contributed to the imperative task of decolonisation, it remained to Mohandas Gandhi to launch a critique that both most creatively addressed the colossal shortcomings in the Western narrative of liberty and also offers the prospect for a far more radical, equitable, and ecumenical conception of freedom. Gandhi had at best an ambivalent intellectual relationship with the Western intellectual and political tradition. He was a relentless if discerning critic of industrial modernity, and, though this takes some by surprise, he did not chafe at describing Western civilisation as 'satanic' when he thought it necessary. He is famously if apocryphally reported, on his last visit to Britain and the European continent in 1931, to have responded to the query about what he thought of Western civilisation with the quip, 'I think it would be a very good idea.' However, if all that should be inferred as pointing to the corrosive influence of nationalism upon him, and, as some of his critics would like to argue, his intellectual philistinism, it must be noted that Gandhi strove for a deep understanding of what he conceived to be dissenting spiritual and political traditions within the West. To add to the formulation I have earlier offered, of how the West colonised its own supposed inferiors—the Irish, Slavs, women, working class, among others—it may be argued that Gandhi was quite firm in his understanding that the West also rendered recessive and marginal its own dissenting intellectuals. Thus, Thoreau became the brunt of jokes as an eccentric who tried to pass himself off as a high-minded idealist when he was in reality, as the author of a recent polemic in *The New Yorker* avers, a miserable misogynist who was 'narcissistic, fanatical about self-control', 'as parochial as he was egotistical', indeed a humourless 'adolescent' suffering from 'comprehensive arrogance'. Similarly, it was the later Tolstoy, who advocated for the religion of Jesus, which he viewed in *The Kingdom of God Is Within You* as a call for radical nonviolence and an anarchist repudiation of state authority, and which he distinguished sharply from the institutionalised religion of Christianity, whom Gandhi embraced. This Tolstoy, a far cry from the lionised novelist, was more likely to be seen as a madman.

Gandhi certainly had much in common with the renowned liberal theorists of liberty in the West. As the founding editor of several newspapers, and as someone who was convicted on charges of having incited disaffection against the British government in India by writing and publishing seditious material, Gandhi knew very well the value of free speech and expression and he upheld that ideal in hundreds of pieces over the course of five decades. Unlike many human rights activists the world over who seek more state intervention to secure rights, even when they understand that the state is often the most egregious violator of rights, Gandhi was profoundly apprehensive of the state and reposed greater confidence in the individual as the agent of social change. 'Any man who subordinates his will to that of the State', he wrote in 1910, 'surrenders his liberty and thus become a slave.' This could have easily come from the pen of Locke, Montesquieu, or Benjamin Constant. Upon being asked by the Austrian journalist Alice Schalek, who interviewed him at Sabarmati

Ashram on 20 March 1928, 'What do you mean by freedom?', Gandhi replied: 'I want the freedom to make mistakes, and freedom to unmake them, and freedom to grow to my full height and freedom to stumble also. I do not want crutches.' Here one detects what appears to be the unmistakable voice of John Stuart Mill.

One might even think that Gandhi drew upon the natural law and natural rights tradition of the seventeenth and eighteenth centuries in Europe. Sometimes he appears to be speaking in the voice of Jefferson and the American Founding Fathers, as is suggested by this passage from 1931: 'Freedom is not worth having if it does not connote freedom to err and even to sin. If God Almighty has given the humblest of His creatures the freedom to err, it passes my comprehension how human beings, be they ever so experienced and able, can delight in depriving other human beings of that precious right.' But if there is nothing more to Gandhi than this, in what respect can he been seen as having withheld his approbation of the liberal view and similarly gone beyond the common anti-colonial denunciations of Western hypocrisy? Though Gandhi's conception of liberty is deserving of a full-length study, it will be sufficient to hint briefly and in the broadest brushstrokes at some elements of his philosophical outlook. First, where Locke, Mill, and other classical theorists principally argued about *freedom from restraint*, Gandhi speaks of *freedom through restraint*. A passage from 1928, where he expounds on the 'limits to freedom', gives some hint of his thinking: 'Freedom, both individual and religious, has always had and will always have many limits. Religion does not hanker after rights, it hungers for restraints and restrictions. Anyone who knows religion and practices it does not think in terms of his rights.' Surprisingly, though Gandhi is celebrated as an advocate of human rights and was invited by the United Nations to issue a statement when the UN Declaration of Human Rights was being formulated, he rarely spoke in the language of rights; when he did so, it was invariably with an awareness that every right comes with a corresponding duty. Gandhi, while of course agreeing upon broader principles such as the unimpeachable fact that every human being has a right to his or her dignity, would very much have been at odds with those in the human rights community. The practitioner of a religion thinks not of rights but, remarkably, *hungers* for restraints: as the author of the second century CE *Yoga Sutras*, Patanjali, would have said, 'the real dimensions of freedom are revealed only in the act of discipline [restraint] which in turn is rendered superfluous by the reality that its practice discloses.'

Why, then, had Indians become enslaved to the British? To this question that haunted every Indian nationalist, Gandhi had a reply that was even more unsettling. To be sure, the colonisers were animated by ambition, greed, the will for power, and much else, but Gandhi averred that the Indians were drawn to them by their own moral failures, their lack of discipline, and the fact that they were seduced by the glitter of the material civilisation of the West. The self-righteous enforcers of political correctness or rather ideological puritans who are found everywhere these days will at once conclude that Gandhi is 'blaming the victim'. There is no reply, at one level, to such a jejune rejoinder. But let us follow Gandhi, in summary. The argument first unfolds in *Hind Swaraj or Indian Home Rule*, an extraordinary work and, I daresay, an unrivalled milestone in the human quest for freedom. True, Gandhi advocates for 'home rule' or self-determination, autonomy from colonial rule, but the word *swaraj* (swa=self; raj=rule) also signifies rule over oneself, or the rule over one's meaner instincts. Before one can aspire to political freedom, much less demand it, one must contain one's baser instincts. Gandhi was to explicate on this often: the language in which he did so might vary, but the intent was always clear: 'The outward freedom therefore that we shall attain will only be in exact proportion to the inward freedom to which we may have grown at a given moment.' This was as true in India or Africa as it was in the US or Europe, and Gandhi did not therefore doubt, as he noted apropos of an exchange with an interlocutor in the United States, that 'even in the land of so-called freedom, the real freedom has still to come'.

The argument has more nuances than is possible to convey here, but it is transparent that the colonisers themselves also have baser instincts—and they too need to be emancipated from their own worst tendencies. If anything, the colonisers are even more enslaved than the colonised: as Gandhi would have argued, the slave never views the slave-owner as less than fully human, but this is assuredly not the case with the slave-owner who does not confer upon his slaves the ontological dignity of a full human existence. 'Let not the 12 million Negroes be ashamed of the fact that they are the grand-children of slaves', wrote Gandhi in response to a request from W.E.B. Du Bois for a message for African Americans, adding: 'There is no dishonour in being slaves. There is dishonour in being slave-owners.' The anti-colonial movement that Gandhi spearheaded to secure India's freedom was at the same time a principled endeavour to free Britain from its own base instincts; it was an invitation, and it is a testament to Gandhi's magnificent ecumenism that some Britons accepted it as such, for Britain to enter into a more expansive world of freedom. It is striking that, at every stage of the struggle, commencing with Gandhi's activities in South Africa, that he was never in want of support from Englishmen and women. They understood, as the world needs to understand, that freedom is indivisible.

7. Freedom's Future

A more thoroughgoing exploration of Gandhi's worldview and praxis yields further insights into the continuing struggle for freedom. The day before his assassination on 30 January 1948, he had prepared a draft constitution for the Indian National Congress, the principal nationalist organisation that had been at the helm of the freedom struggle. It was in part informed by the views that he articulated in public on 27 January, when he averred that 'the Congress has won political freedom, but it has yet to win economic freedom, social, and moral freedom. These freedoms are harder than the political, if only because they are constructive, less exciting and not spectacular.' The message was, predictably, lost upon the leaders of the Congress who were already squabbling over power. Much the same can be said for what transpired in other countries where the anti-colonial struggle led to bitter ideological struggles, often violent, between warring factions. The struggle in India, however, was distinct in that Gandhi was the author of the wholly revolutionary idea of mass nonviolent resistance. That entailed another expansion in the meaning of freedom: there is no freedom unless one is willing to take the suffering of others upon oneself, unless one is willing to bear the cross. The leaders of the civil rights movement in the United States, the anti-apartheid movement in South Africa, and the farm workers movement among Mexican Americans, as well as the proponents of civil disobedience who have blockaded nuclear sites and installations in various countries are among the many activists who have acted on this principle.

The Western notion of freedom has for some time been principally tethered to the idea of the rights-bearing individual. The apotheosis of this idea seemed to have been achieved when the Berlin Wall came crashing down, the Soviet Union fragmented, and what Churchill called the 'Iron Curtain' was lifted. Commentators such as Francis Fukuyama were beside themselves with ecstasy and pronounced 'the end of history': the Western notion of freedom had clearly triumphed, the dignity of the individual everywhere—or at least in Europe, which was in reality sufficient—had been recognised, and the principles of the free market economy, which flow from the recognition that is given to the individual, had been validated as the only basis on which economic exchanges in and among societies can be contemplated. Apparently, on this view, the end of human existence is to be able to choose wisely between fifty varieties of toothpaste—or, as in the United States, between dozens of firearms at the local gun shop. In the aftermath of what is described as the creation of a unipolar world, the United States attempted to push democracy among benighted peoples clearly wanting in basic freedoms. Strangely, nearly every American enterprise over the course of nearly two centuries in the pursuit of 'Manifest Destiny', and to spread the blessings of liberty, has involved coups, the sponsorship of genocidal regimes, or outright war. It is not less ironical that democracy is now in considerable peril in its supposed citadel.

Though the language of 'rights' can be traced back to the eighteenth century, a rights-based discourse only started to achieve prominence in the aftermath of World War II and the creation of a new architecture of global governance which included covenants such as the UN Declaration of Human Rights. States may choose to deny or limit certain rights to individuals, but in principle they are, or may be held, accountable for abrogating rights that are deemed inviolable. The tendency over the last few decades has been to expand the field of rights, such that the right to one's gender, to paid employment, to clean water and air, to what is called 'organic' food, to education in one's own culture and history, to dress as one chooses (or indeed to barely dress at all), to drive fuel-guzzling vehicles, and many other rights have been added to what were once only the right to liberty, the right to freedom of speech and expression, the right of assembly, and the right (extended over time to constituencies once excluded) to suffrage. The field of rights is ever expanding. It may be argued that there is some contraction, too, though such contraction is only another affirmation of rights. Thus, as an instance, we may consider the case recently brought to my attention of a prominent white male university professor who is well versed in the history and culture of Africa, and who is conversant in at least two African languages, who was told unequivocally by an African American student that he has no right to teach African history. Though in contemporary jargon this is termed 'cancel culture', it may also be understood as the affirmation by the student of her right to be taught by a person of African descent.

It may be that, taken to its logical end, rights discourse may yet be productive in ways that we have not yet anticipated or fully comprehended. Courts in India and New Zealand have declared that rivers have rights. If rivers have the right not to be polluted, surely mountains must have the right not to be mined just as birds and animals must have the right not to be deprived of their natural habitats? If the end of this line of reasoning is to produce a far less anthropocentric conception of our existence, then it may be said that a rights discourse offers a richer conception of our planetary existence. Yet, some will view the expansion of the rights of non-humans as possible only by the contraction of the rights of humans, a zero-sum scenario that echoes the narrative of liberty as it has developed in the West. Must our concept of liberty necessarily be attached only to the conception of rights? Rights talk is now part of the global common sense, but is there any common sense that is not socially constructed? It appears that we are from comprehending that freedom, too, speaks in many languages. It is, for example, a general tenet of Western thought that classical Chinese has no word for liberty and that the idea of liberty remains a novelty for most Chinese. However, in reading Confucius's *Analects*, one encounters a passage which suggests otherwise: 'The Master said, The gentleman is not a utensil.' A person, says Confucius, should not be treated merely as a utensil, that is as a means; or, as Kant put it, 'So act that you treat humanity, whether in your own person or in the person of any other, always at the same time as an end, never merely as a means.' Humankind, and the modern West, will have to start thinking about liberty for those who do not speak the language of liberty.

LIBERTY, HYPOCRISY, NEUTRALITY

Naomi Foyle

> And we are free
> Of Europe and Asia alike, at liberty
> To live ... which means to die slowly
>
> *from 'The Sunlight' by Ihor Pavlyuk,*
> *translated by Steve Komarnyckyj*
> in A Flight Over the Black Sea *(Waterloo Press, 2014)*

Bring back 2020. As if climate catastrophe, mass extinction, pandemic and surging inflation weren't enough to be dealing with, Europe, America, and Russia are mired in armed conflict in Ukraine, shattering post-war dreams of peaceful economic union, and pushing the twenty-first century over the threshold into a terrifying new world order. As the media fills with heart-breaking images of rampant atrocities committed by Russian soldiers, themselves being sacrificed wholesale by their leaders, and commentators offer bleak geopolitical prognoses, it feels a surreal privilege to be writing these words from my vantage point – a reasonably comfortable life unfolding on the pebbly shore of a small island. Here in Brighton, much as I have dedicated time each day to fundraising, editing, and translating for Ukrainian friends and colleagues, I can also, and do, read books and the *Guardian*, meet friends, collaborate on creative projects, go for a swim, surf the internet for insightful and informative perspectives on it all. How is it, I wonder, that I am free to shape my days, plan trips, die slowly in the most generous sense of the phrase, when my friends in Kyiv and Lviv, and so many in Gaza, Yemen, and elsewhere, live in fear of being buried alive in their own homes? I am not a political analyst, but as has long been the case for me, taking time to read and think and write about global injustice seems the least I can do with what increasingly seems the arbitrary gift of my time on this earth.

CRITICAL MUSLIM 42, SPRING 2022

What is immediately clear is that, while for Europeans this war still seems unthinkable, for Palestinians, Syrians, Iraqis, Yemenis, Afghanis, Burmese Rohingyas, and others, state terror, war, persecution, and torture have long been a permanent existential condition. The fact that America, Canada, Britain, and Europe have actively sponsored or passively allowed most of this suffering makes it difficult for many people, I know, to join the Western chorus of outrage at Putin's invasion of Ukraine, and outpour of compassion for its blonde, blue-eyed victims. I couldn't agree more that the hypocrisy and racism of both governmental and media responses to the war is staggering. The point of pointing out hypocrisy, though, is surely not to block the road to justice in a stance of self-righteous indignation, but to push forward down that long arcing path – to insist on liberty for all. And so I would like to respectfully urge all who value freedom to view the invasion of Ukraine as an opportunity to build solidarity – against our common enemies of autocracy, militarism, imperialism, racism, hypermasculinity, and other violent, hierarchical, exploitative mindsets, all of which threaten not just our own continued existence as a species.

Liberty & Rhetoric

The language of freedom is, of course, prone to rhetorical flourish. Such clarion calls are not necessarily hollow, however. Across the world, but especially in Europe and North America, Putin's invasion summoned stunned memories of Soviet tanks in Hungary and Prague, and Nazi forces in Poland. In governmental chambers across two continents, Western leaders have stood and applauded Ukrainian President Volodymyr Zelenskiy's insistence that, in resisting Russian occupation, his people are fighting not just for their own freedom but Europe's and the world's. Much as I hate to agree with Boris Johnson on anything, I believe this claim to be profoundly true. Not only are the Ukrainians fighting to defend their democracy, and by extension democratic values, against the palpable threat of totalitarianism, but we only have scant years to save the planet from runaway global warming – as environmentalist Bill McKibben has warned, given the Russian economy's fundamental dependence on oil and gas, success in that struggle depends hugely on victory for Ukraine. McKibben also makes the wider case that fossil fuels feed autocracy: 'hydrocarbons by their nature tend towards the support of despotism – they're highly dense in energy and hence very valuable; geography and geology means they can be controlled with relative ease. There's one pipeline, one oil terminal'. It is frustrating then, to observe that the world itself has not been entirely convinced by Zelenskiy and the West's dramatic declaration of global common cause.

Some so-called sceptics have in fact been poisoned by Putin's propaganda, a different kind of rhetoric altogether, Orwellian in its denial of plain facts, systemically rolled out by trolls and bots in a sinister attack on truth itself. Putin's stated goal in his 'special operation' is to 'de-Nazify' Ukraine and prevent the 'genocide' of Russian-speakers in the Donbas. But it is patently false that Ukraine is a Nazi country that persecutes Russians: the Ukrainian president is a Russian-speaking Jew from the East, and support for the far right has been steadily falling since 2012, when it won ten percent of the parliamentary vote, to six percent in 2014 and just over two percent in the last election, far less than in many European countries, and not enough to cross Ukraine's five percent electoral threshold and enter parliament. It is true that Neo-Nazi militia exist in the country (as they do in Russia and elsewhere), and the infamous white supremacist Azov Battalion has been integrated into the national army. External experts, however, see this as a purely pragmatic move: the public perceives the Battalion as a strong fighting unit, helping to defend Ukraine at a time of need. In addition, the Battalion is small, 1,000 men in a total armed force of 250,000, and since losing its first leader, who left to start a political party, has attracted new recruits mainly on the basis of its tough military reputation. In 2015, only about ten to twenty percent of Azov fighters considered themselves to be neo-Nazi. Still a problem, yes, but hardly evidence of a Nazi nation. Indeed, there's a strong argument that without the continued presence of Russian aggression in the East, this type of group would have long melted away, just like popular support for far-right parties.

As for genocide against Russian speakers in the East, there is no factual evidence whatsoever for this, and international support for the idea is non-existent: the number of deaths in the region plummeted between 2014, when 2,084 people were killed to 2021, when eighteen people died in the conflict. All suspected war crimes, of course, should be fully investigated and brought to account, but it should also be stated that there would be no need for Ukraine to defend the region if Putin hadn't been arming the separatists for eight years. Controversial language laws in the country favour Ukrainian but by no means 'persecute' the country's many Russian-speakers. All education from Year Five onwards must be conducted in Ukrainian, but classes in Russian culture and literature may continue in Russian. Russian-language books are not banned, though must be published in companion Ukrainian versions, placing an extra burden on publishers (though also an extra revenue source). Given its history, it is hardly surprising that Ukraine would seek to protect and encourage its mother tongue, and although restrictive, these laws are hardly punitive, genocidal, or a reason to launch a brutal invasion.

Putin's rhetoric of neo-Nazism and genocide is in fact a classic case of projection, reflecting his own motives and behaviour. As Alisher Ilkhamov argues in a recent academic paper, Putin's authoritarian leadership is marked by nostalgia for a past national 'greatness', complete rejection of liberal democratic values, violent repression of political dissent, imperialist ambitions, racism, and military aggression, and during his reign, Russia has come to exhibit all the hallmarks of a fascist state. Putin, Ilkhamov points out, scorns Ukrainians, whom he terms 'little Russians', incapable of running their own country, and has not even defined 'Nazi', suggesting the possibility that he considers all Ukrainians who refuse his diasporic concept of the 'Russian world' to be fair game for elimination. Certainly, all the tragic evidence from Bucha, Mariupol, and elsewhere in Ukraine, strongly suggests that it is Russia who is committing crimes against humanity in Ukraine. Whether or not, like Ilkhamov, one calls Putin's regime itself neo-Nazi, is beside the point: semantic quibbles must not be allowed to obscure Putin's own distinctive menace, which at this historical juncture threatens the planet itself.

Much rhetoric on the Western left, while less overtly racist, plays directly into Putin's narrative. Given the terrifying vision of an emergent autocratic world order run by oil despots, it is frightening to hear ideologically blinkered arguments rolled out to support a more 'complicated' view of the conflict. Many on the left, for example, argue strenuously that NATO expansion was to blame for the war, having fed 'Russian fears' of being attacked, and in effect forcing Putin's hand. But the invasion of Ukraine makes it blindingly obvious that Eastern European countries have joined NATO out of perfectly justified fears of their own. And far from threatening Russia, the West was operating a policy of appeasement: both NATO and the EU had long refused entry to Ukraine, which they knew would be expensive to defend; even after the annexation of Crimea, Russia was permitted to host the 2014 Winter Olympics; the 2018 Russian World Cup took place during the barrel bombing of Syria; and all the while Russian and Western elites mingled and traded in European capitals in pursuit of mutual enrichment. So there hardly seem rational grounds for these 'Russian fears'—which in any case can never justify a military attack on a sovereign nation.

Rather, this 'pre-emptive strike' against a non-existent threat reflects Putin's strongman tsarist mentality, fascist commitment to geopolitical expansionism, and street gang youth: during which, according to biographer Mark Galeotti, he learned that in any fight it pays to throw the first punch. Apologist arguments that Ukraine somehow provoked the attack because it failed to implement the Minsk Agreements are thin on context. Given that Russia considers itself not a party to the Minsk Agreements, but chief mediator, the negotiations were stacked against Ukraine from the start, making their results impossible to fully implement, even had Russia not violated the ceasefire on what the Ukrainians claim are four thousand occasions.

Such specious arguments from the left all rest on the sweeping assumption that Ukraine has become a 'puppet state' of the US. As such they support Putin's racism, by silencing and insulting Ukrainians, who stood outside, often in the bitter cold, against riot police and snipers in the 2004 Orange Revolution and 2014 Euromaidan uprising, risking and losing their lives to resist Russian control of their country. In the process, they courageously defied anti-protest laws that would have prevented them, among other things, from wearing construction site helmets in self-defence on demonstrations. In response, protestors arrived at the Maidan with pots and pans on their heads. Many also carried the flags of the European Union: and if Ukraine wants to leave the Russian sphere of influence and join Europe, I as an ardent Remainer, certainly cannot blame them. Accusations of neo-Nazism or Western stoogery also fail to recognise the vibrant nature of what Russian-speaking Ukrainian writer Andrey Kurkov calls 'the Ukrainian mindset'. Ukraine, Kurkov explained in a recent talk at the Conduit Club in London, has never, except when under foreign rule, succumbed to 'strongman' politics. From Kyivan Rus' to the present day, when independent, Ukraine has favoured political diversity. Currently, Kurkov explained, there are over four hundred political parties in the country. From my own visit to Ukraine in 2014, where I was taken to an election polling booth in Lviv by my host, political scholar and journalist Lyudmyla Pavlyuk, I can attest to this: not only were there many candidate posters on display, but the voting system was a form of proportional representation. Ukraine, it seems to me, is more democratic than the UK.

Liberty & Hypocrisy

Not all critics of the Western response to Putin's invasion, though, are easy to dismiss. From Palestine and the Global South come fully understandable charges of Western hypocrisy, querying, and diluting what Zelenskiy demands must be a united international response. As Western nations queued up to slap sanctions on Russia, Palestinians rightfully wondered why their Boycott, Divestment and Sanctions campaign against Israel has been fought tooth and nail in North America and Europe, constantly subjected to legal challenge and spurious charges of 'antisemitism'. On social media, Palestinians revisited Zelenskiy's Twitter feed to prove his lack of concern for Gazans under bombardment, while in his weekly newsletter to tens of thousands of readers, prominent Palestinian environmental justice and anti-Zionist activist Mazin Qumsiyeh noted that the 'hypocrisy of speaking of "human rights and international order" [is] not lost on billions of people who see the West's support of colonisation, occupation, dictatorships, and pillaging of resources in dozens of countries even as we speak.' Qumsiyeh and others have good reason to raise their voices. 'What aboutery' might be a tedious and counterproductive game, but it is nevertheless surely the case that the West too has oceans of blood on its hands.

No-one has more cause to be bitter about Western double standards than Syrians, many still fighting and dying in a 'stalled war' that has long dropped from international headlines. After all, as Emma Jane Harrison and Joe Dykes have recently summarised for the *Guardian*, every Russian war crime we see in Ukraine has been inflicted for years on the people of Syria: besieging, bombing, and starving civilian populations and infrastructure, including hospitals, marketplaces, schools, apartment blocks, and power stations; the use of indiscriminate weapons from Grad rockets to cluster munitions, banned under international law; announcing and then targeting humanitarian corridors; all consistently denied in a ruthless campaign to disseminate disinformation globally and suppress domestic independent media. And yet, as Syrian revolutionary-in-exile Adnan Hadad recalls in his recent conversation with Claire Berlinski for *Cosmopolitan Globalist*, even when Assad crossed Obama's stated red line, using chemical weapons against his own people in Ghouta in August 2013 – the West did nothing, America merely repositioning a few warships before Obama infamously backed down and abandoned Syrians to their fate. At most, Hadad asserts, the Americans supplied mainly non-lethal aid to a few rebel groups, which arguably did more harm than good, giving Russia an excuse to bomb anywhere humanitarian aid might be stored. In contrast, as we all know, for Ukrainians, the West provides defensive artillery, economically punishes Russia, and throws open its doors to over four million refugees.

Considering why the West's response to the plight of Ukraine has differed so radically from its disinterest in the suffering of Syrians, Hadad agreed with Berlinski that it was a complex question, involving factors such as Zelenskiy's charismatic leadership, the 'muddying' role of ISIS, the legal difference between an invasion and a civil war, and the increasing unbelievability of Putin's propaganda machine. But both also stressed the ethnocentric nature of the support for Ukraine, for which Hadad blamed the mainstream media:

> ... including outlets to which I contributed when they were covering Syria, like CNN, BBC, and *The New York Times*, to mention a few. Valuing human life equally? Nice words, but these outlets were so explicit about valuing Western lives above all other human life. You could see it in the way they even stopped reporting terrorist attacks on civilians in Iraq and Afghanistan unless a Western civilian or soldier was killed. After years of covering the news that way, why wouldn't you expect your readers to believe, if only unconsciously, that there's a hierarchy of importance in human life? And if you believe that, it's

not hard to believe that some people are just inferior and destined to die in endless wars, so why even pay attention.

Given the rise of Marine Le Pen with her proposed headscarf ban, the xenophobic nature of the Brexit campaign, and Trump's Muslim ban, it's hard to doubt that this Eurocentric status quo is rooted in both racism and Islamophobia. Europe has welcomed its white Christian Slav neighbours with open arms, but – with the notable exception of Germany, after Angela Merkel was confronted by a young Palestinian girl and had a change of heart – threw up literal barriers against Muslims fleeing an equally, if not more, brutal war. Western media coverage of brown or Muslim Ukrainians also reveals these ethnic fault lines. Apart from a brief flurry of interest in 2014, when their fate again became uncertain, the *Guardian*, for example, has barely reported on the situation of the Crimean Tatars, deported by Stalin in 1944, and only able to return after Ukraine became independent. As Andrey Kurkov reports in *Ukraine Diaries: Dispatches from Kiev* [sic], the Tatars were not included in a triumphalist Russian 'history' of the peninsula issued after the annexation, raising fears that their right to return was in dispute. The actual threat has been more subtle: a steady campaign of political persecution against Tatar activists that goes largely unnoticed in the English-speaking media. Meanwhile on the Ukraine–Poland border, according to the EU Agency for Fundamental Rights, Roma Ukrainians have faced discrimination from fellow refugees, who refused to share tents or transportation with them; while as Black Lives Matter activist Shaun King reported in a powerful op ed for *Newsweek*, African students attempting to flee the conflict 'were manhandled, mistreated, deprioritised, forced off buses and routinely told to get to the back of the line'. All this is indisputable. To cap it all off, for many, the charge of Western hypocrisy sticks hard and fast to the 2003 invasion of Iraq. 'How now cry foul?', scoff staunch critics of that illegal, ill-conceived, badly motivated, and fundamentally disastrous war.

But does all this mean Putin is 'just following suit' and no one, especially the West, has the right to try to stop him? I don't think so. I am no cheerleader for American or British imperialism, and opposed both US-led invasions of Iraq, but at the same time I reject cynical or self-righteous reactions to the invasion of Ukraine, which ultimately allow tyranny to run rampant on the grounds that 'everyone is doing it'. As British-Syrian writer and former *Critical Muslim* editor, Robin Yassin-Kassab wrote, with fierce irony, on a recent Facebook post:

> It's hypocritical to complain about the Russian invasion of Ukraine – and Syria, and Georgia – because the Americans invaded Iraq. And it was hypocritical to complain about the American invasion of Iraq because the Russians invaded Chechnya. And it was hypocritical to complain about the Russian invasion of Chechnya because the Americans intervened in Central America. And it was hypocritical to complain about American acts in Central America because the Russians invaded Afghanistan. And it was hypocritical to complain about the Russian invasion of Afghanistan because the Americans invaded Vietnam. Be silent concerning all inexcusable acts of murderous imperialism, comrades. Is that clear?

His vocal Facebook page suggests that Yassin-Kassab is watching the invasion of Ukraine with a mix of anguished *déjà vu* and potent intellectual fury. In his eyes, for all the West is doing, it is not enough. Germany is still buying gas from Russia. Troops pushed back from Kyiv will soon be redeployed in the East, atrocities will continue to mount. Russia, Yassin-Kassab warns, along with Zelenskiy and even the *Observer* editorial of 10 April 2022, will rape, torture, and massacre civilians unless and until it is forcibly stopped. Adnan Hadad similarly fears the war in Ukraine will be long – and ultimately lost to Russia, as the West shrugs and moves on. But at the same time Hadad says: 'I want to believe people will finally get it, how connected our world is, how when something like that, something so grave, happens in one part of the world, eventually it will affect us all, no matter where we are.'

Western leaders are no doubt rueing their craven and myopic response to Russian involvement in Syria, and its annexation of Crimea. Had tough action been taken earlier, instead of applauding Putin at Sochi, there might not now be a bloodbath in Ukraine threatening to spill over all Europe. But self-interest is not the only or strongest reason to support the Ukrainian resistance. Shaun King, on hearing of the mistreatment of African refugees from Ukraine, 'leaned in' to their cause, and what he discovered was that they (unlike the Roma) had overwhelmingly felt welcomed by their Ukraine colleagues and neighbours – it was the police who had abused them. His *Newsweek* op ed is a rousing call to African Americans not to 'harden their hearts' to Ukrainian suffering, but instead to recognise a shared struggle against structural racism, and heed what for him has become a religious credo: Dr Martin Luther King Jr's words 'Injustice anywhere is a threat to justice everywhere.'

Liberty & Peace

Justice, as a principle, is inextricable from concepts of liberty. Though the law all too often works to protect wealth and property, it is when fundamental human rights and freedoms are violated that we most require justice. While all governments are flawed and subject to corruption, and any fixed ideas of nationalism are problematic at heart, so far the human race has widely adopted no better way of safeguarding both liberty and justice than political systems in which leaders are elected, frequently replaced, and subject like all citizens to the rule of law, administered by an independent judiciary and reported on by an independent media. Western nations badly need an upgrade from representative to participatory democracy, a development that might perhaps eventually even challenge the concept of the nation state. But Western leaders at least pay lip service to these democratic ideals, and no matter their own wrongdoings, it is right and necessary that when principles of freedom and democracy are under violent attack, Western nations should find ways to defend them.

A major difference between the illegal invasions of Iraq and Ukraine, after all, is that Saddam Hussein was a dictator and Volodymyr Zelenskiy was democratically elected. That doesn't mean the US-led Coalition was right to forcibly depose Hussein. Although ostensibly a laudable ambition, this was not a justification for breaking international law, which must apply universally, and be challenged in courts, not on the battlefield. And in fact, the invasion of Iraq was a vainglorious smash and grab raid, mainly motivated by the desire to control the country's oil supplies and profit from military and reconstruction contracts (with some looting of antiquities as a war bonus). There was no credible long-term plan to help establish a democracy in the country – and indeed, why should Iraqis have trusted non-Muslim mediators with only a hazy and deeply colonial idea of their history, culture, and language? From the vacuum of power, Daesh arose, only further fuelling conflict in the region. But even though the invasions of Iraq and Ukraine are both illegal and disastrous, and it is right to oppose both, they are not morally equivalent. The difference in the political systems under attack demands a different way of opposing each invasion.

Could anyone of good conscience have supported supplying weaponry to Hussain's Ba'ath Party and the Iraqi Armed Forces to use against the Coalition? Conversely, surely it is reasonable – or even mandatory – to try to help people overthrow autocrats? This is hardly a new argument: even within pacifism and the radical left there are precedents for support of 'just wars' or wars of liberation. As foundational Anarchist philosopher Petyr Kropotkin put it: 'to remain a bystander while a wicked and strong man gives blows to a weak one, is an unpardonable wickedness. *This is precisely what maintains all oppression.*' With his own vociferous support of the Allies in World War One – arguing even against a peace treaty on the basis that it would just solidify the autocratic German status quo – Kropotkin permanently tarnished his reputation in Anarchist circles, but in light of current conflicts his arguments are being sympathetically revisited. Peter Ryley argues that Kropotkin was not, as accused at the time, throwing his anarchist principles on the pyre of his Germanophobia. Rather, he understood that liberty and peace may sometimes be conflicting ideals, impossible to simultaneously uphold, and in such situations, Ryley notes, 'contingency is important. It points away from dogma towards the need to make judgements on specific events at specific times. Judgement is inescapable. It should not be avoided through rigid adherence to predetermined ideas.' Wise words, to which the left today should take heed.

In challenging easy assumptions about pacifism, though, it is vital to avoid the trap of militarism: viewing military intervention as the only or best method of conflict resolution. Taking each case for or against war on its own grounds, and considering the often-catastrophic impact of non-intervention, one obvious conclusion is that international law needs more nuance, enforceability, and accountability. When regimes commit atrocities, whether against their own people or their neighbours, in what ways might it be right to show solidarity and act to protect civilians? While international laws against invading sovereign states exist for a good reason, should they not be subject to universally agreed red lines? Why should nation state parties to an armed conflict have the right to veto, or even vote on, UN resolutions over that conflict? A sincerely concerned world could have practically and financially supported rebel militias against Hussein, if they asked, just as the Syrians did for so long in vain. A serious discussion about amending international law in this regard could develop frameworks for limited and conditional military support from a broader alliance of the international community, including neighbouring states and the UN peacekeeping forces, not just wealthy and economically interested parties. And, as Zelenskiy passionately argued in his 5 April 2022 address to the UN, a credible United Nations would reform itself to ensure full representation of all world regions on the Security Council and prevent the power of veto from being used as a license to kill on an epic scale, perverting and destroying the very concept of international law.

In the case of Ukraine, in the throes not of a civil war or revolution, but a full-scale invasion, there is no current legal or moral restraint on providing military support to the country's resistance fighters. Yes, there has been noble talk on Facebook of non-violent resistance, even comparisons to Czechoslovakia. But legendary as was the Czech civil disobedience campaign against Soviet rule, over twenty years passed between the Prague Spring and the Velvet Revolution. Ukraine does not want to risk waiting that long, or longer, to return to what they have now, and have every right to militarily defend.

They cannot win alone though. While calling out an obvious double standard, urging unstinting humanitarian support of all refugees, and arguing for international law reform, I support Western military aid to Ukraine. As a pacifist by nature and upbringing, whose grandfather died fighting Hitler, an RAF rear gunner and wireless operator shot down over France returning from a bombing raid on the Mannheim central post office, I agree with Kropotkin that some wars are tragically necessary. A Russian win in Ukraine would crush Ukrainian democracy and endanger not only other post-Soviet states and peace in Europe, but a liveable planet. For all those reasons the international community should actively oppose it. Although emphatically not a civil war, Russia's invasion of Ukraine, like its dismembering of the Syrian revolution, is a Spanish Civil War for our times. Much as I also find it painful to agree with Liz Truss, having received on 7 March 2022 – two weeks before the full extent of the rape and slaughter in Bucha became known – this message from my friend

Lyudmyla Pavlyuk in Lviv, I also support foreign fighters joining the Ukrainian army:

> The daughter and granddaughter of a Kyiv professor that we know well are among those locked in basements in the small city of Bucha near Kyiv. People have no food, share their last milligrams of water. The Russian military, in particular the Kadyrovite Chechens, are responsible for atrocities in the area – they kill volunteers, shoot civilians, cut off the channels of departure and food aid, and rape women. If there are people among the foreign nationals who decide to help the Ukrainian army and have experience and skills in anti-terrorist operations, it would be a saving option to involve them in the release of hostages. And, friends, let us pray and help spiritually.

As she requested, I forwarded Lyuda's message to my Labour MP, Lloyd Russell-Moyle (also taking the opportunity to ask him if the recent Amnesty International report on Israel has convinced him, finally, that Israel is an apartheid state), asking him to support permission for British nationals to join the Ukrainian armed resistance. I received in return a cut and paste message about humanitarian aid and receiving Ukrainian refugees. Good to know, but not what I had asked.

In not sending ground troops or enforcing a 'No Fly Zone', NATO has shown strategic restraint, but it is clear that the support provided so far is not yet enough. Ukraine's only hope is to hold out long enough to force Putin to negotiate seriously – and while fifty days into the conflict, with Russia sustaining heavy losses and retreating from the North, it seems they may just succeed at that aim, on the basis of Syria, the worst is yet to come. Russia will inevitably redeploy in the East, and even as I write accusations, albeit unevidenced, of the Russian use of chemical weapons in Mariupol are hitting the headlines. To stop Putin, *The Observer* has editorialised, NATO may yet have to commit itself more fully, to direct intervention in the form of safe havens in the West, provision of tanks and fighter jets, or even targeting Russian forces for committing atrocities.

The risks of such options are clear. The stakes have been raised sky-high, lines previously drawn in the sand now scored into chasms. For all the horror and mendacity of the 2003 invasion of Iraq, Bush and Blair's opening salvo was not a barely veiled threat to drop a nuclear bomb on anyone who opposed them. Though of course the 24 February 2022 invasion was not the start of the war on Ukraine. Putin's warning did not come out of nowhere: its icy impact simply demonstrated what Ukrainians and Syrians had been saying for years, that the West had been napping while Putin and his cronies stewed in their toxic broth of geopolitical resentment and greed, milked the world economy like a barn-raised cow and, entirely unmolested by international law, basked in the afterglow of the successful theft of Crimea while perfecting their nightmarish playbook in Syria. Can anyone doubt Putin will stop at the Donbas?

The challenge will be to stop him without igniting mushroom clouds, the fallout from which will encircle the globe. On that topic, while recalling a story told recently on BBC radio about Putin in his days as a KGB thug, when he dispersed a crowd of protestors by calmly telling a giant porkie – that a tank was around the corner waiting to shoot them – I would like to give the last word to a Ukrainian. Maidan activist and theatre artist Yevhen Nyshchuk, a resident of Kyiv and former Minister of Culture of Ukraine, has regularly visited Bucha and Irpin during the invasion, at great personal peril. On the question of Putin's nuclear threats, Nyshchuk, in a recent interview in *The Scotsman*, said:

> I think they are really the scare stories of a mentally ill person. We suspect that Russia's nuclear power, like much of its land power, is out of service; and we do not think the west should be frightened by this mythology of Russia's great military power.

Calling Putin's nuclear bluff would be an extreme risk. But there are no good options at this point. Ultimately, whoever or wherever we are, we skirt the significance of Putin's war on Ukraine at our peril.

Liberty & Neutrality

Having raised the spectres of all kinds of catastrophe, I must admit that Putin's endgame remains as unclear to me as to anyone – he may well, as Zelenskiy warns, have set his sights on destroying the entire European project and permanently ending the Western hegemony, or he may content himself with annexing the coast of the Sea of Azov in time for his next fake election. Whatever his goals, however, the Gray Chessmaster might have to capitulate – he has overstretched himself, miscalculated badly, and between meeting unexpectedly stiff military resistance, and losing the confidence of his Generals, it is still possible that Putin will lose the war, and hopefully also his job. But in any of these scenarios, diplomacy, however insincere on Russia's part, will almost certainly play a part in determining the final outcome of this war, and all signs so far point to Ukraine agreeing to commit to some form of neutrality.

In the run up to the invasion I was staunchly opposed to this demand. A sovereign nation has the right to decide its own destiny and make whatever alliances it chooses. And how could I, who rues Brexit with all my heart, argue that Ukraine should be denied the right to join the EU, as was Putin's definition of neutrality? After the invasion began, I felt even more strongly on this question: I saw that Ukraine had already in effect declared neutrality and was being violated and betrayed as a result. Post-independence Ukraine surrendered its nuclear weapons on the basis that it would be protected by both its powerful neighbours, but as it is not a member of NATO, such promises from the West were hollow. How might a post-invasion neutrality come with iron-clad assurances of protection in the event of Iron Curtain incursions? While declaring neutrality in itself would not prevent Ukraine from joining the EU, with the right to offer non-military aid to member states, of the five neutral EU countries, Austria, Malta, Ireland, Finland, and Sweden, the Nordic two are currently seriously considering NATO membership.

Now, though, that Zelenskiy himself is suggesting the idea, it needs to be taken seriously. That doesn't mean promoting it. My friend, Lyudmyla Pavlyuk writes:

> If Ukraine loses (I hope it won't), then it could turn out that we need to accept the Putin-imposed idea of neutrality. Or Ukraine could be forced to accept this under the pressure of Western advisers. But to deploy different kinds of theoretical arguments to see something 'good' and reasonable in this idea – no, it is not my choice, my soul opposes it with all its strength and disgust for the imposed decisions.

I entirely empathise and agree with this passionate defence of Ukrainian autonomy. But I do also think that it is worthwhile to examine what the general concept of political neutrality could achieve in this violently polarised world. For the Non-Aligned Movement (NAM), a group of one hundred and twenty developing countries, mainly of the Global South, neutrality represents not just a refusal to take sides in geopolitical conflicts, but a demand for the universal application of international law. And this is a goal that every UN nation ought to be urgently applying itself to achieving.

Founded in 1955 by Jawaharlal Nehru and Josip Broz Tito in response to the Korean War, NAM was conceived as a 'middle way' between Cold War blocs. Nehru and Tito called for 'positive, active and constructive policy that, as its goal, has collective peace as the foundation of collective security.' NAM, which meets every two or three years, is not well-known in the West – the Commonwealth has a far higher profile in the UK, for example. This is another failure of Western media and education, for NAM has been involved in significant decolonial processes, assisting in the foundation of many small independent states. At the same time, some say the group has struggled to find a purpose in the post-Soviet era. David Adler suggests though, that the invasion of Ukraine might just reignite its idealistic fire. Currently, Adler has reported for the *Guardian*, the Global South seems to be Western-sceptic to the core, most countries in Africa and Latin America politely declining to join the sanctions campaign against Russia. Many of these refusals are reasonably argued: 'Neutrality does not mean indifference,' says Pierre Sané, president of the Imagine Africa Institute and former Secretary-general of Amnesty International. 'Neutrality means continuously calling for the respect of international laws; neutrality means that our hearts still go to the victims of military invasions and arbitrary sanctions never imposed on NATO countries.' It is telling, though, that many of these 'neutral' nations are governed by authoritarian regimes propped up now or in the past by Russia. I hope that NAM itself, when it meets again in Uganda in 2023, takes a more considered and activist position, recognising that this war is already causing global food prices to rise, autocracy anywhere threatens human rights and the UN Sustainable Development Goals, and that nuclear threats have no place in global diplomacy.

A vision of collective peace won't come to pass in the fallout of a nuclear conflict in the North. While Ukraine's political status is ultimately for Ukrainians to decide, a reinvigorated NAM, actively involved in UN reform and effective international law enforcement, would challenge both the hypocrisy of the West and the totalitarian regimes currently gathering strength around the globe. In so doing, a vocally neutral political movement could help prevent the world's current volatile descent into a new, freezing cold war on an overheating planet.

Conclusion

I have written on freedom before for *Critical Muslim* and, as then, can only conclude that it is a paradoxical concept. Living in the present moment, as we do, how can we ever tell that our actions are freely chosen? Human actions are all, in some profound metaphysical sense, *fait accompli*. And yet, whenever someone tries to block or violate our freedom of conscience, expression, or movement, we resist. Similarly, as I am sure Muslims experience during Ramadan, we often feel most free not when we are indulging ourselves, but when we are refusing temptation, exercising our will over our instinctive needs. Like the Andromeda galaxy, human freedom is perhaps only visible when we are not directly observing it but forced to look away. Another paradox about freedom is that the stronger our commitment to it, the less free we might sometimes actually feel. I have certainly felt compelled to support Ukraine over the last six weeks, doing whatever I could to help support the resistance.

In my role as Deputy Director at Waterloo Press, I was already editing *The Children of Grad*, a novel by the Ukrainian author Maria Miniailo, translated by Michael Pursglove and Natalia Pniushkova, which went to print in February. It's a gripping novel, about orphans seeking sanctuary from a cruel adult world shaped by war, and I spent time in March promoting it online, giving copies to Andrey Kurkov and English PEN staff at the Conduit Club, and presenting the book at the Ukraine stall at the London Book Fair, in place of the original publishers, Summit-Book, who for reasons that don't have to be explained, could not be there as planned. I also raised funds to buy body armour for Ukrainian resistance fighters, kept in close contact with my Ukrainian friends, and translated daily reviews from the Ukrainian Information Defense – for which I was called a fascist on Facebook. I don't mean to 'virtue signal' – a weird term I don't like. For one thing, I really haven't done anything compared to my Ukrainian friends who are enduring this nightmare, supporting internal refugees, writing eyewitness reports for the army, visiting danger zones to translate coroners' reports on butchered bodies, all the while living on bread and eggs, fearing bad news about loved ones on the front, watching bombs fall from their bedroom windows. But also, in this conflict-ridden world, I think we do need to talk about moral decisions and how we come to make them. For myself, over many years now, I have increasingly found that expanding my personal notion of individual freedom in alignment with concepts of individual judgement and collective liberties has given my small and in many ways fortunate life a sense of greater purpose. I don't know if this essay will change anyone's mind, but I know its publication will mean something to my Ukrainian colleagues. It's been rewarding to feel of some sort of use to them at this harrowing time. Even making a small difference makes all the difference. As the holy books teach us, let's never give up on each other, or the world.

With thanks to Lyudmyla Pavlyuk, Ihor Pavlyuk, Dmytro Drozdovskyi, Steve Komarnyckyj, Neil Swire, Graham Riches and Lee Whitaker for their conversations concerning this essay and its themes.

A PASSAGE TO LIBERTY

Giles Goddard

> The more highly public life is organised the lower does its morality sink; the nations of today behave to each other worse than they ever did in the past, they cheat, rob, bully and bluff, make war without notice, and kill as many women and children as possible.
>
> E.M. Forster, 'Liberty in England' (1935)

On a blisteringly hot day in 1935, the writer E.M. Forster gave the opening speech to the first International Congress of Writers in Paris. His speech feels uncannily relevant today. The congress had been organised by the French author, and later government minister, André Malraux against a background of disintegration and fear in Europe. Hitler was rearming Germany. Mussolini's invasion of Ethiopia was imminent. Franco had taken complete control in Spain and killed thousands of people.

Malraux, a communist who had fought on the Republican side in the Spanish Civil War (1936–39), invited leading radicals to the Congress, including Bertolt Brecht, Louis Aragon, and surrealist André Breton. Amongst such a crowd, Forster's presence seems at first sight surprising. He accepted the invitation out of desperation. The whole world seemed to have become one of 'telegrams and anger', he wrote. He tried to persuade Virginia Woolf to join him in Paris – 'I don't suppose the conference is of any use – things have gone too far. But I have no doubt as to the importance of people like ourselves *inside* the conference. We represent the last utterances of the civilised.' – but she decided not to accompany him.

The speech was poorly received. According to journalist Katherine Porter, a contemporary who was there:

> He paid no attention to the microphone, but wove back and forth, and from side to side, gently, and every time his face passed the mouthpiece I caught a high-voiced syllable or two, never a whole word, only a thin recurring sound like the wind down a chimney as Mr Forster's pleasant good countenance

advanced and retreated and returned. Then, surprisingly, once he came to a moment's pause before the instrument and there sounded into the hall dearly but wistfully a complete sentence: 'I DO believe in liberty!'

Best known for his fiction, Forster was also a powerful advocate in the emergent civil liberties movement. But there are those who question the depth of his legacy on human rights and justice. Re-reading his novels after a gap of twenty years, I am struck anew by how strongly they speak of the tragic consequences of social exclusion, racism, and hypocrisy. His life was one of fear, hope, and enforced compromise. He had one foot within the British establishment and one foot firmly outside. He was a creature of his time but with a passionate vision for a different world. Perhaps it is the enforced marginality of his life which has given his works resonance down the decades: or perhaps the hopeful generosity of his belief that, in the end, it is the 'wonderful muddle' of human relationships that brings life and joy.

He had, by 1935, published almost all his novels: *A Room with A View* (1908), *Howards End* (1910), and *A Passage to India* (1924) are perhaps the most admired. His openly gay novel, *Maurice*, was completed in 1914 but he did not permit it to be published until after his death. By the 1930s he had become known as a champion of civil liberties, an opponent of censorship and totalitarian regimes, and a campaigner against racism particularly as experienced by Indians in England in the 1930s. He broadcasted regularly on the BBC from 1928, and was invited to be the first president of the National Council for Civil Liberties (NCCL), which was founded in 1934. He was also active in the Humanist Society, particularly after the Second World War, and campaigned for the legalisation of homosexuality.

But Forster was not, how shall I say, a typical radical. His speech at the Congress was later published as an essay, entitled 'What I Believe'. Its opening sets out his creed:

> I do not believe in Belief. But this is an Age of Faith, and there are so many militant creeds that, in self defence, one has to formulate a creed of one's own. Tolerance, good temper and sympathy are no longer enough in a world where ignorance rules, and Science, which ought to have ruled, plays the pimp. Tolerance, good temper and sympathy – they are what matter really, and if the human race is not to collapse they must come to the front before long.

He spent little time on economic or structural analysis of injustice and the conditions in society which enable illiberal policies and practices to thrive. His was not one of the voices raised for greater equality: he would not have identified as a socialist, and certainly not a communist. For those who are deprived of the basic necessities of life, Forster regarded such notions as liberty to be irrelevant. Again, from 'What I Believe': 'The hungry and the homeless don't care about liberty any more than they care about cultural heritage. To pretend that they do care is cant.' In *Howards End*, albeit ironically, Forster writes: 'We are not concerned with the very poor. They are unthinkable, and only to be approached by the statistician or the poet. This story deals with gentlefolk, or those who are obliged to pretend that they are gentlefolk.'

A Passage to India broke new ground in its portrayal of colonial subjects, and is often cited alongside Conrad's *Heart of Darkness* (1899) as one of the principal anti-Imperial novels of the early twentieth century. But Edward Said in his seminal work *Orientalism* identifies the novel as a typically Orientalist text, objectifying the Indians and portraying them as servants in a master-servant relationship which Forster fails to challenge.

Said does not quite do justice to the complexity of Forster's thought. True, he was not someone who might have been found mounting the barricades or taking direct action against the Fascists on the streets of London. He was not 'political'. But his commitment to liberty and human rights was intrinsic to his work. The novels are still read not only because of their inherent filmic qualities – it is intriguing that the best film adaptations of his work were made by cross-cultural romantic and filmmaking partners Ismail Merchant and James Ivory, who kept their love secret throughout their life together – but also because they give expression to a profound humanism which few other English novelists have been able to depict with such sympathy.

A Room with a View has many interlocking themes – the visceral importance of art (the hidden passion of Lucy Honeychurch, the young Englishwoman abroad, is manifested in the way she plays late Beethoven piano sonatas), the disempowerment of women, the vacuity of faith – but at the heart of the plot is the disregard in which the relatively low-class George Emerson and his father are held by the ladies of the Pensione Bertolini. Cousin Charlotte – who lives in Tunbridge Wells – has a timorous anxiety about the conventions of her society. It is under the steamroller of convention that she tries to crush the burgeoning love between Lucy and George.

Howards End, published two years later, is a rich and multi-layered dissection of the destruction wrought by the privileges of the wealthy – shibboleths, altars upon which the poor are sacrificed. The novel is a dance between the Schlegels, a family of German origin living on inherited wealth, and the Wilcoxes, first-generation rich and none the better for it. Leonard Bast, upon whom the plot turns, is a clerk who finds himself forced to marry Jackie, a woman who had formerly lived as a sex worker. Leonard's visceral desire to escape from the world into which he was born leads him towards books and art. The chasm between potential and reality is unbridgeable. Beauty and art butter no parsnips. He reads the great nineteenth-century art writer John Ruskin on Venice, yet something is missing:

> ...the voice in the gondola rolled on, piping melodiously of Effort and Self-Sacrifice, full of high purpose, full of beauty, full even of sympathy and the love of men, yet somehow eluding all that was actual and insistent in Leonard's life. For it was the voice of one who had never been hungry or dirty, and not guessed successfully what hunger and dirt are.

Writing in the early years of the twentieth century, Forster saw, prophetically, the motor car as a harbinger of evil, raising dust and stinking out the good clean air of England. He detested the encroaching red rust of London and the onward march of the suburbs through the countryside of Hertfordshire and Surrey. He detested it even more when it emerged in Chandrapore, as evident in *A Passage to India*:

> They reached their bungalow, low and enormous, the oldest and most uncomfortable bungalow in the Civil Station, with a sunk soup-plate of a lawn, and they had one drink more, this time of barley-water, and went to bed ... at Chandrapore the Tuftons were little gods; soon they would retire to some suburban villa, and die exiled from glory.

Forster viewed the Empire with distaste. He was opposed to the occupation of India by the British, and distressed by the behaviour of the Imperial civil servants, plucked out of their suburban milieus and plonked down, to their great discomfort, in the new colonial quarters of New

Delhi or Calcutta. Much of *A Passage to India* is drawn from first hand observation:

> The performance ended and the amateur orchestra played the National Anthem. Conversation and billiards stopped, faces stiffened. It was the Anthem of the Army of Occupation. It reminded every member of the Club that he or she was British and in exile. It produced a little sentiment and a useful accession of will-power.

For me, Forster opened a window into another world. As a teenager in an English public school in the 1970s, struggling to understand my sexuality, I found myself in a lonely desert. Homosexuality had only been partially decriminalised ten years before. There was hardly anything for a young gay man except negative stereotypes on television, snide references to the Bloomsbury Group in the Sunday papers – and *Maurice*. Published in 1971, I still have the copy I bought from the school's paperback bookshop when I was seventeen. Rereading it for this essay I find I can quote whole sentences, and I recall the sense of freedom I felt when reading it for the first time.

> They cared for no one. They were outside humanity, and death, had it come, would only have continued their pursuit of a retreating horizon. A tower, a town – it had been Ely – was behind them, in front of them the same sky, paling at last as though heralding the sea … The song of the lark was heard, the trail of dust began to settle behind them. They were alone.

There is a strong bittersweetness, though, as I read *Maurice*. The bitterness lies in Forster's conviction that he had to keep the manuscript hidden away, just because it had a happy ending:

> Unless the Wolfenden report becomes law, it will probably have to remain in a manuscript. If it ended unhappily, with a lad dangling from the noose or with a suicide pact, all would be well.

Forster lived a life which, while privileged, was also full of fear. Quentin Bailey, Associate Professor in the Department of English and Comparative Literature at San Diego University, describes 1930s England as 'the secure police state of the morally guarded Home Counties'. Homosexuality was criminal. Same-sex activity could very easily lead to prison and social disgrace. Such tolerance that existed was entirely conditional and could be withdrawn at any time. When writer J. R. Ackerley, whose life was more openly transgressive than Forster's, was at risk of arrest, Forster was terrified lest their correspondence should be discovered and scandal ensue. Forster had to live with – a favourite word – 'muddle'. His longest love, lasting forty years, was with married policeman Bob Buckingham, a carefully managed and never openly acknowledged relationship where May, Bob's wife, also became Forster's close friend.

Bailey also references the background of economic power which is unstated in *Maurice* – both the systematic, overt exploitation of natives in the colonies in the name of civilisation and the economic marginalisation of women, the poor, and those who failed to stand up properly for Empire and Nation in Britain:

> Maurice, the struggling homosexual trapped in homophobic England, owes his livelihood to countless colonial and working-class subjects who were too unrecognisable, too foreign, to exist in the world of peace, police, and realist prose narratives.

It is in *A Passage to India* that the ambiguity of Forster's call for liberty is most evident. The book was a labour of love. He had fallen in (unrequited) love with Syed Ross Masood, a young Indian student he tutored in 1906, and his long trip to India via Egypt in 1914 was partly to visit Masood again. In Egypt he formed a relationship with a tram conductor named Mohammed el Adl, a relationship which was to prove a turning point in his life. Previously, Italy had been the almost mythical place where Art and Truth could flourish for Forster. He later discovered in Egypt and then in India a taste of a different kind of freedom, not necessarily sexual but, he hoped, one which could transcend boundaries of class and race, throwing open the potential for profound relationships untrammelled by the conventions of suburbia.

Except it didn't. The inequalities between him and el Adl led inevitably to the end of the relationship, and in India he found himself perpetually caught between the implacable Empire and the complexity of life in India. Dr Aziz, the main character, is a young Muslim frustrated by the narrowness of his life and the constraints forced upon him by the British ascendancy, who mistreat and undermine him as they do all Indians. The novel drips with angry contempt for most of the British officers and imperial bureaucrats. There are few redeeming British characters apart from Mr Fielding, the schoolmaster, and Adela Quested, the young woman shipped out to India in order to marry the bigoted Ronny Heaslop. And, initially, Mrs Moore, Adela's companion, whom Dr Aziz encounters in a mosque near the beginning of the book and with whom he believes he has a deep spiritual bond.

It is opposition to the British which brings Hindus and Muslims together in the book. After the mysterious episode in the Malabar Caves upon which the plot turns, the whole of Chandrapore is united against the unjust treatment of Dr Aziz. Forster was not one of those who believed in the possibility of the reform of Empire so that it could bring a benevolent light to those poor benighted natives. And yet at the same time he seems unable quite to give it up, and wants India to retain a special mystical status:

India a nation! What an apotheosis! Last comer to the drab nineteenth-century sisterhood! Waddling in at this hour of the world to take her seat! She, whose only peer was the Holy Roman Empire, she shall rank with Guatemala and Belgium perhaps! Fielding mocked again.

India is romanticised and somehow unreal. A Hindu ritual overseen by Professor Narayan Godbole is described in rich, mysterious colours:

When the villagers broke cordon for a glimpse of the silver image, a most beautiful and radiant expression came into their faces, a beauty in which there was nothing personal, for it caused them all to resemble one another during the moment of its indwelling, and only when it was withdrawn did they revert to individual clods.

As Said observes, Indians are certainly 'othered' in *A Passage to India*. The word 'clods' may describe the earthbound nature of the participants, but for Forster, as for so many Englanders, they are also an alien people. In the end it proves impossible to leap over the crack which splits England from the colonies. The poignancy of the closing sentences of the book, when Dr Aziz and Mr Fielding try to recover their friendship, is heart-breaking:

'Why can't we be friends now?' said the other, holding him affectionately. 'It's what I want. It's what you want.'

But the horses didn't want it – they swerved apart; the earth didn't want it, sending up rocks through which riders must pass single-file; the temples, the tank, the jail, the palace, the birds, the carrion, the Guest House, that came into view as they issued from the gap and saw Mau beneath: they didn't want it, they said in their hundred voices, 'No, not yet,' and the sky said, 'No, not there.'

So what are we to make of Forster on liberty? Was he at heart a creature of his imperial heritage, or was his advocacy of human rights and freedom of expression part of a wider, more subversive commitment to the re-creation of society? Was he indeed Orientalist or radical, an apologist or a revolutionary?

After *A Passage to India* came out in 1924, no more novels were published before his death in 1970. A couple of plays, some travel writing – including *The Hill of Devi*, an account of his time as a tutor in the court of the Maharajah of Dewas Senior – and collections of essays made up the majority of his output. But his engagement in public life increased as the years passed. He was not only the first President of the NCCL: he was also, from 1959, President of the Cambridge Humanists and from 1963 a member of the Advisory Council of the British Humanist Association.

The clouds were darkening across Europe during the 1930s, and the lights went out with the unleashing of the Second World War. Fascism in Germany and Spain was mirrored by Stalinism in the Soviet Union. Britain, still a great imperial power, was at the heart of the gathering storm. Britain was a country which prided itself on its liberalism but rarely acknowledged the deeply illiberal foundations of its power and wealth – a globally racist empire based on wealth extraction and economic exploitation. Forster was troubled by these developments, as evidenced in his 1935 speech to the International Congress:

Personal relations are despised today. They are regarded as bourgeois luxuries, as products of a time of fair weather which is now past, and we are urged to get rid of them, and to dedicate ourselves to some movement or cause instead. I hate the idea of causes, and if I had to choose between betraying my country and betraying my friend, I hope I should have the guts to betray my country.

Forster's humanism was forged in reaction to the imperial assumptions and rigid class structure of British society – the Schegel sisters 'would at times dismiss the whole British Empire with a puzzled, if reverent, sigh' – and to the political systems of fascism and communism. He resisted the allure of simple solutions and, instead, based his creed on the power of love. *A Room with a View, Howards End* and *Maurice* end with resolutions which overcome the barriers of class, gender, and sexuality: *Howards End* was described by eminent critic Lionel Trilling as 'one of the great comments on the class struggle'. *A Passage to India* closes without resolution, for the fences created by imperial power are too high to be crossed.

Forster had experienced the overreach of power and privilege in too many situations, and believed that the only way to resist it is through the meeting of heart with heart, and mind with mind. John Lucas, Professor of English at Nottingham Trent University, calls it 'an enabling modesty'. 'Only connect', Forster pleads in *Howards End*, and he defiantly amplifies his call for friendship over patriotism:

> Such a choice may scandalise the modern reader, and he may stretch out his patriotic hand to the telephone at once and ring up the police. It would not have shocked Dante, though. Dante places Brutus and Cassius in the lower circle of Hell because they had chosen to betray their friend Julius Caesar rather than their country Rome.... Love and loyalty to an individual can run counter to the claims of the State. When they do – down with the State, say I, which means that the State would down me.

But Forster is no idealistic anarchist, believing that love will conquer everything. He recognises that force is a necessary evil but only of last resort:

> I realise that all society rests upon force. But all the great creative actions, all the decent human relations, occur during the intervals when force has not managed to come to the front. These intervals are what matter.

As for *how* these decent human relations enable human flourishing, he says:

> I believe in aristocracy – if that is the right word, and if a democrat may use it. Not an aristocracy of power, based upon rank and influence, but an aristocracy of the sensitive, the considerate and the plucky. Its members are to be found in all nations and classes, and all through the ages, and there is a secret understanding between them when they meet. They represent the true human tradition, the one permanent victory of our queer race over cruelty and chaos.

He resisted censorship, the mortal enemy of freedom. Of particular concern was the Sedition Act, passed by the National Government in 1934, which would strike 'an open blow against freedom of expression'. The Act, Forster argued, 'encourages the informer, and…can be used against pacifists'. With such an Act in existence, Forster said, it would be easy to set up 'psychological censorship…and the human heritage is impaired'. He greatly admired French novelist André Gide, whom he met at the Congress of Writers and about whom he wrote a piece in 1943, *Gide and George*. He speaks of Gide as a humanist, defined as possessing four characteristics: 'curiosity, a free mind, a belief in good taste, and belief in the human race'.

Forster had a clear eye for the dangers the world faced. He saw that 'the nations of today behave to each other worse than they ever did in the past', yet he played little part in the re-envisioning of Britain which arose out of the Second World War. The Beveridge Report, universal education, the National Health Service were all brought into being without his help.

But today, as Russia wages war on Ukraine and woman and children die in the rubble of Mariupol Theatre, as the Yemen conflict and the genocide of the Rohingya drags on, and confident liberalism seems to be in retreat, Forster's enabling modesty is never more needed. He resisted grand narratives and structural analysis. His novels are stories about individuals' struggles to overcome the destructive power of convention and privilege. They are about the glimmering of light in a world of darkness. Perhaps that is the most that we can hope for. Liberty, for Forster, meant freedom to connect. Only that.

> The greater the darkness, the brighter shine the little lights, reassuring one another, signalling: 'Well, at all events, I'm still here. I don't like it very much, but how are you?'

MY QUEST

Ole Jørgen Anfindsen

In 1965, my parents needed more space for their steadily growing number of children. They found an old house in a suburb called Stabekk, just outside of Oslo. I was seven years old at that time, and this move turned out to have a huge influence on the trajectory of my life through childhood and adolescence. There was an Evangelical church in the neighbourhood, and I was soon enrolled in its Sunday school. There we were told stories of Jesus and His disciples, and God's love for all humans was frequently emphasised. I showed up pretty much every Sunday and have only fond memories from my years there.

During my teenage years, I faithfully attended the weekly meetings of the church's youth group. The religious discourse was now different, to a large degree focusing on typical Evangelical doctrine, including the infallibility of the Bible. This made a very strong impression on me, and by the time I was seventeen years old, I was a full-fledged Bible fundamentalist. So, when I became a youth leader at the age of twenty, I continued – in a radical and uncompromising way – in this tradition.

Although I continued down my fundamentalist path until the early 1990s, my position on certain issues softened a bit over the years. For example, somewhere along the way I concluded that Young Earth Creationism was an untenable position, so for some years I considered myself an Old Earth Creationist instead.

In hindsight it seems unavoidable that this whole edifice had to come crashing down at some point. Being a fundamentalist tends to be challenging, since one must immunise oneself against important parts of reality. Being a fundamentalist with an inquisitive mind is harder still. In my case it proved to be impossible; especially after I finished my education with a PhD in computer science from University of Oslo.

By the time I was forty, I found myself in a deep and painful crisis of faith. Living and preaching the Gospel had been my earnest desire and an important source of joy and fulfilment for most of my life, and I tried to hold on to it for dear life. A complicating factor was that a central leader in my denomination, thirty years my senior and with a PhD in theology from a conservative (more or less fundamentalist) college in the US, had been my personal mentor since my late teens. Our close relationship continued for almost twenty years. I sat under his pulpit numerous times and spent many more hours having face to face discussions with him on topics related to theology, philosophy, and life in general. Sometimes, he would be in the audience when I was preaching; afterwards he would give me advice and constructive criticism to help me develop and mature.

During his studies, my mentor had been told that the doctrine of Biblical inerrancy – that it is without error or fault in all its teachings – was the central dogma without which Christianity would wither and die. I adopted the same view. The fundamental problem with this view is that it cannot possibly be correct. The evidence that the Bible contains inconsistencies and mistakes is strong indeed, and quite a bit of hermeneutical acrobatics is required to work one's way around the associated problems. When this finally dawned on me with full force in the mid-1990s, I felt both devastated and disillusioned.

Having realised that the Bible is not infallible, I started wondering about everything else I had learnt over the years. Might there be other elements in my theology that ought to be questioned? The answer was clearly yes, and chief among them was the Doctrine of the Trinity; the belief that Jesus is the second person in the triune Godhead – that Jesus is God.

Yet, I prayed to God, I kept reading the Bible, and read all the relevant books and articles I could lay my hands on. I fought long and hard, but step by step I was led to my conclusions – kicking and screaming, as they say. The shedding of dearly held convictions, as I have discovered, can be a painful and exhausting process indeed. But sometimes it is the price we must pay in order to make progress. Looking back, I believe I was liberated from an intellectual straitjacket that prevented me from thinking clearly and rationally, which in turn inadvertently caused me to cause problems for other people (not least the youth whose leader I was at that time).

As my crisis of faith intensified during the late 1990s, I started seriously questioning my own religious identity. I was bewildered and disillusioned. For a while, I considered myself an agnostic. I started reading the works of well-known atheists – Richard Dawkins, Daniel Dennett, Sam Harris, and Christopher Hitchens. They all made quite an impression on me, in particular, as a scientist, Dawkins. These authors made a strong case that something is indeed wrong with several dearly held Christian tenets, but they never came close to convincing me that there is no ultimate cause behind the existence of our universe. Indeed, what is by many regarded as the greatest problem in all of philosophy (why is there something rather than nothing?) was dismissed by one of these authors as 'vacuous'. This really made me question the soundness and coherence of their intellectual framework. I felt that their atheism was intellectually unsatisfactory. I can still vividly remember the day when I said to myself 'this just leaves me cold'.

I was wiser, but still somewhat bewildered. I had been liberated from the cold claws of atheism, and therefore knew that I believed in God. Moreover, it dawned on me that I was incurably religious (*uhelbredelig religiøs* in Norwegian). Thus, I took up my old habit of going to church on a regular basis. While this was indeed a blessing for which I am thankful, I still felt a bit out of place since I no longer believed in the Doctrine of the Trinity.

Beyond Anti-Islamic Sentiment

Meanwhile, I had become increasingly concerned about the consequences of Muslim immigration to Norway and the rest of the West. I believed that ethnic Norwegians could become a minority in their own homeland. I was apprehensive of Norway becoming a multi-ethnic society, and felt that our immigration policies were unsustainable. I wrote many opinion pieces in major Norwegian newspapers and participated in debates on national radio and television, criticising our politicians and immigration policies, as well as Muslims and Islam in particular. In 2010, I argued in my book *Selvmordsparadigmet* (*Suicide Paradigm*) that political correctness was destroying Western societies. Five years before publication of said book, my youngest brother Jens and I established the anti-Islam and anti-immigration blog HonestThinking.org (still alive, but now with a different focus). One of the people we attacked and targeted in our writings was Basim Ghozlan, a high-profile Muslim leader in Norway.

Every now and then questions would pop up in my mind. What if Basim Ghozlan's agenda was not of the Islamist strain we thought? What if we were being unfair to him? My conscience told me that I could not just continue this way. Having pondered the issue for a while, I decided to send him an email and propose that the two of us should meet for a one-on-one conversation, to get a better understanding of our differences. Basim has later told me that initially he found my suggestion provocative, and that he did not want to reply to me at all. However, he explains, there was something about my words that made him think that perhaps I was being sincere in my desire to better understand his position.

So, on a beautiful summer afternoon in July of 2005, at 4pm sharp, I showed up on the doorsteps of the Rabita Mosque in downtown Oslo. Basim was literally standing in the door waiting for me, and greeted me with a warm smile and a double handshake. Quite a magnanimous attitude, I thought to myself. A couple of hours later I found myself eating halal pizza and sharing personal anecdotes with a man that I hitherto had considered an enemy.

As the two of us said farewell at Oslo Central Station that evening, my world had been shaken to its core. I knew in my heart of hearts that my understanding of Islam was superficial, and that I had to investigate this religion much more thoroughly. And, of course, I started wondering not only if Islam was a more reasonable religion than I had thought, but also if this faith might provide answers to my many religious questions. I had been liberated from Islamophobia. My Islamic quest had begun.

In the years that followed, I attended many seminars at different venues in the greater Oslo area, including some that were held by student organisations at the University of Oslo. This, admittedly, was a mixed blessing. Sometimes there would be few or no other non-Muslims in attendance, and I experienced something of a culture shock now and then. Moreover, some of the preachers turned out to be of fundamentalist persuasion, and I felt it would be unwise to get myself into such a straitjacket once more. Thus, as the years went by, I still did not feel that I had found what I was looking for.

In addition to Basim, three other men played an important part in my journey: Farrukh Chaudhry, a medical professor at the University of Oslo; Abdul Aziz Ahmed, a Glasgow-based Muslim scholar who visited Norway several times a year at that time; and Timothy Winter, also known as Abdal Hakim Murad, Founder and Dean of the Cambridge Muslim College.

Not long after Basim and I got to know each other, the Rabita Mosque hosted a meeting featuring Tariq Ramadan. During the mingling after the official meeting, I encountered a man who recognised me from a recent public debate where I had been one of the panellists. The man had attended the debate in order to see for himself what kind of Islamophobe I was. Although I was still critical of (certain versions of) Islam, it turned out I was not quite the kind of person he had suspected. That man was Chaudhry, and we soon developed a close, personal friendship. For the next fourteen years or so, he was a very important dialogue partner in issues with my Islamic quest. We exchanged hundreds of emails, shared many meals (at some of the innumerable foreign restaurants in Oslo, or in our respective homes), spent a weekend together in the Norwegian mountains, and met many times for discussions after work. Farrukh was best man at my wedding in 2010.

At one weekend seminar I attended at Rabita Mosque, Abdul Aziz was a visiting scholar. Of the forty or so attendants, I appeared to be the only non-Muslim. However, I was asking more questions than anyone else. During the first lunch break, the Shaykh sat down with me on the floor to chat. This was the beginning of another friendship that proved to be important for my spiritual development. During a later seminar in Oslo, Abdul Aziz invited me to visit him and his family in Glasgow, and a year or two later we found dates that were suitable for all of us. Over the years there have been many more encounters in Norway, as well as one more visit to Glasgow (this time joined by my wife). Abdul Aziz has had a profound influence on me, and I consider him a dear friend.

Sometime between 2006 and 2010, Timothy Winter also visited the Rabita Mosque. I was there to attend his seminar and asked him some questions during one of the breaks. This helped me put some important issues to rest. A few years later I established email contact with him, and I think that on average we exchanged messages a few times per year.

At about the same time, I started reading the Qur'an seriously, but confess I had a hard time making sense of it. This changed when I started studying a relatively recent Norwegian translation (with explanatory footnotes) published by the Islamic Cultural Centre (ICC), one of the major mosques in Oslo. This made a strong impression on me. However, ICC had only completed translating the first sixteen Surahs at that time. Thus, once I completed reading the partial ICC translation, I picked up my copy of *The Message of The Qur'an* by Muhammad Asad and studied it from cover to cover.

This was a major eye-opener for me. Asad frequently interpolates explanatory words or phrases in brackets in the Qur'anic text itself, making it easier to understand the often-elliptical style of the Qur'an. Moreover, Asad's translation comes with an extensive set of notes, which I found very helpful. Thus, step by step, Asad helped me unpack the message of the Qur'an, making good on the implicit promise of the title of his translation. Even more important, Asad communicates in a way that resonates with someone like me with a Christian background. Generally, it seems to me that Asad has succeeded in making Islam's intellectual universe accessible to the Western mind unlike any others. The more I studied Asad's magnum opus, the more mesmerised I became.

My family is an unusually diverse one, representing Judaism, Catholic Christianity, Protestant Christianity, agnosticism, and now also Islam. My wife has a leadership position within an Evangelical denomination. Others within my close circle include a PhD in the Philosophy of Religion, a General Secretary of the Norwegian branch of an international Evangelical organisation, as well as a Professor of New Testament theology. Most of our friends are sincere believers as well. Since childhood, I have witnessed first-hand, within my own family and elsewhere, the blessings of lives lived in submission to God, irrespective of the particular tenets of faith professed by each individual.

Thus, I fell in love with the following verse, along with Asad's explanation:

> VERILY, those who have attained to faith [in this divine writ], as well as those who follow the Jewish faith, and the Christians, and the Sabians – all who believe in God and the Last Day and do righteous deeds – shall have their reward with their Sustainer; and no fear need they have, and neither shall they grieve. (2:62).

This passage – which recurs in the Qur'an several times – lays down a fundamental doctrine of Islam. With a breadth of vision unparalleled in any other
religious faith, the idea of 'salvation' is here made conditional upon three elements only: belief in God, belief in the Day of Judgment, and righteous action
in life.

Given my background, joining a religion that simply dismisses followers
of other faiths as infidels (*kuffar*) was out of the question. Some people
claim that 2:62 has been abrogated by 3:19 and 3:85, but I remain
unconvinced of their wisdom and scholarship. Asad rejects such a view
completely; he does not accept abrogation of Qur'anic verses at all. His
translation of 3:85 is as follows: 'if one goes in search of a religion other
than self-surrender unto God, it will never be accepted from him, and in
the life to come he shall be among the lost'. The phrase 'self-surrender
unto God' is Asad's rendering of the word *islam* in the Arabic text.

The scholars behind *The Study Quran*, another work that I have consulted,
appear to accept abrogation of some Qur'anic verses, but write in their
footnote to 3:85:

> Although some commentators record the opinion that considers 2:62 to have
> been abrogated by this verse, this type of abrogation is not recognized by main-
> stream Islamic Law and Quran interpretation, since only a ruling or legal com-
> mand can be abrogated, not a truth or a report, such as one has here (see
> 2:62c). [...] it does not take into account the more general and universal use
> of islam and muslim in the Quran to refer to all true, monotheistic religion;
> see 2:128c; 2:131-32c; 3:19c; 3:52c; 5:111c ...

In the general introduction to *The Study Quran*, we find this passage:

> The message of the Quran concerning religion is universal. Even when it
> speaks of islam, it refers not only to the religion revealed through the Prophet
> of Islam, but to submission to God in general.

Insisting that the words *islam* and *muslim* (without capitalisation) in the
Qur'anic text should be interpreted in a narrow and exclusivist sense,
strikes me as a prime example of pride and hubris. Thus, the attitude that
one adopts to 2:62, 3:85, and related verses, seems to be an important
dividing line between puritans, fanatics, extremists, and fundamentalists
on the one hand, and reasonable and moderate Muslims on the other. True

Islam must be built on humility, or else the very word becomes an oxymoron. And 3:85 contains a stark warning to those who wish to twist its meaning to serve their own agendas.

Ever since I was a young boy, I learned that truthfulness and a love for truth is the hallmark of anyone who really believes in and submits to God. Thus, I was delighted to read the following in *The Message of The Qur'an*: 'He it is who has sent forth His Apostle with the [task of spreading] guidance and the religion of truth, to the end that He make it prevail over every [false] religion; and none can bear witness [to the truth] as God does' (48:28); and: 'with all this, [remember that] those who are bent on denying the truth are allies of one another; and unless you act likewise [among yourselves], oppression will reign on earth, and great corruption' (8:73). There are many verses in the Qur'an that emphasise the importance of truth, and that warn against, in Asad's words, being 'bent on denying the truth'. This became a central element in my understanding of what Islam is all about.

One cannot be an earnest seeker for year after year after year, without reaching a conclusion. As time went by, I began to perceive this as an increasing urgency. In August 2019, out of the blue, so to speak, I got the following email message from Timothy Winter: 'Dear Ole, I find myself thinking of you. I hope all is well in your life and that you are continuing in your quest. Please let me know if you think there are any questions I might be able to answer.' Encouraged by this coincidence, I swiftly took advantage of his generous offer and sent him questions that were of particular importance to me. Tim provided comprehensive answers, which included this introductory sentence concerning the importance of truth within Islam: 'Islam is indeed passionately committed to truth, and honours those who sincerely seek it out.'

This further convinced me that I was on the right track. A few months later I reached a final decision. On 1 January 2020, I said the *shahada* all by myself; and soon thereafter, told my friends in the Rabita Mosque that I was now ready to confirm my conversion in the presence of others. The ceremony had to be postponed due to the pandemic, but on 14 June 2020 some fifteen people, including my wife Anne and three of her Christian friends, gathered in the mosque for my official *shahada*. It was a memorable day indeed.

What took so long?

In 2005, I was invited to speak at a workshop which was part of an international student conference hosted by the Norwegian University of Science and Technology (NTNU) in Trondheim. Together with twenty or so students from all over the world, I participated in lively discussions there. Among them, a young Muslim from Pakistan really stood out, obviously well informed and intelligent. While most of the students appeared to be of more or less secular persuasions, she was confident in her Islamic faith. Her demeanour made a deep and lasting impression on me. In the following weeks and months, I kept contrasting her confidence with my own lack of poise. A seed had been sown in my heart, and I believe this was one important reason why I contacted Basim Ghozlan of the Rabita Mosque a bit later that year. However, it took around fifteen years before I was ready to convert to Islam. So, what on earth took me so long?

Two different reasons stand out: my relationships to family members and obstacles of a theological and intellectual nature. Members of my Christian family, and some of my closest friends, perceived my Islamic quest as somewhat threatening, or at least as something that created insecurity. If my love for them was worthy of the name, the least I could do was to take their concerns and questions seriously and do my best to ensure that I made a well-informed decision. I came very close to converting in 2013 but realised that I was about to act prematurely. And even though almost seven additional years were spent trying to do everything the way it ought to be done out of respect for my loved ones as well as intellectual integrity, my conversion in 2020 resulted in a devastating blow in the form of a broken relationship. It remains a bleeding wound.

Early on in my Islamic quest I was told that Muslims consider the Bible to be a holy book, second only to the Qur'an, and thus to be read and interpreted in the light of the Qur'anic revelation. Unfortunately, many of the Muslims I encountered seemed not to care much about the Bible. I was left with a vague understanding that only Muslim scholars ought to read the Bible, since ordinary Muslims might be led astray by it. If becoming a Muslim meant I had to adopt an indifferent – or perhaps even condescending – attitude towards the Bible, that would be a showstopper.

Over the years I have met (or read articles and books by) Muslims who radiate joy and confidence, and who appear to have a rich spiritual life. However, I have also encountered Muslims who hardly display such qualities at all – in fact quite the opposite. Even though the Qur'an repeatedly emphasises that God is merciful and a dispenser of grace, some Muslims appear to be obsessed with the minutiae of rules and legalisms.

As far as I am concerned, God gives us rules and guidelines to help us create good societies where people treat each other fairly, to help us establish healthy families for children to grow up in, and to help individuals lead lives that bear witness to humility and God-consciousness. When this is turned on its head, and religion is reduced to a competition among its adherents about who is able to follow the largest number of (more or less arbitrary) rules, then I am no longer interested. Such a religion tends to result in intellectual and spiritual stagnation, places unnecessary burdens on the individual, and hardly promotes healthy, productive, and prosperous societies.

I have also met (or read articles and books by) Muslims who are interested in art, music, culture, philosophy, science, and other products of intellect and creativity. However, I have come across many Muslims who hardly display any interest in these areas. I hasten to add that there are issues of class and resources involved here. Children who grow up with little or no schooling, will obviously be at a disadvantage. The same applies to a certain degree to children who grow up with parents who do not encourage – or even discourage – interest in the products of our God-given abilities. Even so, it seems to me that some Muslims are outright anti-intellectual. This made me question the sincerity of many Muslims, as well the soundness of the Islamic edifice.

Then, there is the issue of intolerance among Muslims. Many are intolerant of other religions, labelling even followers of Judaism, Christianity, and other monotheistic faiths as *kuffar* – infidels or disbelievers. Not only that, but some of them also condemn Muslims who practise Islam in a slightly different way from their own. Certain infamous organisations appear to be leading the race towards the bottom of this pit, while others follow in their footsteps albeit in a less extreme way. There is just too much intolerance within the Muslim *ummah* for comfort. What is it about Islam that causes it to produce so many bigots? For years this question was looming in the back of my mind.

Towards Liberty

My fifteen-year-long Islamic quest has a certain element of liberation to it. I was liberated step by step from many concerns that held me back from becoming a Muslim. A number of authors profoundly changed my perception of Islam from antagonism via scepticism to cautious acceptance gradually, until I became convinced that the Qur'an is indeed a revelation from God. Chief among these is Muhammad Asad. But I am also greatly indebted to (in alphabetical order): Reza Aslan, Charles Hasan Le Gai Eaton, Khaled Abou El Fadl, Muhammad Abdel Haleem, Abdal Hakim Murad, Ziauddin Sardar, and Hamza Yusuf.

It is interesting to note that my story has some similarities to that of Dutch convert Joram van Klaveren. While my antipathy against Islam was never as strong as his (he used to be a member of the Dutch Parliament, representing an anti-Islam party), we were both deeply concerned about the problems caused by multiculturalism in general and Muslim immigration in particular. However, we both felt compelled to have a closer look at Islam, consulted some of the same scholars, and we both became convinced that our respective assessments of Muslims and Islam had been premature, biased, unfair, and unbalanced. Of particular importance is that we both realised that Islam need not be the way various extremists (as well as many critics of Islam) claim it must be. Reading van Klaveren's book *Apostate*, sometime after my own conversion, was a great encouragement to me.

God is the ultimate source of all truth. It follows from the principle of *tawhid* (the oneness of God) that He must also be the ultimate source of all that is good and all that is beautiful (since anything false is in general ugly and no good). This is millennia old wisdom, famously captured in Plato's exhortation that truth, goodness, and beauty ought to be the essential virtues in our lives. We should thus strive to have the qualities of truth, goodness, and beauty becoming ever more prevalent in our lives, as well as in our communities and societies. This, for several reasons, is easier said than done. Even so, we must never give up on these ideals since liberty without truth is false.

POSTNORMAL UKRAINE

Petro Sukhorolskyi

1. Genesis

Unlike some of its neighbours, Ukraine did not want to find itself at the forefront of world history. The contemporary dystopic images that flood the news reaffirm a metaphor put forward by the nineteenth century poet and artist, the founder of the modern Ukrainian identity, Taras Shevchenko, that evokes this tendency towards peaceful hermitage. In one of his poems, Shevchenko describes the real traditional Ukrainian utopia as 'a cherry orchard by the house'. It is a private cosy place on which no one can intrude, at which there reigns a measured, somewhat archaic, order. Similar ideas are expressed by the modern iconic painter and author of satirical and obscene short plays Les Poderevianskyi, who several years ago formulated the national idea of the Ukrainians in the words which can be approximately rendered to translate as 'get off us'.

This ideal image of the future was apparently established due to the centuries of foreign domination in Ukraine. That is why the word 'independence' has acquired extraordinary significance for Ukrainians. It means not just the independence of the state, but something much more important: the self-determination of the people, the preservation of their identity, as well as freedom of person and unconquerable human spirit. It is no accident, therefore, that this very word (*nezalezhnist* in Ukrainian) has become the object of ridicule by Russian chauvinists and propagandists, who link it to 'Russophobia', total dependence on the West, and 'licking the American boot'. It is also remarkable that another Ukrainian word used in relation to Ukrainians, which they hate, is *svidomyi* (conscious).

As a futurist, let alone a simple, sane, and rational individual, it is difficult to describe what has and continues to befall Ukraine. I am in the relative safety of the city of my birth, Lviv. But missiles are falling over northern and eastern Ukraine. Hospitals and railway stations are being bombed. Genocide has been committed in Bucha and other cities. Mariupol has been annihilated. Millions have been displaced and forced to migrate. The only way I can make sense of things is to consider that we are now living through postnormal times, which is characterised by complexity, contradictions, and chaos. But the signs of postnormalcy do not manifest themselves evenly everywhere. In many spheres and regions, the processes and mode of life of the people are not much different from those that were several decades ago. Hence, the questions arise: where are the manifestations of postnormality most powerful and where does the theory of postnormal times best explain what is going on. We can assume that it is where the framework of normality is not so strong, where there are borderlines and transformations, and breaking up takes place, or where formerly there was desolation, and something new has appeared in a short period of time. More often than not, it gets complex, contradictory, and dysfunctional. I think nowhere is more postnormal than Ukraine at present.

Ukraine is often associated with the edge, the borderland, the frontier. Indeed, since a particular moment in history, the line between Moscow's despotism and the societies which share European values and way of life has found a comfortable home here. At the same time, almost everything that we can associate with the word 'Ukrainian' (at least until 1917) is much closer to Europe. It is worth noting that there are many versions of the origin of the name Ukraine. Ukrainians prefer the one that links it with the verb 'ukraiaty' – to cut out, referring to the part of land on Earth where they live or that was given to them by God (the Ukrainian word *kraina* – country – is of the same origin). However, the Russians persistently promote another version linked with the word *okraina*, outskirts. From their point of view, Ukraine is exactly the outskirts of Russia, despite the fact that the city of Kyiv, which is located in the middle of Ukraine (if one measures from the west to the east), is considered to be the cradle of their civilisation. Another important contradiction is that Ukrainians have no doubt that the medieval state of Rus, which existed from the ninth to the thirteenth century, with its centre in Kyiv, is Ukraine's direct predecessor, while Russians believe it is the main root of their statehood and civilisation.

However, there is no special need to delve deep into history in all its various interpretations. Instead, let us focus on the situation that arose after Ukraine gained independence in 1991. Even then, it was quite possible to understand the main factors and contradictions that led to its sliding into postnormality in the following decades. After the collapse of the Soviet Union, Ukrainian statehood was closely tied to the two competing narratives, which were in many respects contradictory. At the core of the first narrative is the idea of the centuries-old struggle of Ukrainians for liberation from Russian/Soviet occupation, which not only aimed at the destruction of Ukrainian national identity but was also associated with numerous large-scale tragedies and crimes. Among them, one can mention: abolition of the Zaporozhian Sich, the semi-autonomous polity of Cossacks that existed between the sixteenth and eighteenth centuries; the slaughter of Baturyn in 1708; the destruction of the Ukrainian People's Republic (1917-1921); the Executed Renaissance of the 1920s and early 1930s, when thousands of Ukrainian writers and intellectuals were killed; the Ukrainian famine and genocide of 1932-33, known as the Holodomor that killed millions of Ukrainians; other numerous crimes of Stalinism before and during World War II, political repressions during the whole Soviet period, and numerous acts of Ukrainian language suppression from the seventeenth century until 1990. The list can go on for pages. The second narrative includes the vision of Ukraine as a continuation of the Ukrainian SSR with all its achievements, including metallurgy, energy, nuclear power plants, aviation, space conquest, advanced science and technical capabilities, and many more Soviet wonders. The first narrative is about passion, the will to fight, and the unconquered spirit; the second is related to income, jobs, material stability, and oligarchic economics.

During most of their history, the Ukrainians politically lacked state-building experience. The previous states existed for short periods of time. The Ukrainian People's Republic, for example, was finally defeated as a result of the treaty between Russia and Poland in 1921. The Ukrainian Cossack state of the seventeenth century, rapidly lost independence after its treaty with Russia in 1654. Therefore, state-building really started in the 1990s, forcing Ukraine to resort fully to the experience of the Soviet administrative apparatus and bureaucracy with all its shortcomings such as absence of the institute of an independent court. This is the former normalcy that was still alive and current at that time, in spite of the collapse of the USSR. Still, many new trends sprang up. Freedom of expression was finally asserted and the tradition of democratic elections was established. Elections themselves gradually turned into the major periodic show next to which football championships and musical festivals became dim and dull. Geographic division of the country was quite noticeable: the western part was naturally against the Soviet legacy and for European integration of Ukraine, while the industrial and Russian-speaking southeast opted for the preservation of ties with Russia. Russia itself was very heterogeneous but, in general, not aggressive and oriented towards friendship with the West, and the US in particular. It generated interesting cultural and political events and figured noticeably all over the post-Soviet space, and therefore was attractive for the majority of the Ukrainians on condition that traumas of the past were left firmly in history.

Other important complexities and contradictions in the Ukrainian society are not unique and are typical of the nations in the process of transit from the Soviet model to the democracy of Western persuasion, Russia included. It concerns the end of the centrally planned economic model, setting up of markets, and transformations in society linked with it. Wholesale dismissals and criminal redistribution of property become common. A majority of people had to overcome the consequences of the breaking down of their daily practices and look for new ways to live their life. Eventually, in the early 2000s, this was overlapped by the attempts to reform different branches of the government in accordance with an idealised, Western model. However, this process in Ukraine became ludicrous: a façade for reforms was created aimed at battling corruption while shifting responsibility to the lower levels of the hierarchy of power. And all this took place against the background of diminishing incomes and the beginning of a grave crisis of the Western model of democracy throughout the world.

One more public shock followed due to an abrupt liberalisation of the informational space accompanied by the appearance and rapid proliferation of the Internet. At first, quite different standpoints coexisted in the information space, more or less civilised dialogue was carried out, and manipulations often were primitive and not aggressive. Alongside this, mass media were overloaded with pieces of news on UFOs, psychics, conspiracy theories, and new radical interpretations of history. This trend, which was rather scarce earlier during the Soviet period, infiltrated the main media trend throughout the 1990s. In addition, numerous new religious organisations emerged, including aggressive and totalitarian sects. Later, in the early 2000s, informational manipulations of public opinion became a much wider phenomenon that remained subtle while growing in complexity.

Despite this, it seemed in the 1990s that Ukraine was stable and predictable. The widespread contradictions in society did not lead to violence. The belief that the Ukrainians are peaceful and tolerant people dominated this period. External threats were not obvious because Russia looked relatively democratic (at least up to the beginning of the Second Chechen War in 1999), and other neighbours were busy solving their own transitional problems. Ukraine renounced nuclear weapons in 1996, and few were against its neutrality. A bloodless exit of Ukraine from the USSR was considered to be one of the main achievements of the day, and the Yugoslav Wars were perceived as a remote nightmare. At the presidential elections in 1994, the Ukrainians voted for a pro-Russian candidate, Leonid Kuchma. But this fact essentially did not change anything. He went on adhering to the neutral status of Ukraine, tried to achieve a political balance between Russia and the West, and did not encroach on Ukrainian-centred cultural policy too much. The 'end of history' had been declared; and it seemed that Ukraine was a shining example of the triumph of liberal-democratic normalcy. But under the surface, a volcano was bubbling.

2. Burst

After the collapse of the Soviet Union, many Russians were frustrated that their country was defeated in the Cold War and ceased to be a Superpower. Part of Russia's political elite, close to the security structures, developed plans for revenge that were supposed to culminate with the return of Russia to the group of world hegemons. The return of the former Soviet republics to Russian orbit was considered to be the first step in this direction. After the outbreak of the Second Chechen War, which ended with the complete destruction of Chechnya, the ruling regime began to implement these plans. During the first year of his rule, Putin changed Russia's national anthem to the well-known music of the anthem of the USSR. While most of the oligarchs were cut off from political influence, many close to Putin rapidly became US-dollar billionaires. These were the first steps in manufacturing a new normalcy.

Fully-fledged attempts at manufacturing normalcy began with the curtailment of freedom of expression. All major television channels were quickly subordinated to the Kremlin and a propaganda machine of gigantic scale was created. Since then, it has been constantly spreading the following messages: Russia is a great power and has the right to an exclusive place in the world; Russian culture, literature, language, people, spirituality, the victory in World War II, and so on, are also 'great'; The West (and especially the United States) is Russia's eternal enemy seeking its destruction; Western organisations are hostile and aggressive (NATO), or unattractive and unviable (EU); the former Soviet republics that do not aspire to unite with Russia are wretched puppets of the West; Russians, Ukrainians, and Belarusians are one people that the West is trying to incite against each other according to divide-and-rule maxim; and, the West artificially invented Ukrainian identity and uses it for the destruction of Russia. Until recently, the West paid little attention to these propaganda messages, despite the fact that Russia spread them internationally.

It is reasonable to assume that the population of Russia was tired of the chaos of the 1990s as well as the horrors of the Second Chechen War. It gladly plunged into the warm bath of state propaganda. The explosions that hit four apartment blocks in Russian cities, including Moscow, in 1999 marked a high point of social tension. The authorities blamed the events on Chechen militants and exploited the situation to justify the Second Chechen War that helped Putin win the presidency in 2000. However, a number of critics of the regime, including former security officer Alexander Litvinenko, accused Putin and the Federal Security Service of the explosions. In 2006, in Britain, Litvinenko was poisoned with radioactive polonium by Russian agents. As Putin consolidated his power and gained more control over the media, social tensions eased significantly. Moreover, the Russian economy improved as, after the lowest point in late 1998, oil prices started to rise steadily reaching the highest peak in 2008. Consequently, the new Russian normalcy manufactured by Putin's regime turned out to be a very comfortable place for many Russians. Meanwhile, the new Russian 'tsar' with huge financial resources at his disposal, enjoying popular adherence, was able to begin implementing his geopolitical plans.

In Ukraine, the situation moved in the opposite direction. In the early 2000s, the domestic political landscape worsened considerably, and many factors pointed to Russia's direct involvement in this. In 2000, Ukrainian journalist Georgiy Gongadze was assassinated, and secret audio recordings in the office of Ukrainian president Leonid Kuchma indirectly indicated the president's involvement in the crime. These events significantly weakened his power and were a major obstacle to his participation in the 2004 presidential election. Instead, pro-Russian Viktor Yanukovych and pro-Western Viktor Yushchenko became the main candidates. The election campaign was accompanied by unprecedented abuses by the government headed by Yanukovych. At the same time, pro-Russian forces actively disseminated information about the geographical division of Ukraine and claimed that for the United States and their allies the Ukrainians in the south and east of the country were third-class people.

Election-related tensions and chaos culminated in the fall of 2004. About two months before the election, Yushchenko was poisoned by dioxins and found himself on the brink of death. The poisoning resulted in significant long-term health problems for the candidate and disfiguration of his face, which later became the subject of nasty manipulations in pro-Russian media. In the second round of elections, the authorities committed significant fraud, resulting in declaring Yanukovych the winner. It could have ended with the complete victory of the pro-Russian forces in Ukraine. But the chaos led to a postnormal burst: the Orange Revolution or the first Maidan, which radically changed the situation and was the first failure and shock of its kind for the Putin regime.

The word *maidan* is of Turkish origin and means square. The name of the protest movement derives from the name of the central square of Kyiv, where the main protests took place. In the remote past, debates on public issues also took place in maidans of Ukrainian towns and cities. The Maidan is a shining example of how a complex system, such as the Ukrainian society, effectively self-organises in postnormal times. This was an unexpected swarm of Black Jellyfish – event and phenomena that have the potential of going postnormal by escalating rapidly – that had the potential to change the course of Ukrainian history. The Orange Revolution brought together office workers, students, farmers, entrepreneurs, celebrities, politicians, and many others. They demonstrated an extraordinary capacity for concerted action and self-sufficiency. People from quite different backgrounds found their place in the Maidan where the outsiders suddenly became leaders, and conventional leaders and celebrities did not seem so bright. It was a place where one could preserve and develop one's identity, in contrast to ordinary life where the dominant system tends to transform people into a plastic pliable mass. There was real creativity: people sang and wrote songs, painted, cooked together, engaged in self-improvement, and gave public performances. There was a high degree of mutual assistance and support among the members of the Maidan. It was a place of large-scale polylogue where participants were concerned not so much with their own interests but with the future of their country and community, the fate of the next generations, and the values guiding people's choices and actions.

It may sound too idealistic. But that is what it looks like from the inside to those of us in the Maidan. But looking from the outside, it is easy to mistake the Orange Revolution for a product of skilful manipulation by influential external forces. Russia's regime itself seemed to have truly believed that the Ukrainian Maidan was caused by using American social technologies. And this significantly hindered the Russians from adequately assessing the situation in Ukraine in the coming years as well as making informed decisions. Indeed, the US and the West have long supported Ukrainian civil society, and NGOs they have been funding, obviously, promoted and took part in the protests. However, their participation, like any other, was not decisive. In the following years, Russia and its allies in Ukraine have repeatedly tried to recreate the Maidan. But the outcome has always been miserable. It turned out that to predict or organise a Maidan was impossible.

After the Orange Revolution, the socio-political system in Ukraine appeared to return back to its normal state. However, this widespread conclusion reflects only a very superficial assessment of the situation. In fact, there had been fundamental qualitative changes in society, the significance of which became clear only a decade later. The Maidan opposed both the remnants of the former normalcy in Ukraine and the Russian manufactured normalcy. However, they were not so easy to resist and overcome. In the period from 2005 to 2013, Russia increased its attempts to significantly influence the domestic political situation in Ukraine using all available levers, especially natural gas supplies on which the Ukrainian economy depended heavily. As a result of numerous political crises and confrontations, in 2010 the same Victor Yanukovych, who had been ousted by Maidan in 2004, did become the president of Ukraine. However, this time he won a fair election and the people recognised his legitimacy without any protests.

Despite its expectation, the new president did not immediately run into the arms of Russia. Rather, he continued the course of Ukraine's European integration, which led to the approval of the text of the EU-Ukraine Association Agreement in 2013. However, a few days before the planned signing of the agreement, and after Yanukovych's negotiations with Putin, the government made a radical foreign policy reversal and announced its intention to integrate with Russia. This shocked Ukrainian society and led to mass protests called the Euromaidan. At first, there had been no evidence of a dramatic change until the Yanukovych's government attempted to forcibly disperse the protests, injuring many participants. This was a turning point – a trigger that launched a second big postnormal burst and deprived Yanukovych of a chance to stay on as president.

The authorities resorted to violence and repression. They tried to take into account the experience of 2004, but they did not understand the essence of the Maidan. They continued their attempts to organise anti-Maidan protests, engaging people with money and involving criminals. Russia supported Yanukovych, but the revolution could not be stopped. As a result of clashes and shootings of protesters, more than a hundred people, known locally as the 'Heavenly Hundred', were killed while about 2,000 were injured. The protests themselves which were originally aimed at preserving the course of European integration came to be called the 'Revolution of Dignity', because people stood and died precisely to preserve their dignity, freedom, and rights. After the victory of the Euromaidan, Yanukovych fled to Russia and early presidential and parliamentary elections were held in which representatives of the political forces fighting for Ukraine's independence and its European integration won a landslide victory – over 77 percent of the votes in parliamentary elections. Russia could not deal with one more defeat and in 2014 started an aggressive war against Ukraine, occupying Crimea and then invading Donbas.

The Revolution of Dignity proved that the first Maidan was not accidental and that its potential in 2004 was far from being fully realised. The second Maidan was much tougher and bloodier and its opponents committed more serious crimes. After this, direct involvement of an external enemy in Ukrainian events became apparent, although Russia denied it for a lengthy period. At the Euromaidan, the postnormal phenomena manifested themselves in all their brightness. Under considerable external pressure, Ukrainians managed to create a new reality in the face of which all aggressive strategies of the enemy proved powerless. Some Ukrainians compare this phenomenon to carbon powder which under strong pressure turns into a diamond. Others talk about a swarm of bees attacking the enemy who had disturbed the hive.

3. Culmination

The acute phase of the war in the Donbas lasted about ten months in 2014 and 2015. At that time, Russia consistently denied any involvement of its own troops in the war despite substantial evidence to the contrary. Instead, it established two quasi-state entities in the eastern part of Donbas similar to the ones earlier established by it in Transnistria, Abkhazia, and Southern Ossetia. After the invasion of Crimea, the manufactured normalcy in Russia steadily moved towards radicalisation, isolation, and the curtailment of fundamental freedoms. Arkady Babchenko, the prominent Russian liberal journalist, calls this process 'pupation or crystallisation of the Reich'. The overwhelming majority of the Russians just kept living in a relaxed state supporting Putin's foreign policy and feeling proud of their president. The slogan 'Crimea is ours' plunged the Russian society into a state of unbridled euphoria for a while. The postnormal lag between the processes in the real world and the manufactured normalcy in Russia kept growing.

The situation regarding human rights and freedoms was also becoming increasingly worse in the parts of Ukraine occupied by Russia. In particular, according to the 'Freedom in the World' ranking by Freedom House, in 2021, Eastern Donbas was ranked seventh from the end right next to North Korea while in Crimea the situation was not much better. It was ranked twelfth from the end among 210 countries and territories. Thus, under occupation it is impossible to identify sentiments and positions of the population of these areas without its liberation and freeing of people's mind from long-lasting propaganda. In its turn, Ukraine was also plunged into a kind of manufactured normalcy in which the war did not seem to exist. The vast majority of people were not directly affected with the tragic consequences of war and continued to live a normal life after 2015. Additionally, Ukrainian citizens have been accustomed to Russia's aggressive rhetoric. It is not hard to understand why many believed that their eastern neighbour, despite its behaviour, was quite satisfied with its territorial conquests and might leave Ukraine in peace.

The influence of the Russian threat on Ukrainian domestic politics continued to diminish. In 2019, the former comedian and actor Volodymyr Zelensky was elected president by a large majority (73 percent of the vote) and his party which had been established immediately before the election won an absolute majority of seats (56 percent) in Parliament. One of Zelensky's key electoral promises was to stop the war in Donbas and to reach peace with Russia through direct negotiations. Thus, the majority of people of Ukraine never imagined they would face another bloody phase of war. Instead, they sought to improve socio-economic indicators and overcome corruption. At the same time, a public consensus regarding the need for integration into the EU was virtually achieved and a majority of the population supported the accession of Ukraine into NATO. Because of such pretended normalcy, as well as confidence of people in the pragmatic character of the Russian political elite, insufficient attention was paid to a potential full-scale Russian invasion of Ukraine, even though numerous military experts had clearly indicated its possibility.

The invasion, which began at about 5am on 24 February 2022 with the rocket attacks on a number of Ukrainian cities, shocked the Ukrainians – although it came as no surprise. For some, such as for the residents of Ukrainian-controlled part of Donbas and for the military, it is simply an extended present. For other Ukrainians, this is a familiar future because images of a war with Russia are ingrained in their consciousness; and have been widespread in media for a long time. Russia has turned out to be a real big Black Elephant – an extremely likely and predicted event widely ignored – not only for many in the West who, despite sanctions, had been developing economic relations with it for many years and had even negotiated the launch of the Nord Stream 2 gas pipeline. But this does not mean that the West did not understand Russia's imperial ambitions. On the contrary, they were well known and many Westerners were even ready to accept them. The most unpleasant and unexpected surprise related to Russia's readiness to disregard and violate all the norms of the civilised world. The existence of a united and cohesive Ukrainian nation that represents strong and organised force also turned out to be a Black Elephant in the early days of the invasion. In other words, before the escalation in 2022, the West continued to rely on obsolete theories and practices that had repeatedly proved ineffective – and not just in relation to Russia!

Russia's large-scale aggression initiated a new spirit of popular resistance. The first weeks of fighting have shown that the Ukrainian army, together with the authorities and citizens, is able to provide fierce resistance to the invader – it brought the inadequacy of the Kremlin's plans and strategies to the fore. In such a situation, the most interesting thing is to understand why it is so difficult for a major power like Russia, with all its resources and unbridled desire to conquer, to cope with Ukraine.

There are four main reasons.

First, it should not be overlooked that manufactured normalcy created by Russia has no historical counterpart. Putin's regime is not a kind of light Stalinism, and in the twenty-first century there are many factors that did not exist in the times of the Cold War. In any case, it is impossible to step in the same river twice; and the result of Putin's efforts has turned out to be rather grotesque. One of the main reasons for this is corruption. Transnational corruption including bank accounts around the globe, instant financial transactions, the possibilities to get a passport through investment, to lobby for any solution by spending vast sums, and to invest dirty money in luxury goods, real estate, yachts, and masterpieces of art worth hundreds of millions of dollars, is a real phenomenon of postnormal times. Corruption is now an integral part of all conventional strategies; and methods of dealing with it are inefficient because it is often impossible even to clearly draw a line between legal and illegal. The insanely high speeds and incredible complexity of the financial world make corruption fluid and elusive. Unlike Putin and his oligarchs, the architects of USSR 2.0, former Soviet officials including the highest in ranks did not embezzle billions, did not live in palaces, did not imagine themselves the nobility of the nineteenth century, did not buy the most expensive yachts in the world and real estate in London, and their children did not study in the best schools and universities in the West. As a consequence of rampant corruption, hundreds of billions of dollars intended for the modernisation of the army vanished into thin air. Obsolete military equipment of various generations has come into Ukrainian land. As it turned out, Russian soldiers have often lacked even basic supplies and have had to eat food from packages expired many years ago or to feed themselves by looting shops and civilians. The prominent Russian opposition leader, Alexei Navalny, made corruption a central theme of his fight against Putin's regime. However, his critics said that if there had been no corruption Putin with his oil and gas money would have been able to build a truly horrible military megamachine against which his opponents would not have had much of a chance. In other words, Russian corruption has become one of the key allies of the Ukrainians. And under the current circumstances, the only real strength of Russia is terrifying weapons of mass destruction designed and manufactured in the Soviet Union.

Second, a major source of the failure of the planned blitzkrieg is Russia's misunderstanding of the processes taking place in Ukraine. There is a big misconception of the phenomenon of the Maidan, which is perceived and portrayed as a product of Western machinations, carried out with the use of Western technologies to manipulate of public opinion. Therefore, the Russians who had powerful technologies of human manipulation at their own disposal, inherited from the Soviet times, and significantly developed in recent decades, were not deeply concerned with genuine social changes in Ukraine. Their propaganda and psychological operations have turned out to be very effective in many situations around the world, including in Ukraine. So, it was assumed, they will work again. However, these tools have proved to be quite ineffective against a people who merge into self-organised networks that are both difficult to control and predict. They can mislead some of the people some of the time. But as is evident, even in this case, a vast number of activists quickly detect manipulations and draw public attention to them. Russia planned the invasion taking into account the Ukrainian reality of 2014 or 2004, or even of the Soviet times. But the Ukrainian society, warmed up by the Maidans and the war in Donbas, has been transforming significantly. It has acquired new characteristics and has reached a new level of consolidation.

So, the endless manipulations of Putin's regime of historic events of the last millennium and those associated with World War II, may influence the Russians. But most Ukrainians were baffled and puzzled by all this. In particular, Putin's attempts to justify the importance of capturing Crimea by the fact that Volodymyr the Great, the Grand Prince of Kyiv, had been allegedly baptised in one of the ancient Greek cities of that region at the end of the tenth century, sounded as if today's Italians were claiming the territory of Egypt by using the facts from the life of the pharaohs for justification. Meanwhile when the current great war broke out, Ukrainians themselves, without any coercion or instructions from above, extracted from the depths of their collective consciousness remote and close historical events to strengthen their identity and gain additional energy to fight. These events include numerous episodes of the struggle for independence from Russia in previous centuries and armed resistance to the Nazi invasion during World War II. This has come as a real shock to many Russians.

Third, observers in Russia and the West have greatly underestimated the emerging complexity and contradictions in Ukraine. This is typical of today's world where perceptions of lesser-known peoples and cultures, whose history can be measured in millennia, are reduced to simple schemes, patterns, and prejudices. The language issue could be taken as an example. Outside of Ukraine, few seem to doubt the validity of a highly simplified and erroneous conclusion that Ukrainian-speaking Ukrainians are for independence and integration with the West while Russian-speaking Ukrainians are for strengthening of ties with Russia. In fact, the so-called Russian-speaking Ukrainians are very different. Most of them are bilingual or have close ancestors for whom Ukrainian was a mother tongue. The younger generations are almost always fluent in Ukrainian. And even if a

Ukrainian citizen is completely Russian-speaking or ethnic Russian, it means practically nothing regarding his attitude to the Putin regime or to modern Russia immersed in the dark dreams and myths of the past.

Fourth and finally, a big surprise for Russia has been the transformation of President Zelensky, whose rating and popularity was continuously declining, into a true leader of the nation in the time of war. Not only did he not back down and panic in the face of the terrible threat, he also gained considerable popularity among people around the globe through his speeches and actions, and canny use of social media. In this respect, Zelensky is a true Black Swan at all stages of his short political career. His participation and victory in the 2019 elections were truly amazing and unexpected. In 2022, he once again managed to surprise the Ukrainians and attract even the majority of his opponents. It is impossible to predict what will happen to him in the future when the current postnormal burst comes to an end. But for now, we can assume that a postnormal leader like Zelensky is essential for postnormal times.

4. Lessons

The world has found itself in the turmoil of the Russian invasion of Ukraine, even as the coronavirus pandemic is still with us. Despite the numerous forecasts, expected return to a 'new normal' has not happened. There are, however, lessons to be learned from what is going on.

To begin with, it is necessary to admit that most of the former approaches and theories have turned out to be inadequate. By relying and leaning on them, the West lost sight of developments in Russia. Focus on oneself and one's own problems frequently blinds us to the reality outside. This is proved by the fact that in numerous forecasts for 2022, both Russia and Ukraine were conspicuous by their absence. Even if the authors of such foresights made mention of the probability of a big war between these states, this fact did not have any impact on their judgment of numerous global consequences that we now face. The same mistakes were made regarding the forecasts of the Covid pandemic.

Similarly, when speaking about various existential threats, global nuclear war is mentioned only in passing without focussing on its possibility. The West seems to believe that Russia is a variant of the USSR and thus former strategies of nuclear deterrence are going to be as successful as they were during the Cold War. But this is not the case. The Soviet Union was a huge industrial machine of the post-Second World War period, with various institutions and checks and balances that kept different centres of influence (at least after Stalin's death) in equilibrium. It was, thus, predictable to some extent. Putin's Russia is a product of postnormal times: it is unpredictable, and functions on the whims of one man, embroiled in the sectarian and apocalyptic theology of the Russian Orthodox Church (ROC). It is not by accident that Putin describes the invasion of Ukraine as 'noble'. For the ROC, the Catholic-Protestant world, and 'brotherly Ukrainian' territory 'lieth in evil' and has to be cleansed of all sins. Even if it means nuclear war. As Putin has declared, 'as martyrs, we shall go to paradise and they will just croak'; and 'why do we need the world if there is no Russia in it?' The Russian-American philosopher and literary scholar, Mikhail Epstein, describes Putin's theology, as 'Satanodicy'. It has long roots in Russian history, stretching from seventeenth century to the contemporary fascist philosopher, Alexander Dugin, who has had considerable influence on Putin's outlook.

Freedom in postnormal times is clearly not just freedom from outside interference or freedom of empty existence in an automated world. It has to be based on values, the real core ones, critically considered and developed in the changing context of our world. How do we see others; how do we live and let live. These existential questions require us to challenge our thinking so that we may rise over the sea of complications and contradictions, and restore order in the chaos of postnormal times. Ordinary people are more sensitive to these questions than technocrats, businesses, and governments. The experience of Ukrainian Maidans proves that an effective self-organised resistance, based on common values, trust, and equality, can be a force for positive social change. Humans are not just biological beings. They tend to create values and lay down their lives to make them real.

LIVING IN FREEDOM

Katharina Schmoll

Lockdown I

Despite it all, I felt a sense of freedom. The wind was flowing through my hair, gently caressing me while I was walking through the fields with my hands open, palms touching the stalks of wheat around me. I was happy. Happy to enjoy the first warming sun rays of spring on my face. To be fully present in the moment. Not thinking about the future. I had established a new routine. Getting up around seven in the morning, exercising, ablution, belated *Fajr* prayer, marking student essays, *Dhuhr* prayer, and then my treat of the day, a walk in the fields of my childhood. Life felt easy. These were the first weeks of the Covid-19 pandemic lockdown and the first days of Ramadan. April 2020.

I had just moved from London to Leeds, taking up a job as a lecturer at the university when the pandemic hit. When in March the French president Emmanuel Macron hastily announced the closing of the European borders, I did not think long before booking a flight and leaving the UK in the middle of the night to go back to Germany, the country of my childhood. Since moving out, I only ever came back to visit my family and the village I grew up in for a few days each year. As a young girl, I had always known I would leave. And yet here I was. Amidst the not knowing, the confusion, the crumbling of any sense of security in the early days of the pandemic, all I had wanted was the comfort of family. So I went home. It took me a few weeks to realise that this was not going to be over any time soon. With every day passing by and new restrictions coming into place, it dawned on me. I was stuck. And Ramadan was around the corner without anyone else around me to share the joys and burdens of that holy month with.

These should have been days where I felt restricted and lonely. In a place where I had often struggled being myself. With a pandemic not even allowing me to escape to the next biggest city for a few hours. During Ramadan, when I could not eat or drink all day. And yet I felt free and happy. Liberated from the constraints of my fast-paced city life. Liberated from constantly making plans for the future. From wanting and having it all. Walking through the fields of my childhood, I started wondering: How much freedom makes us truly happy?

That Ramadan 2020 ended up being one of my most fulfilling ones. I felt at peace. Before picking up fasting in my mid-twenties, fasting from dawn till sunset had been something so alien, so incomprehensible to me. There was a mystical beauty about it I was unable to grasp. And there was a longing. To feel that poise that some fasting Muslims radiated. My first years of fasting were trial-and-error. I was worried my migraines would get worse and I would not be able to go ahead with work. I started fasting gradually like children do. At the beginning I was hardly able to do a few hours without getting headaches. I did not have Muslim friends close by or relatives to explain to me what foods to eat before fasting and to drink plenty of water to get me through the day. I had to figure it out all by myself. It took time, patience, and a lot of willpower to fully reap the benefits of fasting. By 2020, a certain Ramadan routine had settled in. Yet everything was different that year. I was back home and we were confronted with the first ever Covid lockdown. To me, Ramadan was a true blessing that year. But to my non-Muslim family and friends, my choice to fast seemed astonishing. Why add another restriction to the already intense constraints of the lockdown?

The question of freedom and restraint is something many Muslims grapple with at some point in their lives. What exactly do we gain from adhering to the tenets of our faith? Why fast from dawn to sunset when we could share a cup of tea with our friends or indulge in comfort eating instead? As someone who was not born into the faith, I understand both outsiders' prejudices and the blessings of restraint. I have often overheard Muslims trying to explain to non-Muslims how Ramadan can be a relief from modern-day consumerism and the constant availability of everything we desire, and how it reminds us to be grateful for what we have. One could argue, perhaps, that the restrictions of the lockdown had a similar effect. So, why fasting? But with all certainties and daily routines suddenly vanished, the routines of the holy month gave me the stability and spiritual energy I needed. It was not limiting, it comforted me. Sometimes mental freedom can be found in restriction.

Indeed, being restricted to a little flat in my childhood village and the surrounding fields and forests that Ramadan, I was able to block out all worldly aspects of life and fully immerse myself in divine beauty. With my senses heightened thanks to the fasting, listening to the chirping of the birds and the leaves of the tree moving softly with the wind, my daily walks through the lush green fields made me feel so close to God. With the mundane almost entirely cut from my life, that summer I reached unknown spiritual heights. I felt liberated. I felt like I was succeeding. Yet the blissful state did not last. Thank God I had no idea what was coming.

Lockdown II

When I woke up, for the first time in weeks I felt calm. I slowly opened my eyes, gradually giving them the chance to adapt to the light. The blinds were pulled down but the winter sun gently cracked through the edges of the window, covering my bedroom in a soft yellow. I realised it was already midday. Dazed, I tried to find the strength to sit up. I felt endlessly exhausted and empty. But weirdly also calm. Relief. After almost three months of panic, unable to control my breath, unable to eat or fall asleep, my heart rate was finally regular. I took a few deep breaths in, soaking in the unexpected stillness in my head. I pulled away the duvet, slowly put one foot on the ground, then the other. I managed to get out of bed, stand up, and go over to the wardrobe. With every step, I felt relief that I was suddenly able to breathe normally. But then I opened my wardrobe and my stomach started churning. I began to shiver. I took out a few clothes. Skirts, dresses, pullovers. I looked at them in awe. I had never seen them before. And worse, I did not even particularly like them. I went to the living room and looked around. The beige sofa, carefully arranged paisley cushions, an Orientalist painting with an antique golden frame on the wall over the fireplace. I had no clue who had chosen these decorations. I felt a stinging sense of loss and alienation. I went to the bathroom and looked into the mirror. I slightly tilted my head to the side and started studying the face I was looking at. I was looking at a stranger. I did not recognise my face. I lifted my arms and could not feel anything. They were not mine. Everything felt alien, numb, and hazy. As if I was not really there. As if I did not exist. I broke down.

Exactly a year later, in February 2022, I am amazed I am almost able to joke about it. But perhaps laughing is the only way to cope with what cannot be made sense of. Anyone who has ever had to deal with intense forms of depersonalisation and derealisation might immediately recognise what I went through. But that day back then, I had no idea what was going on. I was scared to death. I was going mad. I did not know that I was suffering from a condition one can experience as a result of prolonged and severe stress, panic, and sleep deprivation. It is like your soul leaving your body and this world. Your body's last resort when your mind cannot cope any longer. I wish I had known this state would only be temporary. But I didn't. So, for now, I had to live without identity. Just when I finally thought I had figured it all out, I had to start from scratch. *Who am I?*

I was born in West Germany in 1989, eight months and twenty-two days before the wall came down that had separated the East and West of my country for almost thirty years. I was lucky. I grew up during a period of time that was called 'the end of history', marked by the end of the Cold War and the supposed victory of liberal Western-style democracy. Germany reunified and Europe was growing together. Walls and borders were torn down all over Europe. But it took me a long time to tear down the walls in my head.

I grew up in a stable middle-class environment, with an intact family, in a small German village where everyone knew each other. People had time for each other and life was easy. I had close friends. The quality of housing was high. Never did I have to worry about money or anything else. And yet, there was this question that occupied my mind from a young age. *Why do we suffer?* I can't tell how I came up with this question – my life was fairly normal from what I remember. But this is how my journey of finding happiness and freedom from suffering began. Learning about Islam and Judaism in school a few years later had me suspecting for the first time that I might not be Christian after all. That the answer to my question, my quest of finding happiness and freedom from suffering, would take me somewhere else. But it would take more than a decade until I finally surrendered to the idea that I felt closest to Islam. In the years between, I was falling in and out of love with ideas and worldviews. Buddhism, atheism, nihilism, humanism. Nothing really convinced me. So I continued exploring the world through books and, later, through travelling. And the more I exposed myself to the world, the more it dawned on me that I might never again fit into the world I had been born into. In my mid-twenties, I moved to East London and eventually embraced Islam. For a while, it felt exciting to explore my new life in Britain, to travel all over the world and to meet people from all walks of life. I was becoming myself at last. I was thriving. But my liberation came at a cost. I lost a sense of place and belonging. I started feeling disoriented.

Our identity crises are a quintessentially modern condition, and the consequence of life in our globalised, borderless, media-saturated world, full of possibilities, and choices. Always in need to reassess our place in societies constantly in flux, changing at an ever-increasing speed, unable to provide a stable and secure framework for our existence, we turn to ourselves as a source of meaning. We have groomed the individual as the main pillar of society – with increasingly dire consequences. We have become so individualised, so unique in our identities that it is getting hard to relate to each other meaningfully. The results are frail, insecure human beings and social turmoil, as the sociologist Manuel Castells argued: 'social groups and individuals become alienated from each other, and see the other as a stranger, eventually as a threat. In this process, social fragmentation spreads, as identities become more specific and increasingly difficult to share'. In his three-part magnum opus *The Information Age*, published in the late 1990s, Castells saw it all coming. The identity crises, the polarisation, the instability. Brexit, Trump, Islamic terrorism. I suppose I am a product of our time. The confusion, the anxiety, the restlessness. The inability to make sense of myself and the world around me. I have felt it all.

Truly, I can say it is no surprise to me that in 2018, the controversial psychologist Jordan Peterson managed to write a multi-million copy, global bestseller by advising people on how to bring order into their lives. I ended up cleaning not only my room as a response to my inner chaos and the perceived turmoil around me, as Peterson advised in one of his *12*

Rules for Life, but my entire life. I reacted by limiting my own freedom. Islamic style.

In a borderless and often confusing world, following Islam and its set of guidelines that regulate our everyday lives and provide a group identity one can belong to is appealing. For a while, it was the same with me. I started praying more regularly, fasted more seriously, dressed more modestly, read the Qur'an more often, and said goodbye to alcohol. I turned into a fairly pious person. My focus increased. My insecurities and anxieties lessened. I felt empowered. But then subtle doubts started invading my thoughts, and it slowly dawned on me that I was not feeling so great after all. That I was tired and lonely. That I was so different from other Muslims. Then the second lockdown came and turned my world upside down.

When I managed to piece together a resemblance of composure after the first few days of my dissociative episode, I started feeling fairly normal again to my friends. But to me, even my closest friends were complete strangers now. The disassociation makes you lose all empathy and connection. It was beyond painful to suddenly feel estranged from friends and family. But perhaps worst of all, I also lost my connection to God. For anyone who has been blessed with a strong spiritual connection, it does not matter much what is happening to you or around you. Things happen for a reason. The first lockdown was easy because of my faith. I did not feel trapped by the pandemic, the shackles of the *dunya,* because by then I had mastered focus on the *akhirah*. During the first lockdown, I was often reminded of the words the captive Arab prince and poet Abu Firas al-Hamdani had written more than a millennium ago about – most likely divine – love and longing:

As long as you're sweet, let life be bitter
As long as you're pleased, let all men be wroth
As long as there's a bond between me and you
Let all between me and the worlds be in ruins
If truly you love me, then all things are easy
And let all that's over the dust, be dust

But then the second lockdown came and with it, the panic and the disassociation. Whenever a non-Muslim friend had asked me what Islam and having faith meant to me, I would smile and say, 'It's like your best friend permanently hugging you.' But then the world turned into ruins and that friend left me. All of a sudden, nothing felt easy any longer. I had stopped feeling God's love. His *rahmah*. I did not feel anything. The world had become a scary, soulless place. I stopped listening to my favourite Islamic podcasts. I started praying less until I eventually resigned, giving in to my feelings of separation, giving up any hope I might eventually recover a piece of my spiritual connection. After all these years, Nietzsche had found his way back to me. *God is dead*. I felt enslaved by my mind and imprisoned in the confinement of my London flat.

In the summer of 2020, when the first lockdown gradually eased, I gave up my flat in Leeds and moved back to London to await an insecure pandemic-stricken future surrounded by the comfort of friends. I was glad to have my friends close to me again. But there was this loneliness inside me. A loneliness that first visited me when I had moved to London. I had tried to fill that hole with divine love and books. But it was not enough. I craved human warmth. Feeling someone's body and heartbeat next to mine. The steadying comfort of masculine affection. It was time to get married. But then the second marriage felt within reach and I turned on my heel.

For a few weeks it felt like bliss. Shortly after I moved back to London, I had fallen head over heels in love. It all made sense. We started talking about the *nikkah*. Everything felt great. Until it didn't. One sunny lockdown morning in November, leaves had started falling from the trees and my breath was shimmering in the cold air, I was out for a short walk when my chest started feeling heavy. I tried to catch my breath but my body would not let me. I thought I would suffocate. I went home. I was swamped with work but could not concentrate. With no distraction available, all cafés closed and human interaction reduced to a minimum, my thoughts started spinning in circles until my head began feeling light-headed. After a few days of panic, it started dawning on me. *I can't breathe. I can't breathe in this relationship.* My body intuitively knew he was not the right one for me. But my mind questioned my bodily intuition and a quarrel between the two began. A few weeks later, my entire body felt so tight and heavy I struggled to take in any food. During the nights, I rolled over from one side of my bed to the other, unable to find any rest. At the time, I did not understand why my body was reacting so strongly. As the weeks passed by with me barely able to get any work done, the panic fully started to take possession of me. When a major depression finally started to creep into my already exhausted body and mind, the disaster was complete. And so, my soul decided to leave. When I thought I couldn't get worse, the dissociation began.

Had I realised that I had been physically unwell even before falling in love, perhaps I might have been able to calm myself and at least not worry about losing my job. Had I realised that I had already massively struggled concentrating since my Covid infection. After many hospital visits, I now know that I was suffering from long Covid: intense brain fog which made it difficult for me to process any information or emotion. The panic and depression were just a natural result.

Being able to live again with the brain fog, depression, and disassociation was hard. Not to withdraw from social life despite the intense sensations of confusion and separation. To regain the slightest sense of joy. It required a lot of work and professional help. But even in the darkest moments, I clung on to one of my favourite verses of the Qur'an in which God reminds the Prophet Mohammed of His blessings and reassures him of spiritual relief: 'Verily, with hardship comes ease' (Qur'an 94:5). So I chose to live.

Life after

January 2022. He gently takes my face into his hands and kisses me passionately. It is around midnight, and we are somewhere in a bar in Kensington. American 1920s-style music. Dim light. Leather and plush sofas. Two cocktails on the dark wood coffee table in front of us. I can't stop smiling.

We got to know each other a few months ago. When I was still barely able to function but determined that life had to go on. During Ramadan. Neither of us was fasting. He had never gotten into the habit and I felt physically and mentally unable. He was unsure what exactly he was looking for. In what felt like only seconds ago, I would not have considered giving in – even for a second. I truly believed in the Islamic view on marriage, 'And one of His signs is that He created for you spouses from among yourselves so that you may find tranquillity in them' (Qur'an 30:21). But when I thought I had found such tranquillity just months ago, why did I walk away? Had my almost fiancé really just been the wrong one? Or was I perhaps also a product of our time? As the sociologist Zygmunt Bauman wrote in his book *Liquid Love* about relationships in our modern individualist times: We are 'despairing at being abandoned to [our] own wits and feeling easily disposable, yearning for the security of togetherness …, and so desperate to "relate"; yet wary of the state of "being related" and particularly of being related "for good", not to mention forever – since we fear that such a state may bring burdens and cause strains [we] neither feel able nor are willing to bear'.

How, as Muslims, should we engage with a world where relationships are often fluid and where 'fun' is instantly available via dating apps? With so much instability around me, I was longing for a stable, loving relationship. I valued the Qur'anic wisdom of finding tranquillity in marriage and was suspicious of modern-day casual dating. But for months now, I had lost my spiritual connection, my identity, and my ability to feel any joy. Life was not the same. I felt insecure and vulnerable, and I knew I needed something to lift me up slightly. So instead of running away from this man who was not sure what he could give me, I hesitated. And then, after a bit more soul-searching, I decided to let go and to free myself from the restrictions of my faith.

So here I am. Late in the evening, in my mini skirt, in this bar in Kensington with its American 1920s-style music, dim light, leather and plush sofas, a cocktail in front of me and a very charming man next to me. A man who makes me laugh. Who does not take life too serious. And I feel great. A few lines of my favourite song Rule the World by the DJ and producer duo Gamper & Dadoni come to my mind about two lovers having the night of their life, drinking tequila, ignoring what the world and their lives might look like the next day.

Perhaps tomorrow the world will burn. But tonight I want to taste tequila and feel like I rule the world. To feel light and free and young again. To hell with all these social media imams and the *akhirah*.

Secretly, I had long had a soft spot for electronic music. Particularly as a teenager. But the older I got, the more I felt the need to suppress certain parts of me. The more I explored myself and the world around me, the more overwhelmingly complex my identity became. Especially after adopting Islam, I did not dare to be all of it. To accept and live with the complexities and contradictions within me. Listening to Avicii during the day and then the Qur'an before going to bed? Being a complete natural in flirting but wondering whether it's *haram*? Opting for the *halal* food option whenever possible but then back home guiltily unable to say no to my grandparents' homemade pasta stuffed with pork? The glass of red wine on Christmas Eve? Welcome to my world. The truth is, most people are complex. Because so is life. But chances are modernity and globalisation have rendered some persons more complex and contradictory than others.

As Muslims living in the West, navigating faith and freedom can be a daunting challenge. We find freedom and comfort in restriction but often we also find ourselves confronted with having to justify our choices to the people around us. We are surrounded by a myriad of lifestyles, and it is a natural human desire to blend in and to be shaped by what we see happening around us. Complex and contradictory identities are the result. Making sense of these complexities and contradictions within ourselves can be hard and at times overwhelming. There is an abundance of opportunities to trespass in every possible way, and so we constantly need to make choices about how strictly we want to interpret and follow Islam. In the instances I chose to trespass, I learned to live with the feeling of shame and guilt. But as the years passed by, I more frequently opted to submit, for peace of mind. It is no coincidence that the Arabic root letters for the word 'Islam' are *s-l-m*, the same as for submission (*tasleem*) and peace (*salaam*). Indeed, translating Islam as 'peace through submission' is completely acceptable. And, often, submitting to what can be perceived as God's will felt more natural to me anyway. The virtue of covering up for example. Whenever my mother and I go to the lido in our village, I am prepared for the same discussion. Why do I 'have to' wear a swim dress rather than a bikini like everyone else? Why don't I want to show my beautiful body? For many in the West, it can be hard to accept that for some women, freedom can mean the freedom to cover up rather than having their body exposed. I had always felt uncomfortable showing too much skin. I never completely stopped wearing mini-skirts but mostly, there was a trend towards looser clothes. And the more I covered up, the more I prayed and fasted, adhering to the tenets of my faith, the more I was able to find some peace of mind in this borderless, complex world. I felt liberated. And happy. Or so I thought. But then the second lockdown came and with it the dissociation, forcing me to question the path I had taken.

A few days ago, I found myself standing at home in front of a full-length mirror. I curiously studied that woman in a bikini in front of me. Did I seriously just order a bikini? I couldn't believe it. I laughed, shaking my head in disbelief. *I am wearing a bikini.* And I was loving it.

I had wanted to be liberated from the complexities of my identity and the challenges of life. Submitting to God for peace of mind. But we cannot run away from ourselves forever. Life needs to be lived. Had the Prophet Muhammad (peace be upon him) not advised us to 'take advantage of five before five': youth before old age, health before sickness, wealth before poverty, free time before business, and life before death? Perhaps I needed to be pushed to the boundaries of my existence to reclaim an appreciation for this worldly life again. To allow myself to truly live. To ignore the guilt and shame. To embrace the complexities of this world in the twenty-first century. The truth is, I feel happier now than I have been in a long time. I feel connected to the people and the world around me. Rather than being constantly drained, thinking about *halal* and *haram*, feeling judged, I am starting to be able again to give back. So how wrong can it really be to enjoy some mundane pleasure – cocktails, bikinis, and romance? Even before, I was always the never-good-enough Muslim. What does this make me now?

Just when I thought I had figured it all out, all certainties suddenly crumbled in front of me like sand slipping through my fingers. In the West, freedom has long been the catchphrase of our times. But how much freedom makes us truly happy? And what exactly *is* freedom? Freedom from the shackles of the worldly *dunya*, or freedom to forget about *yawm al-qiyamah*, the Day of Judgement, and enjoy what life has to offer? Throughout my adult life, I have been trying and struggling to find a balance between freedom and restriction. But perhaps, in the end, it is not so much about finding the right degree of freedom but accepting that freedom can and must mean different things at different times. Accepting that life can be messy, that we live in a complex and multicultural world, not seventh-century Arabia. Accepting that life is constantly in flux, with the pandemic perhaps more so than ever before. Why not lean in and trust our intuition about what feels right in the moment? That's what I did. I liberated myself from all the self-imposed religious restrictions and decided to live in the present. To laugh, to feel life, to love. And slowly, very slowly, I can feel my connection to God coming back. Almost two years have now passed since the beginning of the pandemic and, as I write this, another Ramadan awaits us. I can't wait to begin fasting.

HOW *DISTORTED IMAGINATION* CHANGED ME

Jack Wager

What part did I play in manufacturing public consensus about Islam and Muslims? Are my opinions and judgements based exclusively on what I have been taught by my teachers, told by commentators, read on online blogs, and what I have garnered from the media? These questions had been troubling me for some time. And, in these times of wide access to information, what some have termed infoglut, I think it is important for us to continually trace back our own belief systems, to self-reflect upon what motivates our opinions and lifestyles.

I was born in Birmingham, a multi-cultural hotbed, neighboured by many rich cultures of the world; and grew up in a Catholic household. Religion is important to me. But it seems that religion has captivated the media's attention for the theatrical more than ever before. I was born nearly a decade later than the Salman Rushdie affair of 1989, and too young to remember the events of 9/11. But I have known nothing other than the aftermath, the ensuing demonisation of Islam and Othering of Muslims, and polarisation and reactionary patriotism. I noticed a parallel: how we the Irish were treated and subjected to in the twentieth century. If these sentiments about the Irish existed as staunchly today, it would be my family that faces that misrepresentation, and the social consequences that follow. That realisation may have only been drawn from the self-preservation reserved for children, but it did give me a pivotal conclusion early on. The conclusion that discrimination was cyclical and fed on fear, the seeds planted in history but the growing roots hard to cut down. Under these circumstances, the contextual knowledge of reoccurring social debates becomes an asset to possess. I witnessed the controversy surrounding the *Charlie Hebdo* affair in 2015, and wondered how it was and was not related to the Rushdie affair. I found myself drawn towards studying literature and politics of the twentieth century.

After obtaining a master's degree in Creative Writing from the University of Salford, I continued my exploration of twentieth century culture and history, researching and planning my first novel. It will explore the rise of working-class participation in football hooliganism during the 1970s and 1980s, in direct proportion to declining opportunities and stability for men in traditional industries. The treatment of the working class in the media during this time was devastating, and I believe it has left a long-lasting social impact on England that has still not been recognised or debated for what it was. Once again, I saw parallels with the media's treatment of Islam and Muslims.

While looking for potential publishers for my novel, I received a letter of interest from a newly established Manchester-based firm, Vellum Publishing. I met with the owner, Salik Rahman, to discuss my project but soon found we were talking about literature and culture, Islamophobia, marginalisation of certain communities, and other talking points of the day.

I could see by how Vellum approached business and industry with social accountability and long-term thinking; and their ethos of wanting to promote marginalised voices, to enrich debate, and minimise the impact of harmful rhetoric, seemed to align with my passions. I was offered a job as editor at Vellum and started to work on projects with themes that are traditionally unrepresented in literature. This is where I was given the project of editing and updating a book that would come to act as a defining point in my internal anguish and self-reflection. It provided me with historical context that enabled me to make sense of what is going on in today's world, and answer a number of questions that were circulating in my mind. The book is *Distorted Imagination: Lessons from The Rushdie Affair* by Ziauddin Sardar and Merryl Wyn Davies. It would come to act as a big step forward for my own realisations, helping to unwind the twenty-odd years of the media's coercion.

Distorted Imagination was published in 1990, two years after the publication of *The Satanic Verses* and a year after Ayatollah Khomeini's fatwa against Salman Rushdie. In his autobiography, *Desperately Seeking Paradise*, Ziauddin Sardar provides the background of how the book came to be written and eventually published after several mainstream publishers initially accepted the manuscript and then withdrew their offers. The book argues both against *The Satanic Verses*, a portion of which is based on the life of Prophet Muhammad, and the fatwa, and suggest that the real issues raised by the Rushdie affair are not freedom of expression or blasphemy but the survival of a cultural identity. It provides a detailed analysis of *The Satanic Verses* and other works of Rushdie, the notions of freedom of expression, tolerance, and secularism. But more than that, it traces the long history of the Rushdie affair within the concept of distorted imagination: the intellectual tool the West has fashioned to explain Islam and other non-Western cultures.

As some reviewers noted, intellectually *Distorted Imagination* is far superior to anything that the defenders of Rushdie had produced. Bhikhu Parekh, for example, described the book as 'ambitious and complex', with 'a remarkable historical and cultural depth and a wide intellectual sympathy'. Rightly arguing that the Rushdie affair cannot be understood in isolation from the Orientalist discourse on Islam, it skilfully analyses the latter's nature and genesis, and subjects it to a powerful critique. It then goes on to examine the contents and assumptions of *The Satanic Verses* and shows why the book has given such offence.

For me, *Distorted Imagination* was an eye opener.

I grew up in a milieu where the figure of Salman Rushdie was a pop culture reference. Before I was aware of his writing and the reaction to his work, I knew Rushdie as a level-headed figure whose opinion, when sought after by the big media conglomerates, would be framed to be trusted, wise and pragmatic. I first became aware of Rushdie when he would feature on TV with comedians who were notorious atheists, such as Ricky Gervais, where they would ridicule religion rather than intelligently dissect it. They would present religious followers as naïve and unintelligible, and suggest that religion was a disease that has infected the modern world, making it unable to progress. The Western idea of the right to ridicule, I find, has led to an over-representation of ridiculing religion in the media, as if to hammer home the point so these rights to ridicule can never be discussed. I talked about religion with friends who are similar in age to myself, and I recognised that most held the viewpoints of the atheist comedians we often see, with their sets full of religious mockery. I saw in them that the spiritual aspects of why one might follow religion were almost entirely discounted, and the topics we see in the news media became their key reference points: wars, intolerance, liberty. Religion had acquired a whole new meaning to them, far from the roots of community and sanctity. That's where I saw Rushdie's position in the Western operation: he is seen to embody the supposed core value of freedom of speech. This is evident in the pivotal role he had when he reappeared to represent this 'Western value' in the debate surrounding 'no platforming' in universities. Islam's alleged denial of freedom of expression seemed to be a repeated topic brought up by the commentariat. Apart from being rather unimpressed with the antics of atheist comedians, I wondered how we have reached a climate where Islam is viewed as intolerant, ignorant, and divisive? And was freedom of expression absolute and sacrosanct? These were the questions I had on my mind and thought it imperative to track my own awareness of the Rushdie affair, and what it told me about where the West was in the ideological arena.

The historical context provided in *Distorted Imagination* shows how modern debates such as no-platforming, censorship, and personal freedoms are just another stage in the wider operation of imperial domination that has been ongoing for centuries. I particularly found the notion of 'brown sahib' compelling in the contextual explanation of the Rushdie affair and how it progressed. Brown sahibs are native South Asians who not only imitate English lifestyles but have a huge bias towards the West regarding the East. They often talk with an Oxford accent and have internalised colonial ideology to such an extent that they become totally Anglicised. In the first decades of the post-independence world, the brown sahibs were preoccupied with establishing a strong foothold in the countries they had inherited from the colonial powers but now, the second generation of brown sahibs have become writers and commentators and celebrities. Their basic characteristics remain the same, but having acquired global pretensions. This is a very integral stage to track the history of religious freedoms and behaviour. Colonial powers had created a legacy that shaped religious, political, and social discourse that remains rife today. Religion, or shall I say religious following, may be seemingly declining in the West, but it holds a significant influence in geopolitical debates, maybe even more than ever through ongoing cultural operations. With this influence, religion is open to mockery, misinformation, and meandering.

And for brown sahibs, such as Rushdie and V. S. Naipaul, Islam presents an inevitable target for misrepresentation, mockery, and ridicule.

There were a couple of topics that I identified as challenging, forcing me to reflect upon my own beliefs. The first topic was doubt, more specifically the right to doubt. Where once challenges may not have been permitted, secularism gave society a chance to challenge belief. Just as doubt did not come easily into history, so must it be protected. Therefore, everything must be subjected to questioning, including ridicule and abuse. *Distorted Imagination* convinced me that while doubt is essential for belief, it cannot be perpetual or eternal. Reading the book, I also saw that doubt enabled the West to promote secularisation. History has been a back and forth of imperial domination. I focussed my attention towards the *Charlie Hebdo* attacks in 2015, an event I can remember clearly, as well as its media reaction. I wondered how my opinions about the attacks and the rhetoric had changed, if at all, and if this contributed to beliefs I have in reaction to similar news events. I could recall the *Je Suis Charlie* movement embraced by journalists in support of 'freedom of the press,' which had echoes of the Rushdie affair. I could now better understand the reaction within France, with the Republican marches, and the reaction by Britain, with *Charlie Hebdo* winning both International 'Islamophobe of the Year' award (Islamic Human Rights Commission) and also 'Secularist of the Year' (National Secular Society). It helps you to understand the landscape that followed, leading to 2020 and *Charlie Hebdo* declaring it will republish distortions portraying Muhammad – supported by the Western media embroiled in the frenzy of the ongoing trials of those responsible for the attacks. I could better dissect the media reaction to the violent protests. The reaction of French media contained colonial tropes and they turned towards Islam as a whole. Macron himself defended the caricatures and there were popular movements in some Muslims countries – mainly Qatar and Kuwait – to boycott French products, while European leaders supported his remarks. French interior minister Gérald Darmanin called the attack 'fundamentally an act of Islamist terrorism', and Prime Minister Jean Castex said 'the enemies of the republic will not win', pledging to escalate the fight on terrorism. The contextual information on the foundations of Islam, so well recounted in *Distorted Imagination*, could help steer the individual away from getting caught up in such rhetoric, and associating acts of terrorism with a whole religion. Through a post-colonial lens, it's easier to identify the broader ideological warzones that are being fought repeatedly when events like the 2015 attacks arise. Seeing the reaction by the French media to these attacks, I found the idea that the West projects the ignorant image of Islam onto the East vastly more convincing. The book claims that the Western image of Islam is in fact the darker side of Europe: racism, unbelief, sex, hate, domination, ignorance, espionage – and as soon as this point was made I thought of many examples where this was reinforced. This operation served as an insulating device to avoid unthinkable thoughts that could not be allowed to gain credence. Here you can identify the colonial and neo-liberal hangover we face today in the political arena. One of the most significant realisations was how much the cultural operation of Orientalism had affected my own thoughts, and how Orientalism has degenerated to undiluted Islamophobia in recent history. In my Catholic household Western Judaeo-Christian heritage was overtly represented, and I considered it to be the source of all knowledge and philosophy – something I took as self-evident. And the corollary proposition that Islam, and indeed other cultures, made no contribution to knowledge, philosophy, science, and history was almost a truism. The book dispelled this illusion. I recognised that the distorted imagination so consciously created by John of Damascus, Dante, and *The Song of Roland*, and nurtured by countless writers, travellers and philosophers, still shapes the West's understanding of Islam. The operation is still in full swing and I was participating in it.

What do the ignorant images of Islam and Muslims look like? As well as deconstructing the Rushdie affair, *Distorted Imagination* serves a vital purpose in explaining the roots of religion and the history of Muslims and their representations. As the Qur'an is so central to the religious practices of Muslims, background knowledge of the Sacred Text is vastly significant in this climate. Again, I saw how important this was when reading *Distorted Imagination*, as it explained how the Qur'an asks a series of questions, and the answers to these questions are to be found by the use of reason and thought, physical exertion as well as inner reflection, and of course, in the Qur'an itself. Yet, in Western society the connotations of the Qur'an are seemingly worlds apart from its reality. I learnt how the message of the Qur'an is not static, and Muslims do not believe that they have a total understanding of the Qur'an once and for all. However, I realised I knew little of this, despite being exposed to many news stories, articles, and think tank pieces that have claimed to reference the 'truth' of the Qur'an – often for their own gain and depicting Islam as intolerant. The Qur'an allots one-third of its contents to asking the readers to think, exercise reason, read, ponder, and reflect, therefore it is not likely to look down upon other religious texts. Not only is it fundamental because it is believed to be the Book of God but also it is a basic tool of discourse, a vehicle for the dissemination of thought and ideas, a prime instrument of criticism and countercriticism, and a basic means of intellectual and literary expression. Given this central role of the book in Islam, how could Islam be against freedom of expression? This was another breakthrough moment for me in realising how entwined the ignorant image of Islam was in Western culture – everything I thought I knew about the Qur'an had been disproven by *Distorted Imagination*.

I appreciated equally the explanation and exploration of Muslim writers and scholars of the classical period. That their works were made viable by the freedom of expression promoted by Islam, is essential context in the modern date of censorship. That is not to say that no attempts were made by this or that caliph to suppress this or that idea or book. But the overall freedom of expression we see in Islamic history contrasts sharply with medieval European history. The West is often seen to 'defend' its 'freedom of speech' against the East and Islam, both determined to 'colonise the mind'. Yet almost all philosophy that emerged in Muslim civilisation was the outcome of reasoned discourse and discussion. Freedom of expression was not limited to works of philosophy, theology, mysticism, and scholarship but also discovered its expression through literature too. During my first reading of the book, I highlighted the R.A Nicholson quote where he pointed out the evolution of a diverse range of thought 'was accompanied by an outburst of intellectual activity such as the East had never witnessed before'. Literary criticism, as we know it, first emerged in Muslim civilisation, its prime concern was with the analysis of the figures of speech in both poetry and prose to heighten the understanding of the wonder of language. These features are not the products of a people who abuse whistle-blowers and outlaw free thought.

Distorted Imagination crucially offers a literary explanation of the reaction to Rushdie in these terms. The book claims that Rushdie engages in a 'mock trial of Islam as a religion, culture and civilisation'. The novel, the book clarifies, derives from the Western literary tradition to which it contributes. In fact, *The Satanic Verses* was one of three novels the author produced, which defined a new type of author. He would articulate Eastern culture with the style and language of Western literature, and Rushdie is often praised with creating a hallmark of a new era – one of interconnection and interdependence. Therefore, it is important to dissect the reaction to *The Satanic Verses* in this context. The shock and indignation that Muslim response produced in western literary circles, *Distorted Imagination* tells us, emerges from the assumed place and function of art in modern society and the particular place of Rushdie within modern literature. Rushdie was the amalgamated culmination of an international procedure. It is when the nature of this globalising world, the repository of the conscience of Western civilisation, is taken by surprise, that its reaction is indicative of something authentic and profound in the perspective of Western civilisation.

In his portrayal of India, Rushdie keeps to the well-worn path marked out by Orientalism, so in this context, the reaction to *The Satanic Verses* reveals no surprises. The transgression that offended some Muslims was the culmination of a theme Rushdie had flirted with before. He has stated that his works *Midnight's Children, Shame*, and *The Satanic Verses* are a kind of trilogy of themes he knows: India, Pakistan, Islam, and migrants from the subcontinent in England. Rushdie's literary style is essential to be aware of too for this debate. He uses the techniques of 'recurrence' and 'correspondences' in his work, and 'cannot refrain from telling his readers how and what he is about.' Familiarity with the culture he discusses reveals another subtext within his writing, that can be dissimilar to the unschooled readers. Rushdie states that he stands at a particular angle to Islam but his writing, I'd argue, is littered with attack lines formed by the process of Orientalism. His speculative thinking about Islam is shaped not only by the world of Muslim ideas but those imposed upon it by Orientalists. He reduces religion to the secular vision, one where religion is imposed upon them by describers and definers.

I read *Distorted Imagination* a number of times. In the end, I subscribed to the book's claim that 'when examined, Rushdie emerges as little more than the distorted imagination writ large'. He relies upon a historic body of evidence which he presents inaccurately as the most profound level and in specific detail and his writing serves the modern operation of Orientalism. Here, I could pinpoint the similarities between Rushdie's writings and the media's cyclical coverage of migration, immigration, and refugee debates. The book explains that Rushdie's ideas about immigration are one dimensional. Rereading his works, this stuck out to me more clearly within his writing. Rushdie's hints that migration is some sort of notion of being cut free from history, memory, and time is completely at odds with real-world examples, such as my heritage in the Irish community. The world has a view of Ireland that has been crafted and publicised because of Irish migration across the world, not the reverse. There's no denying the discontinuity of migration but Rushdie's view is very narrow in this regard.

The Satanic Verses is essentially a religious book, in the sense that it is about the nature of religion, despite most reviewers treating the text in the context of migration or translation. Rushdie often names his characters similar to key figures in classical Islam, which has become a characteristic of his writing. He mixes facts and fiction, equates the Sunnah with the Qur'an, and totally alters the nature and function of the Prophet as he himself taught and expressed it and as the Qur'an states it to be. Few of his supporters realised this. I found it eye opening to see some of the hypocritical rhetoric being spouted by the West around the debate surrounding *The Satanic Verses*. The novel contains what they expect it to; it confirms all their biases and prejudices.

Distorted Imagination, in my opinion, is an important book that needs to be read and reread by my generation. It offers an important context of religious disparagement, colonialism, and knowledge formation to manufacture consent and cement cultural hegemony. With modern debates often diluted by rhetoric and misinformation, *Distorted Imagination* could act as a reliable and accessible reference of information and analysis that would force the readers to confront their own prejudices, examine the geopolitical landscape of the media, and see through the tropes that represent the Other as barbaric and unworthy. I'm sure it will be a piece of work I will return to at many points of my life, and its information will act as context to the many debates the media will concoct in the future.

In 1989, in response to the protests against *The Satanic Verses*, Rushdie asked his detractors: what kind of idea are you? In 2022, *Distorted Imagination* changed my idea of who I was to become who I now am.

AN AFGHAN SUCCESS STORY

Sulaiman Haqpana

Several important events happened in Afghanistan during the year I was born: 1986. Russia's invasion, which started in December 1979, was coming to an end, and Mikhail Gorbachev, the Soviet premier, had declared he would withdraw six regiments from Afghanistan. By 1989, when I was three years old, the withdrawal of all Russian troops had taken place. At the time, Afghanistan was a significant battlefield for Cold War competitors, and by 1986 the resistance fighters, known as Mujahideen, were receiving sophisticated weaponry from the West, particularly from the United States, the United Kingdom, France, and China through Pakistan. The weaponry included shoulder-fired ground-to-air missiles, which were critical in destabilising the Soviet air force. In the middle of 1986, Babrak Karmal, the general secretary of the People's Democratic Party of Afghanistan (PDPA), was forced to resign and was replaced by Dr Najibullah Ahmad Zai. The PDPA was established as a Marxist-Leninist political party in 1965, and came into power in 1978 with Karmal serving as its general secretary from 1979 to 1986. The Soviet-Afghan War lasted from 1979 to 1989, and after the withdrawal of Russian troops in 1989, civil war began, lasting from 1989 to 1992. The war was waged between the government led by Ahmad Zai and the Mujahideen groups.

This was the Afghanistan I was born into. My parents were from a middle-class family originally from Herat Province, who had, for work reasons, resettled to Kabul in 1975. My earliest childhood memory dates back to when I was about four years old. I remember my father buying me a yellow tricycle. As we lived in a flat, he had to take it out into the playground located in front of our building. We were living in Macroyan Three, a complex of high-rise flats built by the Soviets before the invasion. By the end of the year, the civil war had reached the Macroyan areas. One bright afternoon when I was playing outside on my tricycle, I heard a massive explosion that shook the ground. My elder sister, who was out playing with me, immediately picked me up and took me indoors. At the time I was not sure what was going on, but then the fighting intensified, and I was not allowed outside anymore.

The whole family found itself locked indoors all the time. One evening when we gathered with our neighbours in the basement of the block; it was dark and I was very frightened and there was no power. The water pipes were broken and there was a flood in the basement. I was with the women and other children in a big utility room while the men formed a chain to take the water out of the basement with buckets and bowls. The sound of gunfire and rockets was getting closer and closer, and things were getting worse by the day. So, my father decided to leave Kabul and move back to Herat. That meant leaving our flat and all our possessions behind. I remember reaching the airport, which was under the control of the government at the time. It was the first time I had ever seen a helicopter, let alone flown in one, but we all climbed aboard and flew towards Herat. Herat was much safer then, because the main battles were for the control of Kabul, the capital of Afghanistan.

We resettled in Herat in 1990, when I was four. I was happy that we had managed to get there safely and pleased to meet my cousins for the first time. We became close friends and started playing and drawing together, but it didn't last long as we had to move out of my uncle's house and rent somewhere much further away. I gradually made new friends, and a year later, I was enrolled in a public school in Grade One. The civil war carried on in Kabul and the surrounding cities, but Herat was relatively peaceful during our stay, which lasted until 1995. Life was normal – at least insofar as we couldn't hear explosions and gunfire. I really did not like having to change schools twice when we moved to a new house. Moving house meant losing all the friends I had made, and it felt like every time I made friends with new classmates, I had to leave them. I found it hard to make new friends.

The educational system in Afghanistan was designed in such a way that if students didn't pass their year, they remained in the same grade regardless of their age. Normally, the bullies and less able children would fail, and I was scared of facing them in a new school. There were several instances of confrontations and fights between me and those bullies. I was referred to as the 'class geek' as I normally did well and achieved good marks. Every day, for six days a week, I attended supplementary Islamic education in the local mosque. Reading the Qur'an and memorising sections by heart were part of Islamic studies in the mosque. For me, going to the mosque was like going to jail. My dislike of the supplementary Islamic studies was due to the cruelty of our mullah, the local religious leader. Mullahs were respected by the local people, so every evening one house sent food for dinner to the local mullah. I was taken to the mosque by my uncle, who said to the mullah: 'First, we hand over these children to Allah, and second to you. Their meat is ours, and their bones are yours.' This meant that our parents gave the mullah permission to use physical punishment on us. My uncle's words were a common statement, and they encouraged the mullahs to be aggressive and abusive while teaching Qur'anic lessons. The only person I was scared of was my mullah, and I made sure that I learned what I was expected to learn. 'Anyone who does not memorise their verses will face *falak,*' he declared. It was a harsh system of punishment mainly used in mosques but also in some schools.

The *falak* itself was a length of wood with a rough rope connected to it in the middle. The person who was to face *falak* had to lie on the ground, his legs would be tied with ropes, and two boys would hold each side of the stick. The mullah would use a hard piece of rubber to beat the soles of the feet of the person who had sinned. I faced the *falak* twice in my life. Once when I missed going to the mosque and went swimming with my cousins instead, and once when I did not memorise my verses. The number of blows depended on the level of sin. In the first case I received fifteen blows, and in the second ten. I was unable to walk on my feet after facing the *falak*. It was even worse when I was told to hold one side of the *falak* when my close friend was being beaten. We didn't have the right to say no or object to the mullahs' order. I felt bad for my friends, but it was commonly understood that we had no choice, and when it was my turn, my close friends held the sides of the *falak* for me. When I got home, I started crying and told my parents about the punishment. Their reply was, 'well done to your mullah. You won't be late for class or forget to do your homework again, will you?' A couple of years ago I asked my father why he didn't go and talk to the mullah about not using physical punishment. He said that society at the time required me to obey the mullah's rules.

My niece, who is still in Afghanistan, tells me that the practice is still widespread in the majority of mosques.

In the mosque, we all sat in a big circle and read our verses aloud. The mullah tested each of us one by one, and when we were called, we had to go and sit face-to-face with him and read or recite the Qur'anic verses for him. He would either give us a new lesson or ask us to repeat the same one after he had corrected it. I remember that there was a beautiful girl in our group, whose name I can still remember. The mullah usually kept her until the last, and I remember that she was treated very differently. The mullah would sit her much closer to him, and I sometimes saw that he was touching the girl inappropriately. I was sure at the time that it wasn't a normal thing to do but I was too scared to discuss it with anyone at home or outside the mosque. I was worried that if what I said got back to the mullah somehow, I would face the *falak* again. I am sure other elderly men knew what he was doing, but they were too scared to say anything about it. Now, I wonder about the psychological and social effects of all the bullying and the mental, physical, and sexual abuse that students faced during their mosque lessons. It was not just our mullah who did things like that, many other mullahs were the same.

I attended the mosque until the age of eight, when I was in Grade Two. Then I was enrolled at the Galaxy English Language Centre to learn English. Apart from my time at the mosque, my family's life was comparatively normal until the Taliban came to Herat.

I clearly remember the day, in 1995, when the Taliban captured Herat. I was in Grade Four at the time. We were sitting outside our house when I first saw the Taliban, driving past us in their cars and tanks down the road. In front of our house, there was an old man who was repairing radios. He had his radio loudspeaker turned on, and instead of the everyday music programme we heard the songs of the Taliban with no music or instruments. The verses of the song that I still remember meant that 'the Taliban came to the country, and the people are now free'. As a curious child, I wondered where they had come from. Did they come to us from outside the country? And free from what? What were they liberating us from? Why did they look so different, with their massive turbans, black eye kohl, and long beards? In the afternoon of that day, we were told that the militias that once belonged to former resistance

Commander Ahmad Shah Masoud were hiding in the Khaja Amini public bath. When the Taliban were informed, they went there and killed them all. We went to the public bath to watch what was going on. When we got there, people were bringing dead bodies out to the main road. Lots of bodies were covered with a massive green plastic carpet. I could see human hands, legs, fingers, a small-sized face mirror, playing cards, *pakol* (a hat common in the Panjshir Valley), and many more objects covered in blood. It was frightening, and we ran back to our home to take the sad news to our families. We were shocked. After that we were too scared to go out, even to play. At first, we didn't know whether the schools were open or closed, but after several weeks, they announced that boys could return to school on the condition that they wore a turban. The turban was common among students attending religious schools or madrasas, but we never knew we would have to wear them as a part of our school uniform.

Herat is renowned for having strong winds that sometimes blow for 120 days during the windy season. One morning, I dressed and wore my turban as I was going to school with my younger brother, but before we reached the school a gust of wind blew my brother's turban from his head. Unfortunately, it fell into a stream that was taking waste and dirty water from the households and the public bath near our house. The turban was white, and got very dirty, and we were unable to take it out of the filthy water. I recommended that my brother should go to school anyway, and if the teacher asked about the turban, he could explain what happened. My brother took my advice, but at the end of the school day, I found him crying and red-faced. I asked him what had happened, and he told me he had been taken to the school office and beaten severely by the headmaster, who was a member of the Taliban. I felt terrible.

A few days later, my parents made the decision to migrate out of Afghanistan. Iran was closer to us, but it was obvious that there would be no education available to Afghan refugees there, so my father decided we would go to Pakistan. We had to return to Kabul in order to travel from there to Pakistan, where we settled in Peshawar. Life was better in Pakistan, and my older brother was working in Europe and sent us money on a monthly basis to cover all our living costs. I attended an Afghan private school, where all subjects were taught in English, apart from Persian (Dari) literature. Initially, I struggled with English, but I pushed myself to catch up.

After we'd been there for two years, I started to play *tabla*, a twin headed drum used in a lot of South Indian music. I played its rhythms on anything handy. The idea came from relatives who had a *rubab* (a stringed instrument resembling a lute, the national instrument of Afghanistan), a *surood* (a similar stringed instrument), and a *tabla* in their house. Their son was learning to play *tabla*. I loved playing and I asked my father if I could attend the course my relative was going to. But my father told me that the family was short of money and couldn't afford for me to take the course. I discovered that the course cost 100 rupees per week. For pocket money, I used to receive ten rupees per day, and I liked to buy five rupees' worth of sugar cane in the afternoon on the way back home from school and five rupees' worth of chicken corn soup in the evening. I would rarely miss these two pleasures, but I wanted to find a way to convince my father to let me go and learn *tabla*. I worked out the mathematics and told him that I would use my pocket money and that he would only have to pay thirty rupees extra. 'I won't eat sugar cane anymore, and you're always telling me it will ruin my teeth anyway,' I said. Eventually, my father gave in and granted me permission to attend the course. I was over the moon. After a few months, he bought me a set so I could practice at home. I still practice and play every day.

Life was good in Peshawar. But one Sunday afternoon everything changed. I went to visit a friend to play Tabla, and when I got home my father told me that Ahmad Shah Masoud had been assassinated by Al-Qaeda in Afghanistan. The date was 9 September 2001, and two days later, when we returned from school, we saw the footage of the Twin Towers falling in New York. All the television channels were showing the news of the 9/11 attacks. It was shocking, and we felt enormous sympathy for the innocent people who had been killed in the attacks and their families. A few days later, the news showed a clip of George W. Bush announcing the War on Terror, which meant targeting Al-Qaeda bases in Afghanistan. Bush's announcement was followed by US air strikes that marked the start of a twenty-year US War on Terror in Afghanistan.

A few months later, the Taliban were defeated, and the Bonn agreement was underway. We received a handwritten letter from my uncle explaining the situation in Afghanistan and inviting me to come back as there was a high demand for young people who could speak English to work for both the NGOs and the military forces as translators. I was excited about the idea as

I had just finished school with excellent grades. I spoke to my father, and I told him I was going to Herat to get a job. He was not happy as he wanted me to continue my higher education. I will never forget his words and the promise I made to him in return. He said, 'I am not happy for you to go, as once you get the taste of getting paid in dollars, you will never return to university.' I said to my father, 'Please let me go to work for a few months or years. I can always return to university when the time is right. I promise that I will not give up studies and I will go on to gain a PhD.'

I went to Herat alone and stayed at my uncle's house. My family remained in Peshawar, where my brother was still going to school. I started looking for a job. I made a CV and took it round the new NGOs and the offices that were being established in Herat. There was a post at the International Office for Migration (IOM). I went for an interview, but failed to get the job as they told me that at sixteen, I was too young. I eventually got a job as a Programme Assistant with the International Rescue Committee (IRC) on 15 May 2002. After a year of working there, I was promoted to the position of Programme Officer, and a few months later I was promoted again to the position of National Programme Manager. Work was great. I was doing well and enjoying it and I learned something new every day. I visited the poor and vulnerable people in remote areas. The IRC was a donor organisation with many implementing partners. A large amount of USAID funds were being transferred to the IRC at the time, and being used for a variety of development projects in Herat and the surrounding provinces. At the end of 2003, I joined the United Nations Assistance Mission in Afghanistan (UNAMA) as a Language Assistant. Working for the UN was amazing; it was highly paid and offered lots of benefits. I also had the privilege of meeting high-profile people such as governors, ministers, and community leaders, as we were helping to facilitate the first general election in Afghanistan. After a year, I got a better job working for the United Nations Development Fund for Women (UNIFEM), as their Coordinator. This position was quite senior, and it came with lots of threats. We were funding a safe house – a shelter that a local implementing partner (IP) was running for women who faced domestic violence. We had weekly meetings with a collaborative group called the Commission for Cooperation and Collaboration (CCC). At these meetings, we identified and referred cases to the shelter as well as reviewing other issues based on women's empowerment and gender mainstreaming. One day, we took on the case of a girl who had been the victim of forced marriage and sexual abuse. She was the wife of a Taliban member who lived in a remote part of Shindand. Although the Taliban were not visible in the major cities, they were active and present in the more remote districts, and we were told by the Department of Women's Affairs (DOWA) that this girl had disguised herself in male clothing in order to escape from Shindand and reach Herat by accepting lifts in cars. When she reached DOWA, she was referred to the CCC and offered shelter in our safe house. The case was processed, and the girl was offered a permanent place there.

A few days later I received a call on my mobile phone. A man spoke with a strong Pashto accent. He swore at me and threatened to kill me. He told me that the girl who had escaped and took refuge in our shelter was his wife. I immediately wondered how he knew that she had come to us, and later we found out that the driver who dropped her off had followed her to the DOWA, where our office was located. I was terrified as the man continued to threaten me. I tried to pretend that I had no idea what he was talking about, but he continued to threaten me loudly and aggressively and said that the Taliban would find me and deal with me. I informed the head office immediately, and straight away they sent me back to Kabul. I stayed there for a few weeks, and the Kabul office changed my SIM card.

I planned to returned to Herat after a few months. But I was told that our UNIFEM/WDC office in DOWA had been attacked by a grenade while I was in Kabul. It was clear to me that it was the work of the Taliban, more specifically the man whose wife had escaped and taken shelter in our safe house. I had no option but to resign, as I knew I would be attacked by that man and his Taliban friends, as he knew I was the coordinator for UNIFEM. When he yelled at me over the phone, he accused me of committing a sin by liberating and westernising poor Afghan girls. Indeed, I did not feel safe even in Kabul.

By now, I had met a woman I wanted to marry. She was born in Afghanistan but fled to UK as a refugee. I met her in Herat in 2006 when she travelled back to her homeland for the holidays. I fell in love with her, but I had to go to my mother to see if our families could arrange for us to be married. I had long conversations with my mom and my sister, and we discovered that my fiancée's father was related to my sister's husband. My brother-in-law therefore played a crucial role in negotiating the marriage for us. Eventually, my proposal was accepted. My mother-in-law and my wife travelled to Mashhad, in Iran, where our engagement took place. We travelled to Islamabad, where I had to file all the available evidence and submit an application for a spouse visa to the British Embassy. To my surprise, I received my visa after four weeks. On 15 August 2008, I landed at Heathrow and was greeted warmly by twenty-five to thirty people, all of whom were my in-laws and relatives who were waiting to welcome me. I had never met any of them apart from my wife's family, but from the moment I arrived in the UK my in-laws showed me warmth, kindness, and care. I also managed to get some work: I worked for an insurance company, a mobile phone repair shop, and even took a job in a laundrette and dry-cleaning shop.

But I had a promise to fulfil. I had assured my father that I will pursue higher education – right up to the PhD level. In 2010, my wife and I started to search for the right university. Many of the universities I applied to wouldn't admit me because I didn't have any GCSEs or A-Levels or any British qualifications. My high school graduation certificate and Diploma in Business Administration were not considered as being equivalent to their admission criteria. One day, my wife told me that London's Birkbeck University was offering full and part-time evening degree courses. I wrote to Birkbeck, explaining my situation and telling them what I wanted to study. They offered me an interview, during which I discussed my work experience and showed them all my work and academic qualifications. Birkbeck offered me a place on their BA course in Global Politics and International Relations, starting in 2011.

One evening, during my European Union Integration module I found myself looking at courses at the London School of Economics (LSE) on my iPad. My close friend and classmate, Tiago, was sitting beside me. He noticed what I was doing, and he laughed loudly. 'Hey!' he said. 'You haven't even finished here and you're thinking about studying at LSE? Do you know LSE? It's a really prestigious university.' I smiled at him, and whispered in his ear, 'Dream big to grow big, my friend!' Eventually, I applied to LSE's Department of Social Policy to study for an MSc in Social Policy and Development with a focus on NGOs. Once again, I had to write a detailed personal statement about my work experience and my interests in social policy and development and submit it along with my application. I was invited for an interview, and eventually, I received an offer for a full scholarship. The offer was made on the condition that I achieved an upper 2:1 in my undergraduate degree, which I did! I studied at LSE from 2015 to 2016. It was an intense but very enjoyable period. Eventually, I graduated with a distinction in my dissertation.

My wife suggested that it was not necessary for me to go further. It was time to stop studying and consider finding a job in my field. Life was becoming much more expensive. Our first daughter was born in 2012, and with high rents and living costs, I realised that I needed to work rather than continue my studies.

However, I kept searching for an opportunity to pursue doctoral studies. Towards the end of 2019, I came across the Economic and Social Research Council (ESRC)'s PhD funding programme. Through the Grand Union Doctoral Training Partnership (GUDTP), the ESRC funds thirty-five scholarships on twenty-three pathways per year. The GUDTP is a network of PhD scholarships from Oxford, Brunel, and the Open University. Given my experiences with the mosque school in Herat, I wanted to see how Islamic schooling is conducted in the UK. It was an ideal subject for my research. My initial idea was to apply through Oxford University. However, I discovered that in order to apply through Oxford for a full-time ESRC project, I had to be based in Oxford, and I couldn't move there while living and working in London. My next move was to apply for a PhD through Brunel's Education Department. I exchanged several emails, had long discussions on the telephone; I was told in no uncertain terms that the GUDTP was a highly competitive scheme and my chances were slim. By looking at previous ESRC projects, I saw that the majority of the ESRC scholarships were funded through Oxford applications. But I applied; it was a lengthy process that involved writing a research proposal and a personal statement along with the application. I was invited for an interview where I faced non-stop questions about my past and my motivations for wanting to pursue a PhD. On the afternoon of 6 August 2020, I received an email informing me that I had been successful and that my studies would be funded by the GUDTP. I could not believe my luck; my persistent had paid off!

So now I am in my second year of doctoral research. I combine my study with my love of music; and I believe that I could create a fusion of my musical skills and my academic achievements. This means becoming more innovative and working hard to bring communities together through music. I always use the metaphor that resettlement in a new country should be considered in the same way as the cultivation of a tree. Every day that passes, our roots grow deeper in the new soil, which means that there is a vital need for integration and social cohesion in the society we live in. At the same time, our leaves will grow with our achievements, and our branches will grow by building networks and thinking positively. I have performed in many prestigious venues such as the Royal Albert Hall, the Holywell Music Room in Oxford, the House of Commons, the British Museum, and SOAS.

I believe freedom and liberty from extremism, ignorance, and oppression have to be gained by the individual rather than simply granted to them by others. In gaining these freedoms, we develop dignity that acknowledges the value of others, regardless of their class, religion, race, gender, or abilities. As a child, I learned and memorised *ghazals* – poems – that speak about love and equality, freedom and dignity, by popular poets such as Rumi, Bidal, Hafiz, and Iqbal. The first *ghazal* I memorised as a child is 'Mankind' by Saadi Shirazi. Written eight centuries ago, it is now inscribed above the main entrance of the United Nations building:

> Human beings are members of a whole,
> In creation of one essence and soul.
> If one member is afflicted with pain,
> Other members uneasy will remain.
> If you've no sympathy for human pain,
> The name of human you cannot retain!

ON LIBERTY UNTHOUGHT

C Scott Jordan

Some 250 years of American history is long enough time to go without a revision of some of its foundational tenets. I like to think I am not alone in my anticipation for the long overdue US Constitution 2.0. Since the eighteenth century, a few things have changed and perhaps the highest legal document in the land of the free ought to reflect certain social iterations. Yet, an alarming number of US citizens believe all the thinking that could ever be necessary for such a monolithic entity was completed in 1787. Such mental framework starting points are, well, they aren't much of a starting point at all. In fact, this can be a very destructive hurdle as it threatens to reduce democracy, something having to do with the voices of a contemporary people engaged with one another, to the Indian intellectual, Ashis Nandy's conception of a mere custom, frail and at the mercy of the slightest breeze. And to keep it real for the realists, indeed, it would be quite the ordeal to organise a constitutional convention again. A brief stay on CSPAN will show you how much harder it is for representatives from fifty states to agree on things than when there were only thirteen. So, if you cannot be sold on the whole, how about a taste? For a starter that is sure to tickle the palate, let's try one of the more problematic good old-fashioned American principles that is making quite the scene in our postnormal times.

Liberty, the American variant in particular, has gone the way of far too many Hollywood child stars. Something once so full of promise, a sure hit for all those utopian expectations, now a window into how bad things can get, calling much into question, especially our continued negligence and outdated thinking on mental health and drugs. American exceptionalism, with no small aid from Euro-fascism's abduction of liberal sentiments, has seen to several Enlightenment ideals' rot from a tool for combating oppression into a torture implement for a new ignorant oppression that wears the skin of freedom. Beyond bastardisation, it has become a fundamentalism existentially threatened by anything that deviates from its freedom to the utmost extreme. Its fans, fanatics, bathe in its seemingly infinite contradictions that constitute the bricks and mortar of the house built for individualism.

Give me liberty or give me death. Be free or die. Liberty once lost, is lost forever. Liberty and justice for all. Sweet land of liberty, let freedom ring! Every slogan, either simply empty or repeated beyond the point of anyone remembering any original meanings, spewed through foaming mouths reinforces the converted and lays bare the faults in an already shaky position. And then of course there is the far too often quoted comment of the United States' third President Thomas Jefferson, 'the tree of liberty must be refreshed from time to time with the blood of patriots and tyrants'. Liberty, the name given to the ninety-three-metre woman who reigns over the border between New York and New Jersey, seem incompatible to society itself. Or at least a society that is not at constant war with itself. Imagining ways to reconcile the fundamentalist defenders of liberty with the other values of a so-called Enlightened democratic spirit, community, society, or even civilisation is utterly incomputable. But that cannot be right. How could something so critical have gone so far astray?

At the sight of such reckless disregard, one is left to wonder if the whole thing ought to simply be scrapped. It is too far gone. Yet, we are somewhat trapped, because to do away with liberty would result in an ultimate betrayal of democracy, or worse, to see it as a failed enterprise. To simply widdle away at the excesses in hopes of excavating some purity has a high chance of backfiring and unintentionally justifying the long road to the dark alley we find ourselves in on the matter. This cannot be a simple study in etymology. In the literature and discourse behind postnormal times, there is a new avenue before us. One that does not attempt to see liberty as it stands today in any sort of distortion of reality, but that may help progress it so that it may live again and fulfil its purpose to the good systems of liberal democracy. Values are critical for providing us any agency in our futures and quite a few values in the contemporary milieu are worth saving. To save liberty, we must unthink it.

To clarify, this is not to be confused with unlearning or erasure, though a degree of both can become necessary in pursuit of the unthought. The idea is brought into postnormal times literature by Ziauddin Sardar and John A. Sweeney as they establish the three tomorrows framework for exploring deeper futures. They used the Algerian philosopher, Mohammed Arkoun's coining of the unthought during his investigation of the limits of our worldviews, particularly the notion of Sharia in Islam, on our ability to conceive of external notions. Arkoun's account leaves readers with a need to flesh out this idea to which Sardar and Sweeney happily oblige. They note that the unthought 'is not unthinkable', as though it defies some internal logic or consistency. It is just beyond our ability to conceptualise for a myriad of reasons – the assumptions we take for granted, the paradigms we think and work with, the truisms of our society. All that makes us who we are plays a role in this. Our language, our culture, our education, our senses, our experiences, and so much more define how we engage with the world and shape our thinking processes. Take, for instance, two people. The first is born on land, beholden to the Earthly forces of gravity and the bipedal's desire for mobility. This person is beholden to simple Cartesian coordinates for his or her navigation of the world (north, south, east, and west and all her combinations therein). Suppose a second person is born and lives their whole life in the ocean. Suddenly, the world cannot be said to be flat or planar and a new system of directional navigation taking a three-dimensional approach adds to simple Cartesian planes. The navigation used by the second, aquatic person is unthought to our first, terrestrial person. Indoctrinated with certain worldviews our grasp of reality is left with certain gaps not minded. When we meet people from other walks of life, a beautiful phenomenon takes place and worldviews are broken down like a muscle exerted in lifting a heavy weight, that will, with rest and care, repair larger and stronger. This is why Sardar and Sweeney offer in their introduction to the unthought in postnormal times the need for greater polylogues with others who differ from ourselves, to breakdown the limits of our worldviews or manufactured normalcy. It should also be noted that the unthought comes in a progression (that need not be necessarily linear!) of tomorrows (categories of the future). The first tomorrow being the extended present, that future which is mostly set, determined by our past and present events. The second tomorrow, the familiar future, is the often-mistaken idea of the future given in science fiction films – seeking out strange new worlds, but not necessarily going somewhere entirely outside the realm of our comfort. The unthought constitutes the third tomorrow, this is the end of the line for comfort, where our present mental frameworks do not allow us to go.

So, to get to the unthought of liberty, we are going to have to travel to places outside of our comfort zone and if we are lucky, we just might learn something along the way. To begin this exercise, I find myself travelling to a most uncomfortable piece of my own history. My very own childhood's end. My experience with liberty is rather tremulous.

Liberty is a town. This is not a profound metaphor, but the name of a (actually, several) town(s) in the United States. The one I am speaking of is in the state of Missouri and is more appropriately described as a suburb of Kansas City, a city whose imperially expansive desires would make Russia blush (and Putin would be wise to take a page from this city that has gobbled up significant land claims in two US states and without a military – though US police forces and national militaries differ little these days). For 200 years, this small town in the northland (KC metro areas north of the Missouri River) has taken as its namesake that most sacred of American concepts. And best of all, the name is disgustingly ironic.

Liberty has two historic claims to fame. First, in the 1830s, tensions (or persecutions) occurred between Mormon and non-Mormon settlers in Missouri after the Mormon prophet, Joseph Smith Jr., was revealed a revival of the Christian gospel noting that Jesus would have his second coming soon in the town of Independence (today a similar KC suburb to Liberty, but with more methamphetamine). The conflict was known as the Mormon Wars which ended with Smith and a few other Mormon leaders being imprisoned at the Liberty Jail, one resembling a jail out of a John Ford film. One of the early town heroes, Alexander Doniphan, the man ordered to lead Missouri soldiers to arrest Smith, would defend Smith in a trial. Doniphan, a disgruntled soldier in his own right, looking to get away from the horrors of conflict after a particularly traumatic stint in the Mexican-American War, would win his case. Smith would be spared the hangman's rope but was ordered to leave Missouri should he wish to keep his life more long-term. Liberty for some, see terms and conditions below. Second, an American Civil War later, the day before St. Valentine's Day, 1866, Jesse James, his lesser-known brother Frank, and a gang of outlaws conducted their first bank robbery at the bank in Liberty, riding off with

$60,000. This became the new vocation of the James brothers and their gang after they gave up the less lucrative practice of bushwhacking (irregular military forces that supported Confederate operations in the border states during the Civil War). Bushwhackers continue to this day alongside their Union counter parts, the Jayhawkers, in a highly anticipated annual collegiate basketball game that allows the war to continue ad infinitum and remind everyone of how little progress has been made on racial relations.

These two historical moments give us an insight to the contradictions that have always been embodied within the concept of liberty. The Doniphan and Smith examples hint at almost this requisite need for liberty to remain precious. Perhaps we might forget its importance if it isn't taken away every now and then. Certain Christian theologies are far too accepting of that logical premise. More obviously with the first case, 'liberty for whom' is asked and while the US Constitution guarantees this for 'any person', the reality of this protection and the definition of who exactly is a 'person' remains disappointingly murky. Later in the same constitution, certain people are described as fractions of 'a person' which made matters all the more complicated, luckily that little compromise would eventually be repealed. In the case of Jesse James, the antagonistic relationship between security and liberty is highlighted. This dichotomy, taken as impossibly irreconcilable by most, has been a particular one of interest underlying a destructive contradiction in the US Constitution that has nearly seen the document tear itself to shreds following numerous legislative debates (and those of executive orders) following the 11 September 2001 attacks. This troublesome little idea has far more internal dilemmas that have also not been given their just dues in the intellectual arena.

But history doesn't provide the only contradictions for our little town in Missouri. Today, a cornucopia of Christian denominations make their relatively peaceful home in Liberty. A significant population of Mormons have settled into the land that once gave only options of death or death to their prophet less than a century ago. Abstinence as the best form of sexual education, optional attendance of science classes on evolution, and Jesus being an alright dude keep Catholics, Protestants, and everyone in between cheering together at Friday night football games. For the little things, agreeing to disagree is fine too. Liberty also houses the esteemed liberal

arts college, William Jewell College, which contrasts nicely with the nearby
Ford assembly plant that keeps the blue-collar life force alive (when not
swiftly laying employees off) that has built most of the pro-Trump
electorate throughout the country. Republican, Democrat, well those are
just ingredients we are happy to blend together as filling for that great
American pie. Just remember to vote the same elite families into local
posts, that guns don't kill people (how anthropomorphic!), and to smile at
the occasional minority you see going about their daily life, they are proof
that racism only exists in history. You can take a stroll around the historic
Square where we forget that public lynchings were a regular weekend event
here and that there seemed to be two of everything, one for the whites and
one for the, well, non-whites, until sometime in the 1980s a few farmers'
sons had the wild idea to gentrify and whitewash over all those minor
indiscretions. Support your local small businesses, unless their owners are
paedophiles, then we just make them disappear and everyone gets enough
ice cream to keep us from actually having to deal with any traumas. Fourth
of July weekend, Fall Festival, and the local high schools' homecomings are
sure to be significant events. And if you're feeling extra ornery, you can play
a little game by asking the salt-of-the-earth citizens of Liberty what the
definition of the word liberty is. You are sure to get an interesting
outpouring of responses and almost all of them will be insufficient.

   Although I doubt most of the citizens surveyed in this hypothetical study
have considered the true meaning of the word, I am confident answers will
be provided in abundance. And I would hypothesise a majority of the
responses put forward will be a refrain of patriotic platitudes and bile
painted with a disturbing shade of xenophobia and nostalgia for a fragile
patriarchy. How correct or incorrect the response is not important.
Indeed, the answer requires a far more philosophical exploration than one
might intuit for a seven-letter word. And then there is the issue of trying
to define the word by distinguishing freedom and liberty. Often the two
words are used interchangeably, and I am not entirely sure this is incorrect,
at least in all cases. I cannot give you a clear differentiation myself as I
suspect they may come from the same essence. But based on its use in
English, I would offer that freedom is the broader term for 'uninhibited'
while liberty is the legal ability or authority to exercise said freedoms. In
that case, rights and liberties are essentially synonymous. This discussion

could go on and should as it is important for us, communicating beings, to seek better understanding of what we are saying, but my point here is not to say I am right and others are wrong (if I am to refer to the postnormal literature, we are all a degree of both).

The point is that languages change, and they should be allowed to change. I partially stand against certain language institutes who seek the preservation of their 'pure' language. The French Académie Française is one of the most famous for this pursuit. But anyone who has even glanced at the history of language knows there is nothing pure about any of the languages as they exist today. I suppose one could reduce one's national language back to a series of grunts and moans, but what does that accomplish? Now, having said that, yes there are a great number of languages in the world that are under threat and while I believe in the flexibility of language, I also recognise and appreciate the identity grounded in the languages we speak. So, yes, I believe in preserving languages as cultural and identity stalwarts, but if a language cannot adapt and learn and change, then I cannot feel sorry for its ossification and death. And how are we to call ourselves a globalised world seeking something resembling plurality and peace without borrowing and exchanging words, building a language together. And I admit that's rather radical. The old way is you learn my language or two languages punch it out until one is more dominant. I recognise the irony that the English language is no stranger to this old way. But I would argue, every language needs new words for a better understanding of changing circumstances.

While language ought to and can be quick to change (as soon as a thing is invented, a word is usually instantaneously needed to identify it), sentiments are not so quick to change. Certain constitutionalists will ask 'what would the founding fathers think?' This question is usually asked by someone who thinks the Constitution is a document set in stone. I am the other kind of constitutionalist that thinks both language and laws need to have the flexibility and elasticity to change along with everything else. Recall the Nandy comment I began this piece with. In fact, the other constitutionalist asks this question because they do not wish to think. Ironic because I believe the founding fathers would be rather upset that Americans have opted for not thinking in the contemporary period. So, if this question is put to me with a sly smile of self-confidence, I may scratch my chin and say 'well, well, what would the founding fathers think of nuclear proliferation? They wouldn't!' The founding fathers, mostly white male Protestants living at the end of the eighteenth century could not have conceived of such a weapon. Hell, even the guys who had built the first nuclear bomb, watching it, from a comfortable distance, detonate in the Jornanda del Muerto desert in 1945's New Mexico, could hardly conceive what they were dealing with, what it would mean, how things would forever change. It was the unthought, but I like to think the founding fathers were not afraid of the unthought. I mean, damned fools they were, thinking that Americans would continue thinking into the future!

The thing that always gets me about these sorts of debates is that certain people fail to see the founding fathers' own admittance to their limitations. It is easy for us to turn our national heroes into their deified superhuman caricatures, but they clearly built a system that was meant to last, not keep everyone in line. Their failure to resolve the slavery issue and prevent the slow simmer towards civil war, less than a century later, are prime examples of this reality. Numerous arguments and commentaries around the framing of the US Constitution point to the fact that there is no perfect system and the high likelihood that in a generation the whole process would need to be done again. Several of those present at the constitutional convention had only a decade earlier signed their name to the most treasonous Declaration of Independence in resistance to perceived tyranny. Why would they break from one tyrant to construct a new one? But here we see where the founding fathers made a massive underestimation and set us on the course towards today.

The rise of communism and the Cold War has clouded the American mind to the point of forgetting that the US itself is a revolutionary endeavour. And there is one law to revolutions whether they are launched by young intellectuals in Moscow or Shanghai or Philadelphia or Paris, the revolution continues until it burns itself out or evolves into something new. Look to the Communist Revolution in China. The Communist Manifesto, read without context, provides a wonderfully terrible template that requires only the inputs of a few data points. For communist forces, they became the proletariat, leading the noble cause against the bourgeoise, who began as the Nationalist government under Chiang Kai-shek. After the communists, under Mao Zedong, had taken control of mainland China, the leaders of the party were wise to note that it would not be long before the uneducated farmers that filled their masses could see the party leaders themselves as the next bourgeoise putting down a new proletariat. So, they needed to keep the revolution going or deliver on bringing prosperity to the world's most populous country. Seeing the infeasibility of the latter, they opted for manufacturing a new bourgeoise – the smart people, those dastardly intellectuals. And suddenly a revolution against Nationalist oppression became the Cultural Revolution. And so, this cycle would continue for every generation up until today. The higher-ranking members of the party may or may not have been aware of how well Mao or other leaders' policies were working, but as long as the revolution was kept alive, the order was maintained. The problem today is that now China has its first leader born after Mao's rise to power and where an unspoken understanding of Mao's failures were corrected quietly as the propaganda was kept on repeat, a new generation aware only of Mao's greatness wonders why so much divergence has taken place from Mao's vision. But will Xi Jinping be able to determine the next disposable bourgeoise and keep the revolution going for another generation?

Surely the great United States of America could not allow itself to play into such a cyclical historical trap. There was but one tyrant whose name made good American boys spit at the sound or thought of: George III. And maybe also his Parliament. Okay, at the very most, the entire Kingdom of Great Britain, colonies and territories sold separately, batteries not included. But surely every American child from 1776 until 2022 knows that America was only faced with one tyrannical threat, whose butt it thoroughly kicked and forever after remained the land of the free. We at least made it to the second president before we started calling him a tyrant. And pretty much every president since, perhaps with the exception of James Polk, earned that moniker from someone in the US or her territories. While the template is not as linguistically impressive as those of the communists, to revolt against a tyrant has become a generational tradition in the US, also continuing up to the contemporary period. Tyrants were first foreign oppressors denying liberty to cheap tea, then those in the North denying the liberty of owning other human beings, then those monopolies denying the liberty to compete with them, then foreign tyrants denying the liberty of others abroad, and then those who denied our curiously domineering form of liberating others – the terrorists. Finally, only 250 years later we finally figure out who the real tyrants are. For we have found the tyrants and they are us. Thank you very much Twitter.

And now for the ultimate irony. The US was manufactured as an anti-tyranny. How could this be possible, you may ask. Well, I answer your question with another. Who is the sovereign in the United States? I cannot be mad at those who believe it to be the President or Congress. That is the conventional sentiment of sovereignty that all these years later remains hard to break from. But the sovereign of the United States, those who give legitimacy to its government, are, in fact, the governed. It is the first line of the preamble, 'We the people...' And I have to hand it to Thomas Jefferson and John Locke, it is a rather unthought idea for a Western nation to have as its sovereign, instead of one ordained representative of God (a monarch), the vested interest of all of God's representatives, the people. But to be fair, language again changes quicker than sentiments and it took a very long time to settle who those 'people' were exactly and even today, questions of citizenship remain a fiery political talking point. While a tyrant in the conventional sense should be impossible with regards to upholding the constitution, our revolutionary need to overthrow the tyrants reveals that the American people are tyrants to themselves. Yet another beautiful contradiction. Suddenly, my hearing 'we are legion' every time the phrase 'my fellow Americans' is uttered by a politician makes a whole lot of sense. And social media does a fine job of reinforcing this point.

But before we can pass into the unthought of liberty and, in a nice two for one deal, tyranny, there is a major impediment that has risen in the last few decades that currently undermines my desire for progress and stands as a much larger existential threat. In order for fundamentalist devotion to the concept of liberty to survive and even thrive, it needs a home – a safe place. In the course of America's cyclical history of tyrannical revolutions, it makes sense that anarchy is brought into the conversation. What better to oppose all tyranny, especially that pesky tyranny of the majority, than good old-fashioned anarchism. The problem is that true anarchists stand as a fundamental contradiction to a society and, by convention, the nation-state world order. So, these chaps tended to not be easy to talk to, taking violent and destructive approaches to their freedom of expression. Once an ideology is formed, it can never really die. Anarchism, except in that utopian and passive hue it took among hippies in the 1960s, does not bode well for its followers. In order to keep the glorious anti-tyrannical revolution burning, a few of them made the ultimate compromise to put away their firearms and explosives (those will be needed after the inevitable apocalypse) and agree to the barest minimum of a state structure only allowed to protect the liberty of its citizens. These folks became the founders of the Libertarian Party. Those extremist defenders of liberty now had a home and a name. Soon it would have political legitimacy.

I am not the first to rage against America's *de facto* two-party system – a frank and clear insult to the outgoing wish/harbinger of the first US President George Washington. But when the closest thing we have to a competitive third option is the Libertarian Party, I pump the breaks and begin soul searching. The Libertarian Party is intelligent, clever, and most dangerous. It is entirely too easy to wave the Libertarian banner if only to voice a complete and utter exhaustion with the Republican and Democratic parties (which spare no expense in keeping that feeling on American sleeves). They claim to be the party that breaks the mould and convention of US politics when, in actuality, they are the most disgustingly out of date version of it, unable to move in time. Aside from the belief that society can prosper without taxes (without an alternative paradigm proposed), or that humans left to their own individualism will come around to a profound collectivism, their entire party platform makes me feel like *1984*'s Winston being asked by O'Brien how many fingers he is holding up. Interesting and potentially most dangerous, is that Libertarianism prides itself on existing outside of a standard moral framework. On one hand such freedom allows multiple ethical systems to fit into the party, but on the other that means the ideology could simply thrive without any ethics whatsoever. And such an arrogant, confident denial of reality is a demonstration of power. We saw it take main stage under the presidency of Donald J. Trump. But it has been particularly attractive to young, white, educated, ironically close-minded, male Americans for far too long. All rooted in a fundamental definition of liberty that numerous free speech kerfuffles from Salmon Rushdie's *Satanic Verses* to contemporary French politics demonstrates is past its sell-by date.

It is critical that not just Americans, but all Western thinkers, especially those not of the West but informed by Western disciplinary norms and conventional global (Western) educational systems, consider the unthought of our outdated principles. There, of course, will be many ways to do this and new ways are always encouraged. But to break beyond an understanding of the convention and breach the unthought, it will be of value to explore a variety of polylogues concerning liberty and how it is seen in other worldviews and mental normalcies. Since Western notions of democracy have been hailed seemingly by all and sundry, where one might think democracy would come into conflict with Eastern ideologies, such as the often-proclaimed Asian Values or in terms of Islamic republics, the reality is that these other value systems' understanding of Western 'democratic' values can vary and actually bring in some interesting insight. Specifically, I feel Islam's approach to liberty has a lot to offer the Libertarian dilemma.

When one really puts liberty under high resolution of both the Western and Islamic worldviews an interesting detail arises. Both concepts of liberty assume a degree of responsibility. Libertarianism is often criticised for its reckless desire for freedom, its freedom from everything, including responsibility for what one does. Largely this is a major problem that has arisen, particularly in the freedom of speech debates – and is abused by both the left and right. Yet, the Western Enlightenment thinkers whose treatises Libertarians throw at their opponents, mention this sense of responsibility, but somehow this was lost in the radicalisation of the ideology. The responsibility one bears for their liberty resonates stronger in the Muslim tradition because of a key difference between Western and Islamic approaches to liberty. For Islam, liberty is internal. One of the most established mentions of liberty is the liberty God gives to humans to take care of their own affairs and to build a stronger connection to their community, the Earth, and God. The freedom and liberty in Islam derive from respect and dignity, so the fundamental rights to free movement, right to safety, right to freedom of thought, education, and religion, and even right to privacy gain primacy. In Western discourse of liberty, the notion is much more external: it comes out of one's individualistic value over the dignity respected in others. The struggles even become different. For Islam, liberty is a self-struggle, I must overcome myself to bask in the freedom God has endowed. For the Western tradition, liberty is a dog-eat-dog man-to-man conflict. I must fight for my liberty and defeat the tyrants who would seek to take it. The perceived secularisation of Europe only cranked this up. God, as seen by others was a sort of tyrant I must overcome. While liberty allows Muslims to be free to seek their God, it allows the Western thinker to take up his independence from God (in some interesting theologies this is what God wants). Yet, as I shift from Camera One to Camera Two on these two lenses of viewing liberty, there is an interesting commonality that tethers the two, which I think reveals a key to seeking the unthought of liberty.

Both the Islamic and Western approaches to liberty are liberty *from*. Liberty from my animalistic or sinful nature or liberty from oppression or tyranny. Whether internal or external, they have a fundamental mechanic that is the same. Which if problematic, creates issues for both approaches and at least to seeing liberty as a higher principle. To liberate for both worldviews is to break. Fundamentally this is violent, which should at least feel problematic. But it then gives any preternatural tendency towards liberation an instinctual need to break things. And so, if one of your highest principles calls on you to break – liberate – and when that act does not go to plan, we can do nothing but despair. And in postnormal times where complexity and chaos accompany all these contradictions I've spoken of, the act of liberating/breaking only produces more problems. It fundamentally betrays the complexity of the system and becomes a Sisyphean trap. So are we doomed?

I believe not. For while the Islamic and Western view give us some interesting insight into how to break from our conventional concepts, they are not unthoughts of each other. And indeed, while many more polylogues on liberty specifically can be done adding in notes on Chinese, Hindu, African, and many other perspectives to the discussion, a strict diagramming and comparative analysis could fail to get us to the unthought. So, I put forward a far simpler approach to bringing liberty into a better, perhaps more preferred future. First, we must heed the responsibility at the heart of liberty. If you follow my definition of liberty as this authority or ability to practice one's freedom, the responsibility inherent is that you do not disrespect the liberty of others – taking from the respect towards dignity of others from Islam, but something even the Libertarian may be amicable towards. 'Don't Tread on Me' comes to mind. And instead of this strangely capitalist idea of Liberty as a commodity, we can stop seeing liberty as something that can be lost, further adding to its inherent inalienability within at least human beings (we can deal with posthumanism at a later day). Finally, the simple move comes here: Instead of liberty *from*, we look at liberty *with*. Liberty *with* then represents a societal approach to freedom that transcends the violent contradictions of liberty earned or gained in conventional democratic histories. Liberty *with* is cooperative and open, multicultural as a path towards plurality. It is coexistence and acceptance of each other guaranteed by respect and the need for humans to live amongst each other in societies and open civilisations. Liberty *with* allows us to learn from one another and progress. It provides for freedom of speech towards mutual understanding that discourages the weaponisation of hate speech for belittling, alienating, and othering. The unthought comes in taking liberty from this adversarial conflict and transforming it into a collaborative creation. We do not have to be alone. No longer do we need to take to liberating crusades on social media cancelling others or PC policing. Instead, we can learn and experiment again without the fear of manufactured oppression and homo tyrannus.

Freedom, rights, and our identities are going to be major intellectual battlegrounds in the very near future. Far too much domination in the realm of thought has come from others; and worse, the non-thinking thought of others – the regurgitation of old and less than useful ideas. And with the rise of artificial intelligence and algorithmic 'thinking' or decision making, everything looks to get a whole lot worse. Contrary to popular belief, knowledge and wisdom are not necessary roads that intersect, or exist in the same block, neighbourhood, borough, even city limits. But breaking beyond our comfort zones and seeking out truly new approaches and navigations, such as is found in exploring the unthought, we can find new ways of getting over the next horizons without losing ourselves in the process.

ARTS AND LETTERS

THE NATURE OF THE GAME

Marjorie Allthorpe-Guyton

This is a Venice Biennale like no other. Deferred for one year by a global pandemic, the pleasures of this long-anticipated expression of art and freedom, of renewed access to art, people and to Venice, is overshadowed by a world-devastating war in Europe. Venice has never seemed more fragile and threatened, and not just by rising seas. The newly restored Russian Pavilion is shut down; the curators and artists cancelled their participation in protest at Putin's War. Grim daily reports of the human tragedy of Ukraine bring into focus the realities of making art in conflict zones worldwide and of the significance of the diasporic artist. It has inevitably shifted perspectives of this Biennale whose curator optimistically claims that 'art and artists can help us imagine new modes of existence and infinite new possibilities of transformation'.

The Biennale has an overwhelming 1,000 or more works, and the main exhibition is a triumph, presaging hope over doom, with a cogent vision. One that is driven, not by some revanchist feminist militancy, or New Ageism, but from the position that the impulses of art are limitless, that the artist aspires to freedom, to live in a state of nature and that Man is not the measure of all things. The guiding light for these ideas on freedom, fluid human identities, on relations with the nonhuman and the earth, is not so much Hobbes' *Leviathan* but the philosopher Rosi Braidotti. Her interdisciplinary writings, especially on the Posthuman, underpin the show in the Giardini Central Pavilion and in the vast Arsenale, curated by Cecilia Alemani, the first Italian woman to be invited to this privileged role. She is not the only first in a Biennale that breaks new ground. The majority of the 213 artists from fifty-eight nations selected by Alemani are women, many unknown to an international art world. She takes further the approach of *The Encyclopedic Palace*, curated by Massimiliano Giorni for the 2013 Biennale which attempted to break down the divisions between professional and amateur, insider and outsider. Alemani includes gender non-conforming artists and hitherto unrepresented indigenous artists in an exalted, exuberant feast of work, so rich in material, unfamiliar imagery and ideas that even the most seasoned critic is confounded. Prevailing notions of an avant garde, market-driven international art, of global difference between East and West, or indeed North and South, are upended. But how far is this challenge to critical orthodoxy also met by the eighty National Pavilions, now spread across the entire city of Venice, with their habitual inequality, their national, racial, and cultural divisions? At this point of world crises, is this exhibition the sea change that might shift the dominant Eurocentric axis and fully open up the Biennale to a multipolar world?

Katarina Fritsch, *Elefant / Elephant* 1987, wood, polyester

The show opens spectacularly in the gold frescoed, mirrored Sala Chini of the Central Pavilion with a life-size green polyester and wood elephant by the German artist Katharina Fritsch who is awarded a Golden Lion for Lifetime Achievement. As Alemani quips, 'How can one help but note that, among elephants, the leaders of the herd are always female?' The beast's mirrored reflections disorientate the Biennalist before she embarks on a dizzying journey through the labyrinth of the exhibition and beyond to the National Pavilions. The exhibition title, *The Milk of Dreams,* is taken from a children's book by the British-Mexican surrealist Leonora Carrington (1917-2011). Carrington's voracious intellectual interests, in gender, the unconscious, the nonhuman, alchemy, myth and symbolism, and the ironic ambiguities of her art and writing, are common threads through the three themed sections: *The Witches Cradle, Corps Orbite, Technologies of Enchantment.* New works are shown alongside five capsules of historic works underlining the prescience of early twentieth-century artists whose works resonate contemporaneity.

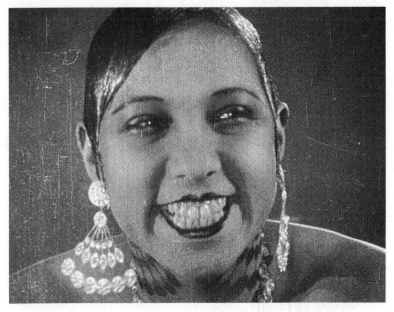

Josephine Baker, *Dans Revue des Folies Bergére, danse avec plumes* (still) film 1925

Paris in the 1920s and 1930s was a cross-cultural crucible which offered some freedom from racial and cultural norms. A silent film shows a bare breasted Josephine Baker (1906–1975), plumed and jewelled, brazenly dancing the Charleston at the Folies Bergère in Paris, 1925. Robed women are painted in riotous colour with Maghrebi motifs by the Algerian Baya

Baya Mahieddine, *Femme robe jaune cheveux bleus* 1947, Gouache on board
Mahieddine (1931–1998), who was born Fatima Haddad, taken up at an
early age by a French intellectual and later feted by André Breton.

Paris also welcomed the African American Lois Mailou Jones (1905-
1998) whose painting *Africa* (1935) is an icon of the Harlem Renaissance
and the *Négritude* movement which embraced the beauty and the fact of
'blackness'. It is a forerunner of the new wave of black figurative painters
shown in the Arsenale such as Zimbabwean Kudzanai-Violet Hwami
(b.1993), who represented Zimbabwe at the 2019 Venice Biennale and is
a recipient of one of the four grants for the inaugural Biennial College Arte
2021. The black female subject is magnificent in the monumental sculpture
of Simone Leigh. Leigh's *Brick House* confronts the viewer on entering the
cavernous Corderie of the Arsenale. This eyeless woman-house, a towering

sixteen-foot bronze, black sculpture, exerts a defiant female agency. It is a play on cultural archetypes, from West African vernacular architecture to the overtly racist Mammy's Cupboard, in Natchez, Mississippi where the restaurant, in the shape of a giant African woman, is entered through the skirt. Leigh is the first black woman artist to represent the US at the Biennale. The Pavilion is unrecognizable. Leigh's *Façade* covers the entire imperial neoclassical building with thatch, a direct recall of the West African Palaces recreated as icons of the colonies at the 1931 Paris Colonial Exposition, sparking coruscating criticism for its racialised premise.

Simone Leigh, *Brick House* 2019, Bronze

Simone Leigh's ethos is driven by an emancipatory black *femme* collectivity. But her costly sculptural practice, figures from clay to bronze, is that of the traditional male *atelier* and the work is readily absorbed by the international market. It is a trajectory British artist Sonia Boyce, winner of the Golden Lion for Best Pavilion, eschews in *Feeling Her Way*, a collaborative project which questions inequality, value, and notions of success. This is a visually complicated and noisily dissonant show with videos of five accomplished black women musicians singing freeform alongside a wall-based archive. *The Devotional Collection* is Boyce's transcultural memorabilia of over 300 under-recognised black women musicians. Jagged glitzy gold seats, pyrites 'Fool's Gold', are inspired by none other than *Goldfinger,* sung by the legendary Shirley Bassey. This 'aural origami', as the critic Adrian Searle aptly describes it, is play with an underlying gravitas. This is work that is not readily consumed, by the market or the audience. The artist initiates but is not present, she is off stage, freeing encounters between her collaborators and the audience, which is high risk and, for the artist and viewer, liberating. It answers Boyce's question: 'As a woman, as a black person, what does freedom feel like? How can you imagine freedom?'

Boyce is the first British black female artist to be bought by the Tate and to become a member of the British Royal Academy. Her long-time friend and neighbour in Brixton, London, Zineb Sedira, is the first French woman of Algerian descent to represent France in the adjacent pavilion at the Biennale. Her selection was contested by allegations that she supported the BDS, the pro-Palestinian Boycott, Divestment and Sanctions Movement, which she vigorously denied: 'I am an artist, not an activist.' The warmth, humour, and emotional power of her show *Dreams Have No Titles*, with film, performance and visual theatre, attracts the longest queues and is worth the wait. Her work is unashamedly autobiographical. For Sedira, the personal is the political. As an immigrant, a Muslim, a woman, and a mother, she deals with transmission, on the possibility of hope and freedom from the colonial yoke through transnational solidarity, cross-generational and cultural communication. She found this in independent revolutionary film, in the first feature length colour film produced in the newly independent Algeria, a co-production by Saadi Yacef, one of the leaders of the Algerian revolution, and the Italian director and anti-imperialist activist Ennio Lorenzini. *Les Mains Libres* (1964) premiered at the Cinema Afrique in Algiers in 1965 and was never shown again. In her twenty-five-minute film for the Pavilion, Sedira inserts clips from the film with her own re-enactments, herself as actor and filmmaker. She creates a sixty-second film set bar with mirror ball and live dance performers and recreates a set design from the film, *The Battle of Algiers* (1966) by Gillo Pontecorvo. She presides as a cardboard cut-out in a remake of her Brixton sitting room with her sixties furniture, books, film posters; the archaeology of a rich transcultural life.

Zineb Sedira, *Dreams have no Titles* 2022

France has a strong presence in this Biennale, a sixth of the artists in Alemani's exhibition are French nationals or living in France. From Lebanon is the Beirut artist Ali Cherri who is the artist in residence at The National Gallery, London. His work is born of trauma, of geographies marred by violence and its impact. *Of Men and Gods and Mud* (2022) is a searing and beautiful three-channel video of the human devastation wrought by the building of the Merowe Dam in Northern Sudan and of the transcendent power of the human imagination to create from chaos. Outside are Cherri's three mud *Titans,* animal-human figures based on ancient Assyrian Lamassu gods. The film's voiceover says, 'If the gods made us in their own image, then the gods, too, must have been made of mud.'

Easily overlooked in the vast Arsenale is *Chillahona* (2022), a quiet and compelling three-channel video by Soadat Ismailova, from Tashkent, Uzbekistan who lives and works in Tashkent and in Paris. Slow paced, close framed shots of a young woman are filmed in the underground cell (chillahona), a place of isolation and meditation, in the Mausoleum of the Sufi Sheikh Zaynudin in Tashkent. Nearby hangs a *Falak,* a Tashkent embroidery with symbols of healing and fertility. Ismailova (b. 1981) is one of the most acclaimed artists from Central Asia of the post-Soviet era to have established international careers and cosmopolitan lives and yet remains invested in her home country. In 2021, she set up the research group Davra dedicated to documenting Central Asian culture and the educational programme, CCA Lab, at the Centre for Contemporary Arts, Tashkent. Her award-winning works are deeply engaged with the culture and especially the lives of women of her native region.

Noor Abuarafeh, *Am I the Ageless Object in the Museum?*, Video 2018

The archive is also central to the work of Noor Abuarafeh, born in Jerualem 1986, and living in Palestine and the Netherlands; she unpacks the collection as a tool of nation building, subject to omission and distortion through state and private interests. The video of zoo animals, *Am I the Ageless Object at the Museum?* (2018), brings into play notions of entrapment, displacement, evolution, taxonomy – emblems of Palestine itself. Nearby, laid like relics in a long vitrine, are small hallucinatory images of imprisonment by the revered Sudanese artist Ibrahim El-Salahi who now lives in Oxford. El-Salahi infuses Arabic calligraphy, Islamic spiritualism with modernist abstraction. These small spidery drawings on medicine packets *Behind the Mask* (2021) were made during illness and long pandemic confinement. The work echoes the artist's six-month term in 1975 in Khartoum's grim Kober Prison where possession of even scraps of paper was dangerous.

Ibrahim El-Salalhi, *Behind the Mask* 2021, pen and ink

Migration, marginalization, and opposition are the condition of the émigré, of indigenous artists, and of the artist as activist. In an historic first, the Nordic Pavilion in the Giardini is given over to the Sámi, the indigenous people of the Fennoscandian region which extends across the Nordic countries into the Kola Peninsula in Russia. Sámi artists Paulina Feodoroff, Maret Anne Sara, and Anders Sunna work in performance, sculpture installation, painting, and film, telling a savage story of violence against a minority, the criminalization of tradition, of loss and healing, if not recovery. This recognition comes, though, almost thirty years after the seminal project *Disrupted Borders* (1993) curated and edited by the artist Sunil Gupta which included *Imaginary Homecoming,* archive portraits of Sámi people presented by Finnish photographer Jorma Purinam. The Chilean artist, poet, and activist Cecilia Vicuña is shown in the main exhibition; her paintings with animal and fantastic imagery, celebrate South American indigenous peoples whose rights she has long fought for. Vicuña was forced into exile during the CIA supported overthrow of Allende in 1973. Her series *Precarios*, small provisional sculptures of found materials are allegories of political and personal struggle. In *Llaverito (Blue)* (2019) she paints woman as a liberated Blue Lady, who she wickedly describes as the 'old troublemaker', both holding keys to all pleasure and as 'ladilla', a crab louse that bothers incessantly. Vicuña was awarded a Golden Lion for Lifetime Achievement.

The diasporic experience is not that of the nomadic artist, the privileged immigrant who is free to cross cultures and live in two worlds, or more. Belgium-born Francis Alys has lived in Mexico for the last thirty years and this year represents Belgium. *The Nature of the Game,* from his ongoing series *Children's Games*, is one of the must-see shows of the Pavilions in the Giardini. Alys's short films of children playing, with ball, kite, and skipping stones, from countries across the Global South, are life enhancing, intimate snatches of the child's universal capacity for joy and resilience. His main artistic territory is the ambiguity and indeterminacy of everyday life, as he says '…as both actor and subject… I can go to Afghanistan and choose to live… borders are becoming more difficult to cross… children are the main protagonists of my recent work… the last years in places of direct combat, refugee camps… finding in those situations' strategies of survival… in Mosul playing the banned game of football without the ball...' Or , as in *Papilote* (2011), flying a kite without the kite. Under the Taliban kite-flying was banned. Alys's relative freedom of travel and wealth is not shared by most of the artists who live in these countries. These disparities and the impact on artists' work were raised in the critical reception of the Iraq Pavilion at the 2013 Biennale where, arguably, the artists were subsumed by the curatorial project – the Pavilion as art object.

Francis Alys, *The Nature of the Game*, Papalote, Afghanistan, film, 2011

Each edition of the Biennale mirrors the world dis-order. Of the ten new entrants at the Biennale of 2013, only two, the Ivory Coast and Kosovo, are present this year. Iraq is absent. Other issues aside, the high cost of participating, a minimum of $200,000, is a challenge even for rich nations hammered by Covid's economic impact, flight bans, and quarantine restrictions. For Asia and the Global South, the problems are multiplied. Private sponsors and patrons step in, not always with good outcomes. Of the five new entrants this year, Namibia was wrong-footed by agreeing a dismal proposal from an Italian entrepreneur which led to a petition from the country's artistic community, cancellation of the project and the withdrawal of a patron of African art and generous sponsorship from travel company Abercrombie and Kent. Namibia is one of five debuts including Cameroon, Nepal (50 percent funded by Rubin Gallery, New York), Oman, and Uganda. Kazakhstan, Kyrgyzstan, and Uzbekistan have their own pavilions for the first time.

Raiya Al Rawahi, *Speed of Art* 2017-2022, Video

The Biennale mercilessly exposes these relative disparities caused by poverty, conflict, political ideology, or censorship. Azerbaijan shows seven interesting women artists, five living and working in Baku, the others in Berlin and San Francisco. Their works are not well served in cramped, first-floor rooms off San Marco. Both Syria and Cuba are shown in ill-signed buildings on the Island of San Servolo, which is a long wait on a wet day for the vaporetto boat. And the work in both is disappointing. In contrast, Saudi Arabia and the Sultanate of Oman make strong shows in the Arsenale. Muhannad Shono, based in Riyadh, fills a vast space with his ominous great snaking *The Teaching Tree,* of blackened palm leaves. Oman has three generations of Omani artists; in the video by Raiya Al Rawahi, *Speed of Art* (2017–2022), the acclaimed artist Anwar Sonya speaks on human values and the dangers of the slavish use of technology. A timely and impressive conceptual project is Singapore's Pavilion, *Pulp III: A Short Biography of the Banished Book.* Through film, a paper maze, and published collected narratives from across the world, Shubigo Rao presents her award-winning project, the first solo woman artist to represent Singapore. *Pulp 1* was published in 2016. The visitor is encouraged to take one of the 5,000 copies of the book, disseminating these multi-layered stories of censorship, loss, protection, and survival. A banner bears the detail of a painting by Rao, *Confetti: Ashes at a Fascist Parade* (2013), a recall of book burning as a weapon for the destruction of freedom of thought and cultural identities.

This is well sited next to the Ukrainian pavilion. The work of the artist Pavlo Makov, born in Leningrad, and living in heavily bombed Kharkiv, was driven out through Austria by the curator. *The Fountain of Exhaustion* was conceived in 1995 as a reflection on the post-Soviet social situation in Ukraine. A pyramid of funnels channels water till it runs dry at the base. Makov now sees the work as a metaphor for the exhaustion of Europe and democratic states. The artist and his team, temporary escapees from the war, were besieged by press who later flocked to the collateral event for Ukraine presented by the PinchukArtCentre and Victor Pinchuk Foundation with the Office of the President of Ukraine and Ministry of Culture and Information Policy of Ukraine. *This is Ukraine: Defending Freedom,* was conceived and installed in less than four weeks, replacing the sixth edition of the Future Generation Art Prize funded by the Pinchuk Foundation. The exhibition, in the great church of the Scuola Grande della Misericordia, is a powerful show of new work by three artists living in Ukraine and three historic works, including the now renowned Maria Prymachenko.

There are works in solidarity by international artists, including the father of Russian conceptual photography, the Ukrainian Boris Mikhailov. The French artist JR shows his blown-up photo of a child, *Valeria,* which he had installed forty-five metres along Lviv's main square: 'I wanted Russian planes to see who they were shooting at'. These are all surpassed by 'Mothers', a project by the Ukrainian *MirrorWeekly* photographers: a wall of 300 photo portraits of women who lost sons in Donetsk and Luhansk in 2014-2015. Vitrines carry Yevgenia Belorusets' compelling daily accounts of her life, trapped in the war zone. Nikita Kadan installs debris of disaster, objects of evidence collected in Kyiv, 'the smashed remnants of everyday lives'. Kadan spoke powerfully of the multiplicity of identities of his generation: 'We want the right to be diverse'. At the formal opening attended by the Mayor of Venice and the President of the Biennale, Ukraine's President Zelenskyy gave a live streamed address: 'If you are free yourself, how can you understand other people who fight for their freedom?... Every single one of these questions is about art.'

JR, *Valeria*, Photograph, detail, Collateral event *This is Ukraine: Defending Freedom* 2022

Few may have made their way to the modest Montenegro Pavilion off San Marco where the Contemporary Art Centre of Montenegro presents five artists alongside works from The Art Collections of the Non-Aligned Countries, part of the Non-Aligned Movement (NAM) formed in Belgrade in 1961, a transnational political project of the former colonies and developing countries from the Global South. There is a curious little *objet d'art* sculpture *The Silver Palm Tree* by an unknown Iraqi artist and a lithograph of the *Dove of Peace* by René Portocarrero, a gift from the Cuban artist Moisés Finalé in 1985. This small show is a sequel to the exhibition *Southern Constellations: The Poetics of the Non-Aligned* held in Ljubljana in 2019. Presenting the heterogeneous artistic production and extensive cultural networks of these countries, it aimed to show that, in the words of the late Slovak critic Tomáš Štrauss, 'The undivided artistic map of the world, or at least one that is not separated into Western and Eastern hemispheres, is simply more colourfully and richly populated than is generally assumed.'

Perhaps Alemani's *The Milk of Dreams* and the Biennale 2022 may also make some small rupture in the Cold War map.

HOORIYA

Robin Yassin-Kassab

1

Her name is Hooriya. Her father named her so for the freedom of the nation, given her birth shortly after a war had ended when such words were in the air. And he named her so also after item number two in the party-state slogan: Unity, Freedom and Socialism.

He was a professor of economics, a highly educated man, and he walked past bus stops and through markets with his head raised and tilted back so as to view humanity from a greater distance, so as not to sniff its filth too closely. Although almost always he drove. He was a man who made a show of being irritable and snappy in public, though in reality the public eye always kept him calm and reasoned, but who in private, in the cockpit of his German car for instance, a car far too wide and clean for the alleyways, would erupt in paroxysms of purple fury, spitting, punching the steering wheel, screaming Pimp! and Whore! He was a man who had struggled to arrive at his station. A man who wore glasses years before he needed to. A man who spoke of his dignity often.

She was surrounded by speech. Shouting teachers and chattering students. Patriotic songs from the schoolyard speakers and Friday screaming from the mosques. Sermonisation and pontification. Building and demolition work. Drills and hammers. Clashing pipes. The gas bottle man. Cars in convoy.

It was noisy outside and noisy in. The TV blaring. The maid clattering the dishes. Hooriya's mother on the phone – clucking, sighing, tutting. Her father shouting at her brothers to say their prayers. Sometimes they dared each other to call back: Why didn't he say his prayers first? Then her father raised his volume. God understood he was busy and tired from his work, not like these lazy failures who he would disown, who he would thrash first, let them see if he wouldn't.

The five of them plus the maid lived in a flat on the fourth floor of a twelve-storey building in a respectable area of the capital city. There were cracks in the walls of the stairwell but the walls of their home were decorated by curling plaster embellishments, like cake icing. Chandelier-style electric lights were hung from the ceilings. The little kitchen and the larger living room both led to a balcony closed off with folding plastic walls to prevent people looking in or out. It was a place for hanging washing to dry, not to enjoy the view. The maid slept there when the guest room was occupied. Hooriya wished she could sit on the balcony and watch the street and especially the sky like the people she saw when she walked to and from school. Some of the balconies in the neighbourhood were still open, and the people sat on them singly or in family groups, drinking coffee, smoking, talking, staring out.

The sky was hazy blue in the daytime and darkly red at night. It was red on account of pollution and dust, so her elder brother told her. He said the sky stretched upwards for only about a hundred kilometers, which was three times less than the distance to their father's ancestral village. If there were a good motorway laid up there vertically a car could drive it in an hour. After that it was outer space: stars and silence, unimaginably vast distances across which no sound could be heard. Sound is a vibration travelling through the particles of the air, but space is a vacuum, airless.

The atmosphere at ground level, meanwhile, was highly pressured. Every move she made was under heavy observation. As there was sound here, so were there ears. The only ones who laughed in the flat were her brothers, and only sometimes, only briefly. Her mother didn't smile except scornfully. Her mother didn't care for her, it seemed. It seemed in fact that she found Hooriya immensely irritating, too irritating to engage directly. Instead she alerted her husband:

Have you seen your daughter?

Which was enough to provoke a fierce slap across Hooriya's face, a flaming brow and cheek.

She didn't understand it. Her mother's notifications and her father's slaps were unaccompanied by any explanatory discourse. There were never arguments, as such. No accusations; no answering back. Occasionally she deduced her crime by context. Sometimes she'd spilled something, or forgotten something, or put on the wrong coat for the weather. Other times she hadn't. The aggression was unaccountable, as impenetrable as a law of nature or the will of God.

Her friends spoke of their mothers with an easy, unforced love. Why couldn't she speak thus of hers? There was no answer to this question, unless she'd done something bad she'd then forgotten. She thought she must have. Some badness in her early history, at the root of her, some kind of moral disease.

She was trapped, in any case. She'd leave if she could – her home, her life, her darkly flawed self – she'd happily abandon them all. But she didn't know where else she'd go if she were free to walk out. Not knowing an alternative was the worst part of the imprisonment.

After school, sheltered in her bedroom, in the quiet, focused by warm lamplight, she wrote stories about a girl who studied hard and prayed to God. This girl was an orphan but God loved her and helped her. He made it possible for her to travel in many foreign countries, to meet kind people in each, to visit mountains and waterfalls and botanical gardens. On one of her journeys a wonderful man fell in love with her, a doctor, a man who cured children. She married and lived with him in a cottage by a lake.

She drew pictures to supplement the stories. Pencil lines and crayons to colour them in. The girl, with her long hair and lashes. The man in his suit. Trees and rivers and cottages beside a lake.

Every so often her mother ransacked her bedroom. One day she found the notebooks in which the stories and pictures were kept. Look at your daughter, she told the professor. What will people call you. The father of the novelist.

He came to her room with the notebooks in hand. He tore each sheet into thin strips, carefully. The strips rained from his fingers like confetti. Shouts issued from his open mouth. Then he raised his empty hand and let it shudder above her head. She cowered and quaked. He left the room, slamming the door behind him.

She wept for a long time. Afterwards she washed her face in cold water. She leaned against the bathroom door breathing into a towel.

Guests arrived. The maid was away on her annual holiday.

Bring fruit, her mother commanded. Sliced, on the crystal plate. Or are you busy writing novels? She grabbed her wrist and pinched it hard. Wake up now. One mistake and I'll kill you.

Her fingers shook as she washed and sliced the fruit. The segments were clean and neatly proportioned. She reached for the crystal plate from the highest shelf but nudged it too fast. It fell, almost in her fingers but not quite under control. It bounced on the table top and cracked, and then as she watched and breathed the crack fissured and spread, until at a critical point of damage the plate shattered in her horrified hands. Silently it broke. She gasped. Please God. She screwed her eyes shut, bit her lips, drove her nails into her palms. Show me you are here. Show me you are with me.

She opened her eyes. The plate was intact. Not shattered. Not even cracked.

As she served the guests a spaciousness surrounded her. Her steps were tranquil. It was as if she were viewing herself from above, from an angelic perspective.

This happened. She has interrogated the story. She hasn't made it up.

2

She grew up; she left school and went to university. Her parents chose French as her subject. She'd have chosen art, or literature, or astronomy, if the decision were hers. She wasn't much interested in French but she enjoyed the university's broader horizons. It was here she met, or better, was noticed by, the man who would soon become her husband.

He passed notes and cards to his friend who passed them to her friend who passed them to her.

His name was Ameer. He was his mother's prince and commander – though his father had educated him with fists. She didn't know that then.

He loved her for her pure heart, he wrote. For her innocent eyes. For her modesty. Her religion.

He had contacts in a city in the Gulf where everything was clean and well-organised and anyone who worked hard got rich. This was where he intended to take her.

He wasn't rich. She knew this would trouble her parents but it didn't bother her. On the contrary, she'd prefer to work alongside her husband, to build their future together.

One day outside the languages building he approached her directly. Under the statue of the president in scholar's gown – the Supreme Student – he pushed his green eyes into hers. Unexpectedly, he seized her hand. His electrical touch. A little box pressed into her palm, as hard and angled as a star. For you, he said. The first gift.

Inside, nested in a bed of foam, was streaked lapis lazuli – 'like your eyes,' he'd written, 'like the sky' – on a silver chain.

She put it on in the women's toilets, covered it up with her high-collared shirt. Nobody could see where it nestled, but she felt it. It burned against her breastbone and her cheeks burned into a high colour too. This is love, she told herself. This is love, thank God, and it's my arrival into adulthood. Somebody loves me and I love him back.

When she arrived home her tingling lips were still curving, her cheeks still swollen with smiles.

Her mother glanced then glared. She drew in her chin and snorted.

Have you seen your daughter? She's plastered in make-up. Everyone will be talking. The professor whose daughter is painted like a whore.

Her father whirled from his study, flapping his hands. Whore! he repeated, and slapped her hard. Hot cheekbone throbbing, not smiling, and a salve of sticky tears. Of course she wasn't wearing make-up. She never did. The injustice was terrible.

But it didn't matter now. Her freedom was coming.

Three months after graduation, once he was sure of the job in the Gulf, Ameer and his parents visited the flat to formally seek her hand.

'What kind of family is it?' her father asked when they'd gone. 'We've never heard of them. No reputation at all.'

Her mother rolled her eyes. 'Who else would take her?'

3

So she was taken.

The wedding night went wrong. She was tense, certainly. And he wasn't kind. She didn't understand what was happening, or what wasn't. There was the overwhelming sense of an obstacle to be overcome, a mountain hidden in shadow.

It's your fault, he said in the end, getting up.

And he swore. And he slammed the door – reminding her of her father's door slamming and of the day the notebooks were torn. Much later he came back. He stared through grainy darkness at her firmly shut lids. And then he climbed into his side of the bed, careful not to touch her. After a while she felt him fall into sleep.

She was living on the twenty fifth storey of a forty-storey tower. You could call it a skyscraper. The twelve-storey block she'd lived in at home had been one of the highest blocks in the country, which is what made it so modern, so respectable. In this city, however, twelve storeys was really nothing much. And in this respect her life had improved. She'd gone up in the world, literally. The elevator was fast and weightless. She experienced the luxury of expansion. Before she'd had one bedroom as shelter – now on these heights she had four bedrooms, two bathrooms, a dining room, a kitchen, a salon. If it was she who owned them – which it wasn't – though in the daytimes she was alone in this realm, a solitary elf flitting spontaneously from chamber to chamber. Just her and the air-conditioning droning.

The balcony which attached to the third spare bedroom, unlike the balcony of her youth, was open to the air. To the white glare of afternoons and onto a purplish curtain at night. She stood out there whenever she had a free moment, clutching the rail and gazing at every angle. The sky downwards was soon tangled in aerials, dishes, balconies, terraces, streets, intersections, shops, petrol stations, schools and car parks, but upwards it reached on forever – first through the atmosphere, then outer space. She'd jump if only she could fall upwards, she thought. If God thought to reverse gravity for a moment, if the natural tendency of things were ascension.

The heat of the day in the car parks was suffocating. The car interior was icy cold, the shopping malls were cold, the flat was cold, but the car parks were unbreathable.

He said he needed money. He said he couldn't afford to keep a princess like her in such a big flat. But she'd never asked for a big flat. She said she'd be happy anywhere so long as he was comfortable. She suggested they move somewhere smaller but he said no, it was too late, they had to stay.

She gave over her dowry to show how she loved him, that he could trust her and relax. She sold her gold so he could invest.

I could work, she offered.

You wouldn't be able.

I could teach children. I could work in a shop.

No wife of mine is working in a shop.

Anything, then. In an office.

What she'd like to do actually is be an astronaut. She laughed at the thought, though her face remained immobile, her eyes steady, though she made no movement or sound. She laughed inside a hidden room he didn't know existed.

Anything, she said. You choose.

You can't work. You wouldn't be able.

She heard this phrase often. Other things she wouldn't be able to do included: driving, taking a taxi, choosing her friends correctly, flying home by herself, remembering names, managing a bank account, interpreting scripture, understanding business, telling a joke.

He brought her maids, one after the next. She learnt their complicated names, and then the names of their children so far away, before he found fault with them, after a fortnight or a month, and sent them away, each in turn. She didn't know why.

She asked him not to bring any more maids, she'd rather do the work herself.

In her dreams each night she arrived at solutions which when she awoke were immediately forgotten.

4

He'd overcome his initial sexual reluctance, even if she hadn't. This aspect of their life was now managed as a monthly encounter. It was another monthly biological necessity, a duty paid to her embodied nature – that is, to God or the fate that had designed her as a woman. It always hurt. And after a while she became pregnant, twice. Two long stretches of nausea, fear, alienation from the body. But she bore two children, which justified almost everything.

A boy then a girl to serve, to pour herself into, to cherish and protect, to laugh with and hold to, loving them as she'd always wanted to love, with energy enough to create a new world of warmth, colour and kindness, a weighted world of the deep and the real – and these children, these in particular, were kind, the boy and girl both, because kindness births kindness, and because God is kind.

But as for the other world, the one she couldn't yet escape:

It was during the first pregnancy that she discovered Ameer's disgusting DVDs. One was in the machine so she switched it on. It made her face hot; she'd never seen anything so obscene. Never heard anything as ugly as those cries.

She didn't plan to mention it but it coiled in her chest and throat like an indigestible worm, and as soon as she saw him, as he threw his keys skittering across the table top, it retched its way out of her mouth.

He wasn't ashamed, only paused for a moment, rotating his head in surprise.

What do you expect? You think I'm satisfied with your ugly face? Your flat body? I need more than that.

The words were like a whip. She reminded him of God.

I'm a man. God knows that. I can't help my instincts.

He shook his head more violently, lips parted, eyes staring in shock at the stupidity which didn't allow her to recognize this.

Nor could he help leering after women in the supermarket. He followed the most vulgar women, all strap-pressurised busts and buttocks, painted eyebrows and black-lined lipstick, the kind who sometimes returned his gaze and even outdid his ogling, as if she, Hooriya, were invisible to them. Such monstrous types – though she knew that wasn't her business, that wasn't the point.

Tearfully, trembling, she requested he respect her dignity just a little bit. Why did he have to humiliate her so?

I'm a man, was his usual argument. I'm a man and you are ugly. Women like me. What can I do?

Past an obstruction in her windpipe she asked: Why did you choose me if you don't like me? Why did you love me if you think I'm ugly?

He cracked a mirthless laugh: You think I ever loved you? You think that's what I needed you for? You don't understand how the world works.

She stumbled weeping through the sliding balcony doors. The sun drooping low in the sand-coloured sky, sweat bursting prickling from all her pores, and a sadness so deep, more profoundly vertiginous than the drop to the concrete below. She'd have followed his orders happily if he had only loved her. She gasped, fought the soupish air for breath.

Water was dripping from the air-conditioning, and domestic air was wafting from the flats below – a misplaced staleness, the exhalations of these bitter interiors – and there was faint noise rising from the city, car engines running generators humming alarms bleeping, but the sounds denatured and swirled together, their edges cut off by distance.

She tried for silence. As if to focus on something, but she didn't know what. As if to hear a whispered answer. She didn't know even what the question was.

The more she tried the less silence there was. The more the sounds that entered her awareness. Amplified music dulled through space, screeching tyres, a policeman's whistling. An upward river of human noise.

She whispered a prayer. Give me silence, my God. No human love is necessary. Just peace and quiet, please God, if you are with me.

5

Silence is the most precious of possessions. It's what the rich buy. The richer you are, the bigger the sound buffer you wrap around yourself, in the form of multiple rooms, thick walls, vast gardens, security-enforced exclusion zones. Conversely, the poorer and weaker you are, the more you must live in noise. Prisons lie at the furthest extreme of this spectrum. In prison you're forced to hear the clanking of bars, the slop of buckets, the cursing of guards, the screams of your fellows as they're beaten and raped. She'd heard whispers about it. She could imagine it.

In the absence of silence, she used the Quran. And if not the Quran the TV. At least she could choose the sound that filled her ears.

On the TV she watched protests spread from one country to another. This is what she was watching on the day she developed the power to control sound. People dancing on hope, singing, laughing, crying, chanting, presenting themselves for sacrifice. Something remarkable was happening. She didn't watch the news channels usually but this something, this birth or becoming, she wanted to understand.

Ameer walked in clutching a phone to his ear. Yes... Yes... Yes... he told it. He stood so his body obstructed the screen. His face was expressionless. He fumbled for the remote with his free hand, and muted the sound. As if he couldn't see her sitting there. Yes... Yes... he said. He laughed very loudly. Smileless.

She rose, left for the bedroom, lay down. Soon the volume was up again, but he'd changed the channel. She turned to the wall and visualised a switch.

In her dream he continued saying yes to his phone. Then he turned to her and barked. Mouth cracked open and yaps floating out. There was the switch. So she muted him.

Afterwards she found she could mute him in the waking hours too. More or less. Then when his mouth moved it made only a slight crackling. Noise without meaning. Words which drew no blood. He spoke and she smiled. She smiled until his speaking faltered. He gave a questioning look. Then his eyes hollowed and his cheeks lengthened into a shape which expressed something like fear.

She returned to drawing pictures. As in her girlhood but deeper she probed with her pencil point until she poked through a paper-thin portal and into their dimension. As she drew she was there, beside the lake, beside the lakeside cottages, crossing a bridge over a river, in the green fields and rolling foothills, on the sweeping jagged mountaintops, amid the swirling stars, the sky.

She passed him in the kitchen, or in the corridor. Sniggering into his phone. Sometimes cheap women's perfume on his clothes. She saw the side of his face in the car, on supermarket trips. At the door, as she delivered the children to be driven to school.

Their monthly encounter was discontinued. The sacrifice of her body. It was she who ended it, with a withering look. One look on his approach so effective he raised no question thereafter. Next day when he was at work she shifted her clothes and notebooks into the spare bedroom, with its access to the balcony. In the evening she told him.

This is mine, you understand?

But that's not quite the point she wants to make.

I mean, this isn't yours. You have everything else, but not this. Here you can't come in. You have no right.

His eyes widened. A dark hole where his mouth had been.

You understand?

He withdrew, backing off, gaze down, hands raised.

He doesn't pester her these days. In return she ignores him.

She floats up. Quieter, colder, the higher she goes. Flakes of silent snow.

On TV she has watched the crushing of the people's hopes. The rejection of their sacrifice.

No TV in her room, but a bed, a chair, a table, a row of books. Love poetry from another planet. Saint-Exupery's Little Prince. The perspicacious Quran, the beautiful words.

And tacked to the walls are decorations. The names of God. A picture of the Milky Way her elder brother sent. He's a doctor in Berlin now. A photograph of him and his half-German children arranged before the dome of the Berlin Planetarium. Photographs of her own children. The boy who will work and the girl who will marry, she'll pass them on to other people, each to their respective fates, unless God wills otherwise. Because they are not hers, the children. She doesn't own them. These are the fatal facts. And it's good she doesn't own them – because, for one example, the girl is stronger than Hooriya was, cannier, wiser to the world. Stubborn, her father calls her. She makes her mother smile.

And there's a photograph of her younger brother, who is in prison after protesting, ringed and enmeshed in bloody noise. And a photograph of her parents. Her father slowed by a series of heart attacks. Her mother who telephones on Thursday nights, who says she misses her...

It's a long time ago, she thinks. It doesn't matter to me now.

Nothing need matter. These days it's as if her mind is multi-storey. While her hands are busy with slicing, chopping, washing, drying, ironing, folding, she takes the elevator upwards. Lips moving, vocal cords resonating, but she herself is in silence, far above the haze.

At night she closes herself outside on the balcony. She lies down on her back, on dust and air-conditioning spatter. Then she rises. Up through the ether. She finds the road of the drawings, walks past the lake, the lakeside cottages. One night not so far away she'll resolve never again to descend.

FIVE POEMS

Ihor Pavlyuk

Translated by Steve Komarnyckyj

From the Moment

I studied how to write with blood
I didn't know what to write about,
I saw my living death,
Drank to her health,

Together we kissed the bars of the body.
We yearn now to be on the moon,
So I can reveal the earth,
That seduced my angel,
In the dusk of an inn,
The twilight of other people.

I have ceased to be afraid
Of the gift of life,
The laws of the lawless,
The apple bereft of blood.

Crosses seem happy,
Cats smile, and meander,
The town wanders through villages
Like destiny.

From the moment someone writes
With foreign blood,
They must write with their own,
I find no bloodlessness in history,
With the thorny word, stringent as salt.

The Bread of Childhood

Grandmother's pyrohy oozing cherries, the soil
Fragrant with spring,
These are the heart's embroidered memories
Touched by the cry
Of a crane.

I sit beneath fir trees and recollect
The sacred village evenings
Grandfather spoke of to me.
'They were truly rich,' he said.

'Something good has been lost since ancient times.
But what?
A song? The ring of a sickle,
Life rolled along like a round loaf until time bit
Into it...'

Twilight thickens.
I leave the forest in a dream.
Cranes seem
To dance in the meadow, my childhood
Is delicately embroidered
With stalks of wheat.

The Sunlight

Dedicated to the Ukrainian poet, Mykola Vinhranovskyi (1936–2004)

The sunlight
Glides into the sea,
Coagulates like mercury,
Makhno's horses you glimpse in a dream,
The children of nature, lost as the wind
Pray to the river's icon.

The well of the Steppe holds gold light in the depths,
Swallows preen and fly.
I yearn to my homeland,
Having no mother,

The wooden boards and frescoes of a church,
The shared sky, the Cossacks anguish
For Paradise
And we are free
Of Europe and Asia alike, at liberty
To live... which means to die slowly.

The crystalline current of living poetry,
A stellar voice of the sea

The sun ray passes
Like a razor through the heart,
Into the throat

Makhno's horses
Fly on pinions of wormwood,
The lycanthropic solace
Of liberty has passed,

The earth is your paradise, the power
Of beauty
Eternal,
Child of nature.

From Polissya*

Christmas Polissya. A drip feed. The deepest cold.
The saline heart bears the scars of journey,
The herbal infusion will not cure the soul
Which you lost because you guarded it most.

You study how to smoke and curse,
Protect yourself against the onslaught of deluges.
Write books, plant trees,
Fashion your house like a nest above the river bank's twists

And then physical training and prayers…
To the Goddess of your ancestors…
The Bible… The Quran…
And honourable glory, blood drenched,
That mist, by the jetty, the mist…

The rural village choir,
Kermesse.
You calculate the numbers of stars flying through the rain.
It is easy again, it is arduous again
At thirty-five.

The village and the town.
Our own and foreign…
I have seen all, I have tested all to destruction.

I love life,
Infinitely deep and unforgiven,

Christmas
Polissya.
Birthday party guests,
The whole drama that we did not conceive
Though we play our role, our own, our own too…

The roads are scars,
Thresholds are scars,
Adieu.

The Word Is Not an Apple

The word is not an apple,
But the last leaf of the fall.
I converse with the autumnal forest using the language of gestures,
The smoke of my fatherland seeps down to my bones…
I sow my lyrical blood as seed,
A naked voice…

Like the crucified I do not love the mesh
Of trade, religious fanatics with their blank eyes,
The inane hiss of politics…
I yearn for the nocturnal rain,

And yet linger, tangled in waves of fragrance,
From an angelic violin that cries with an imperceptible smile,
Remembering bright, kind, and somewhat inebriated Uncle Vasyl
Gathering nuts in Polissya.

I want to write a song that is like the world
Of all who came or who will come.
Then sleep in grass, as in a wolf skin,
While my genes dance, awaiting resurrection.

First published in *A Flight Over the Black Sea* (Waterloo Press, 2014). 'The Bread of Childhood' was a Guardian *Poem of the Week* on 12 Oct 2020.

*Translator's note: Polissya is the poet's native region in Ukraine. It straddles the borders of Belarus, Poland, Russia and Ukraine and several Ukrainian regions. Its culture is a living museum of ancient Slavonic and Ukrainian traditions and its very name combines the ancient words for marshland and forest. Here, as civilisations and states washed over them, people preserved a culture that stretches back to the pre-Christian era. Ukraine, despite the depredations of totalitarianism, can offer Europe a view of its own past before missionaries spilled across the continent with bibles and crucifixes.

WAR POEMS

Olexander Korotko

Translated by Andrew Sheppard

Kyiv, March 2022

No. 1
In the blood
embroidered shirt,
and the sun,
in the fog.
From night
until morning
columns of
tanks
churn
our Earth.
Smile no more
children,
the field groans,
the wind moans
and bombs
pierce
our air.
We have to live
with this pain –
will have to live

with our
truth
and your lies.

No. 2
On the gentle shoulders
of spring
on the soul of my motherland —
of my unbroken
country,
there was not just the
shadow of war
but death
with eyes wide open.
Do not ask
occupiers
what will happen to you
when your dreams
explode
from the bombs that fall
on our villages and
towns.

No. 3
What a long winter!
Oh just don't go
crazy.
And the sound of a siren —
calls of a shofar horn
saved the humble
in moments of nightmare.
And the wax-like snow
fell and fell
from the Motherland of Heaven
to the Motherland of Hell.

No. 4
What different
fates —
we have a war,
and time
painted
in colour red,
you, in Europe,
have peace,
and time,
because of fear
flies over you
white flag,
and heart
of stone,
alas,
you have one
for everyone.

No. 5
It is not your
sun,
it is our
Sun
is in mourning today.
These, our Killed,
have become our
Saviour Angels.

No. 6
Eyes burnt by tears,
of our children and mothers.
I hear how moans
from wounds my Earth.
And sleep in the arms of the night
sisters of time —

uninvited death
and tremulous life.

No. 7
We swallowed the bait
of sleeplessness
the way we could.
We didn't have time
to look around.
Like a howl,
sirens began their
hurdy-gurdy.
Time is torn to shreds.
Who could believe that
life has been rent
into before and after.
Horizon's veins
have swollen.
Death
burst open doors.

No. 8
Night from morning,
the soul of the people
is heavier than clouds.
WAR.
Hush,
for God's sake be quiet,
sleeping baby buggies
of
dead children.

No. 9
Mariupol
A deathly pale
moon

froze over the city,
bent in posture,
reading the funeral
prayer.
This city is encircled, but
the city is no more.
Nothing but groans under the
THEATRE rubble.
The theatre of war
remains, but
THE THEATRE IS NO MORE
It has become
a monument,
a mass grave
for those hearts
that stopped beating
forever
in its stone arms.
Do not ask
where sleep is harder
— in the cellars
or on the downy,
feather beds
that are the clouds.

No. 10

Russian soldier,
what did you forget
in my land?
We had grief enough
without you.
You would do better
to pity mommy,
when
parcel '200'
arrives for her;

when her tears
will sprinkle
your lifeless
face.
Russian soldier,
you would do well
to spare mommy;
since yourself
you could not save.

No. 11
Do not trust
silence.
It's scared,
and looks around
to both sides.
Do not believe
the WAR is
all to blame.
It suffers too,
no less …
…than us.

No. 12
Tin
Soldiers of
Europe,
wake up,
while it's
not too late.
This is life,
not a game.

No. 13
Protect the sky.
Not only

are we
being killed
in this war,
our souls too
are
perishing.

No. 14
People of the world,
stuck in
a monotone
routine
like a street
wench,
do not yield access.
They want sharpness,
emotions
over the edge.
Well, help yourself,
see first
the cover of
TIME magazine,
then turn
to reports
about Ukraine
on CNN.
And now
imagine
a bomber
circling
like a black swan
over your
head.
I know you are for peace,
but only for yourselves
in EUROPE.

No. 15

Here is the military
field hospital.
You understand the conditions?
So-so,
but human.
And he is one of them –
of the wounded, of course.
A simple soldier,
forty-five years old,
he is covered in bandages and blood
frozen reminders
of himself.
Without saying a word,
he suddenly rises
from the bed and, as it were,
apologetically, he says,
somewhere in the abyss,
into the void – emptiness –
'Well, how much
can kill?'
Then he lies down
on the bed
And quietly, imperceptibly
dies.

No. 16

In the landscape
of divine love,
as in human memory,
these cities,
Irpin, Chernihiv, Mariupol,
remain beautiful –
as they were before the war.
NOW, here's the view
from space –

everything looks blacker than the night.

No. 17
Irpin
Do you remember the river
Irpin,
that was barely visible
on the map?
Spilled, it became the sea –
furious grief!
Call her after
Wars
from that world, and from this
too.
CALL her please
after the war.

No. 18
What kind of people are you?
What a strange people.
We came on tanks
to save you,
but for some reason you
are not happy.
There is no fear or terror
in your eyes.
Look to the West.
They tremble like aspen
leaves in a breeze,
repeating like a mantra
'None of our soldiers,
not one of our soldiers....'
Is it hard for you to understand
world order,
and the proper order of the earth?
We kill you with brotherly love,

and they kill you with European
friendship

No. 19
It was like a battle,
of which there were already many.
The soldiers marched in single file,
cursing with terrible,
wild obscenities.
But how else? In war,
war is like war.
There was no fear in their eyes,
our children walked on courage,
walked on their Earth.
No one thought that they would die,
not before their time.

No. 20
We have not
gone
anywhere;
are not
leaving.
This is our
War,
this is
our
Motherland.
Our house
is destroyed,
but it is still
our House.

REVIEWS

CHINESE 'RE-EDUCATION'

Maha Sardar

The massive human rights violations perpetrated against the Uyghur community in China have been largely undocumented and hidden from worldview. Only in recent years has the brutal reality emerged: the state-sponsored cultural eradication and forced assimilation of Muslim Uyghurs. Muslims make up the majority population in the Xinjiang Uyghur Autonomous Region located in the northwest of China. They include Uyghurs, Kazakhs, Kyrgyz, and other communities who are ethnically Turkic and who have their own customs and languages, making them distinct from the dominant Han Chinese. An Amnesty International report in June 2021, based on the testimonies of numerous survivors highlighted mass imprisonment, torture, and persecution of the Uyghurs amounting to crimes against humanity. The organisation's Secretary General, Agnès Callamard, described their plight as 'a dystopian hellscape on a staggering scale.'

Gulbahar Haitiwaji's heart wrenching account of her internment in a Chinese 're-education' camp provides further evidence of the horrors committed by the Xi Jinping regime. It is a personal account by a Uyghur woman who describes her terrifying encounter with the Chinese authorities. Presented in a diary format, her memoir takes the reader through the details of her ordeal, recounting her time spent in a Chinese prison and then in a 're-education' camp where she endured 'hundreds of hours of interrogation, torture, malnutrition, police violence, and brainwashing'. The visceral details make for very uncomfortable reading.

Haitiwaji was born in Ghulja, Xinjiang, in 1966. She studied at the Urumqi Petroleum Institute; and after graduation, she worked as an engineer at an oil company in Xinjiang. Her husband too was an engineer. But, as Uyghurs, their lives in Xinjiang became insufferable. The Chinese government launched a systematic assault on the autonomy of Uyghurs. Job adverts unashamedly declared 'No Uyghurs' in their fine print, checkpoints, police inspections, interrogations, intimidation, and threats became routine. The community lived on 'borrowed time, in a state of partial freedom' that could be ripped away from them at any given moment. Uyghurs became synonymous with dissidents. These state strategies were allegedly designed to remove 'political dissidents' and the threat of 'radical Islam' and separatism. However, Haitiwaji was neither politically active nor particularly devout.

Like so many other Uyghurs, Haitiwaji and her family sought refuge in the West. Her husband Kerim managed to travel to France; and successfully claimed asylum. Haitiwaji and her two daughters followed in May 2006. The family lived in France for ten years.

But in November 2017, Haitiwaji received a phone call from a former employer. Under the guise of a pension related issue, for which she had to sign documents, she was asked to return to Xinjiang. Although initially reticent, eventually Haitiwaji agreed to returned to China. Her instincts proved right; shortly after arrival she was arrested, interrogated, and eventually detained.

Gulbahar Haitiwaji and Rozenn Morgat, *How I Survived a Chinese 'Re-education' Camp: A Uyghur Woman's Story*, Canbury Press, Kingston Upon Thames, 2022

During her interrogation she was shown a photograph of her daughter, Gulhumar, outside the Place du Trocadero in Paris, holding an East Turkestan flag. Gulhumar had attended a demonstration against Chinese repression of Uyghurs organised by the World Uyghur Congress in France. The interrogating officer branded Haitiwaji's daughter a terrorist, and Haitiwaji was guilty by association. For the Chinese authorities, Uyghurs who had moved to the West posed a threat to the regime. This single photograph formed the basis of the entire case against her.

Initially detained in a county jail in Karamay (where she was assigned to cell 202), she had no contact with her family at first who were largely left in the dark about her whereabouts. Haitiwaji and other detained women had their identities stripped, were forced to wear orange jumpsuits, even having their names replaced by numbers. Their lives were largely confined to their cell rooms where the natural light was forcibly shut off, replaced by unforgiving fluorescent lights which suppressed any sense of night or day. Their every move was monitored by surveillance cameras. The crackling voice on the speakers would shout out the commands for the day. Every detail was controlled – even the cooks, who served up the standardised daily sustenance of stale bread, a greyish gruel, and one egg a week, were deaf and mute, chosen for their discretion.

Punishments were meted out for non-compliance. Everyday life was dictated by a series of rules: speaking Uyghur is forbidden, praying is forbidden, hunger strikes are forbidden; and failure to recite the rules by heart would lead to reprimand. In one instance, Haitiwaji recalls being chained to her bed for twenty days. Systematic physical and psychological torture reduced the detainees to a zombie-like existence. However, throughout her degrading experiences Haitiwaji maintained a quiet defiance and dignity. She found comfort in the small things: daily yoga practices in her cell, the lingering smell of perfume on her bra, and prayer. Having never thought of herself as a particularly religious Muslim, Haitiwaji turned to God in defiance. These 'little acts of resistance', as she described them, kept her inner strength alive, in the face of unbelievable repression and cruelty.

A glimmer of hope appeared when Haitiwaji was told she would be tried in a court. This was short-lived. The farcical trial lasted just nine minutes, with neither legal representation nor independent judge. She was sentenced to seven years in a re-education camp. By this time, she had already been detained for a year.

She was moved from prison to a 'school' in Baijiantan where she spent eleven hours a day in the 'classroom', a room no bigger than 500 square feet crammed with up to forty other women. But this was no school. In the re-education camp, the only thing on the curriculum was Chinese indoctrination. Singing patriotic songs, regurgitating Chinese dogma, and pledges of allegiance to the Chinese state were the order of the day.

The women were still forced to wear jumpsuits, this time upgraded from orange to blue in colour, and were compelled to undergo physical education – in reality, a form of gruelling military training. Han soldiers would bark commands ordering the women to march around a room to the point of physical exhaustion. They were required by spontaneous order to keep still for prolonged periods of time. Those who faltered and collapsed were quickly removed, never to be seen again. A scenario eerily reminiscent of the popular Netflix Korean series *Squid Game* – but these women were not here voluntarily, and this was no game.

In the prison, Haitiwaji and the other detainees were largely left with their own thoughts, with boredom and monotony as companions. But the pace of oppression was quicker in the re-education camps. The miliary rules were designed to break them with a strict regimen and 'daily life came down to a triangular ambit: cell – classroom – mess hall.' The disappearance of students and the late-night echoes of women being tortured became commonplace. Haitiwaji became numb to the horrors around her. The toll of the repression and intense programme of indoctrination started showing its effects. Following a forced sterilisation, her spirit began to weaken. Memories of her prior life started to fade, and she began to lose sense of the woman she once was. She realised that the aim of the camps was not to kill those incarcerated but to break their will power, to make them 'slowly disappear'. The programme of de-personalisation, which was targeted at crushing a person's autonomy and ability to think freely, was working.

Naturally, Haitiwaji's detention had an obvious, collateral impact on her family members. Her sister, Madina, was also detained for a period. Her husband and her daughter campaigned tirelessly behind the scenes to raise international awareness of Haitiwaji's predicament. The unsung hero of this book is her daughter, Gulhumar, who became a fearless activist and campaigner for her mother's release back in France. She conducted her own investigation, gathered evidence, and liaised with the French foreign ministry. She even appeared on prime-time French TV proclaiming her mother's innocence and openly reprimanding the Chinese government. Gulhumar's sterling efforts were largely responsible for her mother's eventual release; along with political pressure and a trial, which ultimately found her to be innocent.

Haitiwaji recalls how, in August 2018, the world discovered the existence of the secret re-education camps. Satellite images of the camps began to appear on global news networks. The United Nations took action and, for the first time denounced them, making an obvious comparison to internment camps. The scattered accounts of survivors also began to surface, shining a spotlight on these atrocities. The Chinese government's initial response was a blanket denial of the existence of the re-education camps or that any abuses had been committed in Xinjiang. These denials were coupled with a total refusal to allow independent international monitors to investigate the camps. Considerable resource was channelled towards continued concealment.

But the truth, in the face of mounting evidence, was becoming difficult to resist. Having initially denied their existence, the Chinese authorities later described the camps as 'vocational training and re-education programmes' that aimed to alleviate poverty, increase employment opportunities, and combat terrorism threats. Western democracies, which had up to now remained largely silent on the issue, took notice. The US declared that China has committed genocide and crimes against humanity against its mainly Muslim minority in Western Xinjiang province. Canada and the Netherlands joined in the condemnation. A few Western countries responded with sanctions including restriction on trade with China, and punitive measures against certain individuals and companies. However, given China's economic muscle and political sway, these sanctions have had little effect.

In contrast to the West, the Muslim world turned a blind eye to the genocide and cultural annihilation of the Uyghurs. At its Forty-Eighth Session, held on 22-23 March 2022 in Islamabad, Pakistan, the fifty-seven-nation Organization of Islamic Cooperation (OIC), addressed the plight of the Rohingyas and the Palestinians but ignored the Uyghur genocide in China. Instead, the OIC chose to honour and entertain the Chinese Foreign Minister, Wang Yi. Pakistan's former Prime Minister, Imran Khan, has repeatedly refused to say anything on the Uyghur issue. On the contrary, Pakistani politicians have heaped praise on China for its 'economic development and progress' in Xinjiang. Turkey, the traditional ally of the Uyghurs, due to strong linguistic, cultural, and religious ties, was initially persuaded by 50,000 or so Uyghurs who have settled in the country after fleeing the persecution in China, to speak up. Turkish President, Recep Tayyip Erdogan, described the situation in Xinjiang, in 2009 as 'genocide'; and even sought to internationally shame China. But it has all been rather quiet on the Turkish front since then. It seems that majority Muslim states either lack the courage to confront China or do not care much about the plight of the Uyghurs.

Not surprisingly, despite the emerging international awareness, China's oppression against Uyghurs continues unabated. And it is not just confined to detention or re-education facilities. It is part of a wider campaign of the subjugation of ethnic minorities and their forced assimilation. Restrictions on movement, separation of family members, arbitrary arrest, mass surveillance, which includes the collection of DNA and other biometric information, are all state strategies designed to control and suppress the Uyghur people. There is a clear and concerted effort to erase Islamic traditions and ways of life: a prohibition on beards, headscarves, Uyghur names, banning religious ceremonies, preventing attendance at mosques, even the destruction of mosques and other important sacred sites. One to two million Uyghurs have been detained in a network of high-security indoctrination and prison camps in Xinjiang since 2017.

So, the Chinese government needs to be called to account. Haitiwaji's terrifying portrait of her time in Xinjiang, before and after her internment, clearly shows that a modern-day ethnic cleansing is in full swing in China. It is an affront to human dignity that should shake us all to the very core. *How I Survived a Chinese 'Re-education' Camp* is not just an urgent and compelling read. While twenty-four-hour news cycles and the instantaneous and shrinking attention spans of social media push the popular attention given to the plights of others back and forth across the globe, Haitiwaji's tale urges us to look deeper than the headlines. Through reading these narratives, a truth often left hidden by the state of our contemporary world is lifted. And it is not just for awareness that we seek out these narratives, but it is our moral duty to stand up in defence of communities faced with such criminal injustice as the Uyghurs.

SHRINE JOURNEYS

Nur Sobers-Khan

Quratulain 'Annie' Ali Khan's *Sita Under the Crescent Moon* is not an easy work to characterise: memoir, pilgrimage account, ethnography, auto-ethnography, poetic meditation on the lives of women and shrines across Sindh and Baluchistan, and an archive of stories otherwise untold. A tapestry of narratives, images, observations, histories, personal reflections and spiritual travelogue – a pilgrimage account by a female pilgrim of other female pilgrims and their stories and sacred – and not so sacred – spaces that they inhabit.

Khan was a computer engineer and journalist, well-known in Pakistan as a model frequently seen on television adverts and MTV videos. She became famous for her writing with her pathbreaking 2017 article, 'The Missing Daughters of Pakistan,' which investigated the stories behind a series of horrifying femicides that had taken place in the preceding years, published as the cover feature of *Herald Magazine*. Her stories for the travel website 'Roads and Kingdoms', especially 'A Railway Pilgrimage in Pakistan', published in 2015, and 'A Hindu Pilgrimage in Pakistan', published the following year, were evocative travelogues that drew profound but subtle connections across the range of her work. For instance, through references to the dismembered body of the Hindu goddess Sati ('truthful', 'virtuous'), falling across South Asia to create a sacred geography including the pilgrimage site of Hinglaj in Baluchistan, which features in her articles as well as *Sita Under the Crescent Moon*.

Sita Under the Crescent Moon was the subject of many readings, events, and workshops when it was published in 2019 after a fire in her Karachi apartment led to her tragic death in 2018. The book is the fruit of Khan's travels across the provinces of Sindh and Baluchistan to seek out the stories of women and their spiritual practices, their relationships and hopes and lives. These stories are weaved in a collection that both searches for Sita/

Sati, the divine feminine in Pakistan's landscape, and finds her in the many women she encounters along the way. The theme of the goddess Sati/Sita, women's bodies and the sacral landscape was to become a recurring theme throughout Khan's writings.

Divided into seven chapters, *Sita Under the Crescent Moon* has a forward and an epilogue by Professor of South Asian studies and mentor to the author, Manan Ahmed Asif, who edited the work for publication. The book opens with several quotations from the celebrated Urdu novelist and academic, Qurratulain Hyder, the most relevant of which to the contents and stories of the book is perhaps, 'all is momentary, all is pain', from the 2003 novel, *River of Fire*. The first chapter brings together images that give a glimpse of the author's life, her childhood in Karachi, family and her pilgrimages through Pakistan; the initial pages are a kaleidoscope of the themes that will recur throughout the book. The text reads like an improvised musical performance of poetry, autobiographical reflections, participant observation, storytelling and sobering aphorisms summing up harsh realities that cut the reader to the quick. In a prescient moment that opens this first chapter, the author recounts taking a statuette of the goddess Durga from a family friend's house as a prelude to her visit to the revered Hindu Hinglaj Devi shrine in Balochistan, presaging the importance of the figure of the goddess throughout her work and setting the scene for her pilgrimages and conversations.

Annie Ali Khan, *Sita Under the Crescent Moon: A Woman's Search for Faith in Pakistan*, Simon and Schuster, New York, 2019.

The second chapter, 'The Serpent Moon,' is set in Lyari, a neighbourhood of Karachi that had just emerged from decades of political and gang violence when the author attended *dhamaal*, a healing ceremony of the Shidi community. From this setting in the densely populated urban centre of Karachi, the author travels to interior Sindh to the shrine of Gaji Shah, which is only visited by women. Telling the stories of those accompanying her on her pilgrimage, the author recounts the dream sequences of Afshanm, her fellow traveller to Syed Gaji Shah, (known as the king of jinns), whose oneiric visions were intertwined with the shrine. Upon reaching the shrine, she describes the space and its *jinnat ki kothi*, or empty guesthouse reserved for *jinns*, and the stories interwoven with the structure of the shrine. The voyage continues from Gaji Shah to Sehwan Sarif, the ancient Sivistan, or abode of Shiva, and site of the wildly popular antinomian Sufi shrine of Sayyid Usman Marwandi (1177-1274), popularly known as Lal Shahbaz Qalandar. For Khan, it seemed 'to be the Mecca of the shrines of Sindh'.

As in the healing ceremony she recounted in Lyari, and in Gaji Shah, the *dhamaal* at Sehwan Sharif is a trance ceremony meant to cure the participants, many of whom are women, of their natural and supernatural troubles. While Sehwan has a reputation for voluptuousness, sensuality and the violation of the bounds of propriety, it is also a site where tragedies and traumas are played out and embodied during the rhythmic trance ceremony of the *dhamaal*, taking place every evening at the time of maghrib (sunset) prayers. Khan describes one young female participant in the healing ceremony, whose trance she observes together with her travelling companion, Naz: 'The girl lay there, sobbing and trembling. The mother gave the girl some water and then, together with another woman, carried the girl away to the side of the courtyard. I looked at Naz and in the reflection of her teary eyes I found myself crying. Life was simply impossible.' From Sehwan, Annie and Naz's journey continues to Thatta to the shrine of Lal Shah Bukhari, and to Shah Aqeeq's shrine in the Keti Bunder Wildlife Sanctuary and Naag Baba's shrine, telling the stories along the way of the women she meets and who are her travelling companions to these sacred sites.

The chapter 'Karachi Waali Sita', or the Sita of Karachi, tells the intertwined stories of the women caretakers of the Miran Pir shrine, where only female visitors may enter. Khan describes her unexpected path to the shrine: 'This shrine is invisible to the world. I had only discovered it because of a small reference in a book on Baloch culture. It mentioned the ritual of leaving water in desolate places for birds to drink. Once collected after the birds had had the water, it was given to children who did not speak or stuttered. It cured them. It led me to finding the shrine tucked away, in plain sight, behind the busiest marketplace in all of Karachi.' In a remarkable chapter, the author recounts the experiences of the shrine's female caretakers, their enmeshed life-paths, disagreements, struggles and affections. The vicissitudes of their careers at the shrine play out against the formation of the nation state of Pakistan after Partition and increasing government interference in sacred space from the 1960s until today, as the masculinist encroachment of literalist understandings of worship continue to impinge on the site of the Miran Pir shrine.

The following chapter, '9 Moons,' tells the story of Faqira, caretaker of the Shah Pari tomb at the Miran Pir shrine, and explores the sacred spaces where women possessed by *jinns* seek relief, and '3 Moharram' tells of the author's search for the Satiyan – divine women, Sita/Sati – in the shrine of Shah Noorani in Balochistan, detailing the journey from Karachi to the remote auspicious site. There the author has an encounter with a personality whose story will figure prominently in the rest of the chapter, a young woman named Zahida, whose intense relationship with the Shah Noorani shrine draws the author in. Together the two women explore together the intricate built environment of the Shah Noorani shrine and Lahoot La-makan's sacred landscape, carved into mountains, rock formations, caves and streams, and traversed with bridges and ladders. Zahida's story and her delightfully complex emotional world makes up the remainder of the chapter, in an unflinching picture of this young and idiosyncratic and unconventional female devotee of Shah Noorani and her frequent visits to the shrine from Karachi, describing the texture of their long bus rides to visit the shrine: 'On the front seat by the window in the Ladies Section of the bus to Noorani, Zahida made herself comfortable, plugging her headphones into her cellphone, setting up on the wide screen of her phone, for playing back to back, videos of songs featuring the actress Sunny Leone. Zahida told me the actress was said to have sex for money. She had enough videos of Leone to last us half the ride.' Zahida's history of loves, difficult marriages and family bonds, interlaced with stories of her pilgrimages to the shrine, creates an intimate space of female devotion.

The second-to-last chapter, 'Sita Sati' recounts the author's journey to Tharparkar, the desert region that borders India to the southeast of Karachi. Annie Ali Khan's search for Satiyan takes her to the shrine of Mai Mithi, which soon leads to many other sites of women swallowed up by the earth to preserve their honour, much like Sita in the Ramayana, the inspiration for this chapter, and indeed, the author's entire search through the sacred landscape of Balochistan and Sindh. The chapter closes with the local mythology of Joma, a young mother who becomes a Satt (or Sati) by burning herself on a funeral pyre after her betrayal by her mother – mirroring the author's work in the investigative piece 'The Lost Daughters of Pakistan', in which young women are killed, often being set alight with fire, stabbed or kidnapped, by their own mothers – and concludes with her observation of the Brahmin women's funeral by cremation in Tharparker.

The final chapter returns to the author's own story, recounting her childhood in Nazimabad, and bringing the tales of Satiyan and the story of Sita into the drawing rooms of Karachi's city dwellers and morphing these themes to fit the context of the urban middle classes – the woman who turns up naked at a police station, brutalised by her husband, or the other lady who dies burnt alive when her nylon nightclothes catch fire from a candle during an electricity blackout from load shedding. Telling the story of her father and grandparents after their journey to Karachi in the aftermath of Partition, the author concludes with her reflections on her place in her family, and her family's place in the landscape of Karachi.

The book's epilogue, written by Manan Ahmed Asif, provides some background to its genesis, and Annie Ali Khan's journey writing this remarkable work: 'In September 2015 she began to work on a project that consumed her to her last moments. She began to work on lives of women in Karachi (first in Lyari) who were destitute, oppressed, at the mercy of the men, and yet were powerfully enacting forms of sociality and faith-healing that were astounding to behold. She began to document these lives with photographs, then interviews. As she followed these women, her geography expanded: first other neighbourhoods, then lower Sindh and Thar, then Balochistan. Over three years, she traced, carefully, life after precarious life.' The remarkable book that resulted from these journeys, these acts of collecting and documenting, in parts of Sindh and Balochistan where it is very difficult to travel, much less as a single woman, is many things – by turns magical, lyrical and poetic, by turns devastating and crushing in the realities and stories it recounts. It should be read by anyone and everyone who has an interest in shrines, the creation of sacred geographies, women's life stories and pathways and spiritual practices. Khan's original subtitle for this book, 'A Quest for Pakistan's Satiyan, women buried or burned alive then worshipped as a goddess in the Islamic Republic,' captures the many layers of contradictions that this remarkable work contains within its pages.

WAYS OF BEING FEMINIST

Samia Rahman

An agonising feature of writing is the knowledge that, particularly in our digital age, once a piece of work is 'out there', there is no taking it back. This is true of any online presence (and at this point I cannot emphasise enough the relief of growing up before social media rendered teenage tantrums digitally indelible). An unfortunately worded and polemic tweet by a 17-year-old Twitter user that may compromise their career ten years later, or a casual 'like' of a Facebook or Instagram post that turns out to have dubious unintended inferences, all have the potential to wreak havoc with a carefully curated reputation.

Could this be because we are in denial of the capacity for the written word to embody space for growth? It is assumed that an argument presented in print or online is a firmly held position, an immovable declaration of all that resides in the writer's mind and heart, not an engagement with discourse that invites interrogation. In the Narratives issue of *Critical Muslim*, Nicholas Masterton of the Turner Prize-nominated research agency Forensic Architecture, an independent organisation that investigates human rights violations, discussed how the findings of their investigations are disseminated into the public realm, through courts, reports and social media. 'The output forms the advocacy, and it is here that the work takes on a life of its own, generating criticism and feedback.' A huge part of the project, Masterton says, 'is how it lives outside the laboratory and continues to inform narratives relating to the crime scene'.

Rafia Zakaria, *Against White Feminists*, Hamish Hamilton, London, 2021

Whether it is a collection of paragraphs, images, or a set of data, the assumption that what is being presented is a fleeting stop-off point in a journey of continual evolution, usually prompts resistance. Often it is assumed that we must have a fixed position on an issue, or an idea that we will eternally clutch to. How many times I am asked to offer my position on a particular issue, or state the Muslim Institute's position on the same issue, or explain where Islam stands on such and such. But to be liberated from dogma we must be open to having our minds expanded and our opinions challenged to a point where re-assessment is not an impossibility. A re-appraisal of an idea that we once held on to, perhaps even strongly, is a constructive way to navigate the complexity and contradictions of what it means to exist in our often-incomprehensible world.

Conversations with fellow writers reveals this is a common discomfort when sending a concoction of wordplay out into the universe. There are episodes in any writer's career, particularly when starting out and eager to impress, the pressure to break a story, to uncover sensational scandal, and demonstrate your credentials as the purveyor of unique access to a community or organisation's singular worldview, that can culminate in a piece that causes the older, experienced version of the writerly self to cringe. Now that most of what a writer has ever authored can be dredged up online, it is exhausting to imagine that we can be labelled according to a long ago polemic.

This crossed my mind when I first came upon Rafia Zakaria's blistering book *Against White Feminism*. A Pakistan-born-and-raised US attorney, Zakaria is a columnist for *Dawn*, Pakistan's oldest English-language newspaper. It was for this outlet that she wrote, in 2014, an opinion piece on the UK Rotherham grooming scandal, titled 'Demons of a British Ghetto'. It garnered a not insignificant amount of infamy at the time for perpetuating myth and half-truth with a few breath-taking generalisations thrown in. Beginning as it would go on: 'They [so-called Pakistani ghettos in UK towns] are the underbellies of Britain; streets where the organisation and sterility and order of the Western world are suddenly suspended. Here, people take chances with the rules; throw rubbish in the streets, double-park, let their toddlers roam wild, jump before cars.' With rhetoric more suited to a *Daily Mail* hatchet job, it seemed incongruous that Zakaria would, some eight years later, write *Against White Feminism*; a riveting, insightful and quite brilliant work.

Perhaps she had submitted a column that was re-written into unrecognisable tabloid fodder by a salacious-seeking editor. Or perhaps the book speaks very much to the image white feminism demands she configures herself into. Perhaps, against her own instincts, she felt the burden of white feminism to caricature the misogyny of brown men and carve a role for herself as part of the project to save brown women. After all, as she is at pains to point out, white feminism does not require the protagonist to be a white woman, but indeed anybody serving to sustain the white feminist agenda. 'A white feminist is someone who refuses to consider the role that whiteness and the racial privilege attached to it have played, and continue to play, in universalising white feminist concerns, agendas and beliefs as those of all of feminism and all feminists.'

Such is the potential for liberation of a writer from the ideological constraints of a previous work, that any misgivings I had about Zakaria's book, based on her 2014 *Dawn* column, melted away as I turned the pages. She begins by relating an anecdote that illustrates the censoring of the self that women who do not conform to white feminism's vision of emancipation subject themselves to. The scene is set in a wine bar, where Zakaria is (not) drinking with a group of middle-class white US feminists, while simultaneously trying not to betray her faith-based reasons for being teetotal, as that wouldn't fit the *Sex and the City* vibe. Her personal history is traumatic – she fled an abusive arranged marriage – but tries to gloss over the messiness, suspecting that her life story would only fuel white feminists' belief that they need to rescue oppressed non-Western women like her from their patriarchal contexts by liberating her from all her cultural baggage.

This anecdote stung because it reminded me of a white feminist friend, who asked me to proof-read her novel about a teenager diagnosed with a life-threatening illness, who spends long periods in hospital. He is Muslim, 'but that's incidental', my friend informed me. She and I both studied literature at university and I know she is a talented writer. Her children attend inner city London schools, with a sizeable Muslim cohort. Her views are progressive, liberal, alternative, and embrace the multicultural dynamism of inner-city London. I begin reading eagerly, tasked with checking the authenticity of the Muslim references in her work. She writes beautifully. I expect nothing less.

What I do not expect is to be taken aback by the bluntly two-dimensional depiction of the protagonist's mother. A hijab-wearing caricature, she does not visit her son in hospital because she is daunted by the prospect of travelling alone on public transport. She has never ventured far from home. She is a cliché, encompassing every negative stereotype of the disempowered/oppressed/submissive Muslim female. I explain to my friend my shock.

She counters that the character is based on the Muslim mothers she sees at the school gate of her children's school. 'They' don't seem to leave the local area and are very traditional apparently. I ask her how she knows how these women live, how they would behave if their child was ill in hospital, has she ever even had a conversation with them? No. These are women she has observed from a distance but does not know at all, yet she draws on her liberal sensitivities to imagine their lives. She tells me her horror at one day seeing one of her sons' school friends playing football with his siblings in the street, without a coat on, and despairs at the socially impoverished upbringing he must be enduring. The pity. I remember playing out in the street with my siblings and other children when I was a small child growing up in Bradford, and can't comprehend why that would lead anyone to think my mum was oppressed, or could imply that she would be unable to leave her neighbourhood to visit me in hospital if I was ill. Why would she be any less than a white mother whose children never played in the street, never straying from a garden that fenced them in or a local park, kept safe from all imaginable and unimaginable harms, with their mother watching over them and ensuring they always had a coat on, frequently going on play dates and having sleepovers?

This is the crux of Zakaria's frustration with white feminism. When it comes to who gets to define what it means to be liberated, the assumption is that the Western-centric lens through which female emancipation is viewed is the only ideal, and any other mode of struggle is a compromise. The book's strength lies in Zakaria's ability to systematically analyse such assumptions, excavate their history, and then challenge the racism and class-bias inherent in the ideology.

Crucially, Zakaria distinguishes between white feminism and white feminists. She is quick to clarify that her problem is not with white women who happen to be feminists. In fact, she starts many interviews that she has given since the book's publication by explaining that no, she does not hate white women. Her project is an attempt to extricate the whiteness from feminism and to value the different ways in which feminism is a lived reality across global communities. White feminism prizes rebellion over resistance. Rebellion equates transgression, individualism, consumer capital and sexual wildness – all of which are valid life choices women must be free to make. But there are other paths that strong women tread, which involve endurance, resilience, collective political activism, and building and sustaining community. Deciding that a woman cannot be liberated if she doesn't follow the model of white feminism infantilises and negates the many achievements of women who follow a different trajectory.

As if to perfectly illustrate this, the Muslim Institute's social media recorded its most heightened activity a couple of years ago when I shared on Twitter a video of the all-female, teenage, hijab-wearing Indonesian heavy metal band 'Voice of Baceprot' playing 'Sugar', a song by genius Armenian-American band 'System of a Down'. I loved the video and revelled in the endless likes and retweets. However, there is no escaping that all the white liberal rejoicing at this 'rebellious' group of young Muslim women 'shattering stereotypes' and 'sticking it to the patriarchy', centres white feminism's image of liberation. Zakaria describes this as the great lie of relatability, with its implied claim that there is only one truly neutral perspective, which considers itself to be the original starting point against which all else should be measured. Subversion must take the form of what white feminism regards as rebellion. Anything else is a misguided enabling of the misogyny of brown and black men perpetuated upon brown and black women. True liberation can only be realised through embracing, becoming and performing white feminism.

This construction of relatability compelled Zakaria to contort for so many years in discomfort, presented as it is with the illusion that apparently this was the only way to be a feminist. Relatability is, as she states, just subjectivity dressed up as objectivity. Having experienced the reality of abuse and oppression, forced to run away from her home and seek the support of domestic violence services, finding herself a destitute single mother, she did not find liberation in the spaces that white feminism expected her to reside in gratefully. Those spaces, whether they were women's groups, or the board of Amnesty International, expected her to conform to their narrow white feminist agenda where they always knew better: 'there is a division within feminism that is not spoken of but that has remained seething beneath the surface for years. It is the division between the women who write and speak feminism and the women who live it; the women who have a voice versus the women who have experience; the ones who make the theories and policies, and the ones who bear scars and sutures from the fight. While this dichotomy does not always trace racial divides, it is true that by and large, the women who are paid to write about feminism, lead feminist organizations and make feminist policy in the Western world are white and middle-class.'

This division is part of a greater fallacy within liberal circles that it is enough to simply be well-intentioned, because this well-intentioned urge is the only way to save black and brown women from black and brown men, because only black and brown communities harbour oppression and misogyny. White liberalism is the utopia in which black and brown women may enjoy the heady freedom that white women in the West have fought so hard to achieve, and which women from other parts of the world can only dream of enjoying. According to the National Coalition Against Domestic Violence's 2022 report, a sobering one in three women have experienced domestic violence in the US, yet the offence is not viewed an honour crime. Instead, honour crimes are perceived as far away problems, not found in the West. This distortion fuels a desire to liberate women from the shackles of patriarchy, which turned out to be a ruse to invade Afghanistan, so women could throw off the burka and gleefully frolic in mini-skirts. The policing of women's bodies knows no end of creativity, with the latest culture war that seeks to pit the rights of trans women, who are among the most marginalised groups in society, against women who deny their right to exist in spaces of chromosomal-designated exclusivity. Does this mean women with androgynous features, women who wear the face veil, women who don't fall within heteronormative boundaries carved out by white feminism, will be required to constantly prove they are women? Zakaria forensically situates the transphobic moral panic of our contemporary times as yet another example of white feminists crowding out the many alternative ways of 'doing feminism' that exist.

Third wave feminists criticised their second wave sisters for their elitism and lack of intersectionality, but continued the pattern of exclusion to the detriment of meaningful solidarity and allyship. As Zakaria points out, to claim that women's rights began with the suffragette movement, denies the involvement of women in the sub-continent in the fight for liberation from colonial occupation, and other acts of political activism and agency. These were strong women who fought for the emancipation of their communities and were just as much feminist pioneers as Emmeline Pankhurst and the women who were pivotal in the suffrage movement.

Against White Feminism is an important book, one which will prove uncomfortable reading for many, and will no doubt make some angry and defensive. In the same way a writer's work is a continual process that lives and exists through engagement, evaluation and criticism; feminism, specifically white feminism, must embrace critique so that it can concede space excessively taken up by the centring of white women's agendas, and make room for a greater plethora of voices that authentically encompass all the ways to be a woman and a feminist. Just as Masterton describes the findings of Forensic Architecture's investigations as continuing to deepen understanding of the crime scene, through the system of corroboration and feedback once the findings are released into the public realm, ideologies such as feminism, that seek restitution in flawed and unequal societies in continual flux, must also try not to succumb to the allure of codification. If white feminism is the crime scene, Rafia Zakaria's stunning critique is the feedback that can inspire introspection, growth and a journey towards truth. More importantly, this book, or 'call to action' as Zakaria describes it, should be received in the spirit that it is written; with the interests of equality, justice and global feminist solidarity, at its heart.

ET CETERA

ON LIBERAL TYRANNY

Shamim Miah

May you live in interesting times.
May you live in an interesting age.
May you live in exciting times.

Ask anyone about these proverbs and chances are they will tell you that it originates as a Chinese curse. Yet they will be wrong. No one has been able to authenticate or confirm the saying as having originated in China. But whatever their origins, there does appear a sense of truism associated with the curse, especially if you follow the recent global, social and political trends – from Brazil, the US, Britain, Hungary, India, China, and Russia, politics has become more tribal and autocratic. More significantly, the election of the former president of the US, Donald Trump, and the politics surrounding Brexit in the UK seem to have opened the door to popular support of 'liberal' tyranny. In fact, these interesting times reflect a much wider postnormal epoch characterised by complexity, contradictions and chaos, 'an in-between period where old orthodoxies are dying, new ones have yet to be born, and very few things seem to make sense'.

The world we inhabit has fundamentally changed. The received wisdom associated with liberal utopia, which predicted the end of history, can no longer be used to navigate the complexity and contradictions, that unfold in real time. In Britain, we have seen how, during the fall of Kabul to the Taliban in August 2021, Airbus A330 – a flight chartered by the UK charity Nowzad – was able to fly out from Kabul Airport with the direct intervention of Prime Minister Boris Johnson. This was not the only chartered plane to leave Afghanistan. Most Western citizens made a quick exit, fearing 'victor's justice' from the Taliban. Unlike the other flights, Nowzad's Operation Noah's Ark was unique because it was not airlifting humans to safety – rather it was prioritising animals, especially cats and dogs from remote places in Afghanistan and bringing them to the UK for sanctuary. Whilst the British government was quick to support Operation Noah's Ark, it refused to grant asylum to Afghans who had been employed as British Embassy security guards through a private Canadian company called GardaWorld, which offers private security 'services' to the global neoliberal privatisation of war. The embassy security guards were notified via telephone that they would not be eligible for asylum claims because they were employed as 'contractors'. A war that started with liberal expansionist aims of spreading democracy, rule of law, and the empowerment of women, ended with an Airbus A330 chartered plane carrying 173 cats and dogs to sanctuary. The liberal paradox was further highlighted, in hindsight, through the European Union's high court ruling in April 2020 on Poland and the Czech Republic for breaking EU law for refusing to host Syrian refugees.

More recently, in April 2022, we witnessed the landslide victory of Viktor Orban's popular nationalist and conservative party in Hungary. The Fidesz's spectacular victory puts Orban's self-styled ultra-nationalist 'illiberal democracy' at the heart of the EU. Meanwhile, in Canada, Justin Trudeau's Liberal Party was accused of liberal tyranny in early 2022, following the Emergencies Act, which imposed a ban on public assemblies. The act was a response to peaceful demonstrations in Ottawa, which saw over four hundred trucks and other vehicles gridlocking the streets around Parliament. The protestors were responding to federal regulations on Covid rules requiring truckers crossing into Canada from the United States to be vaccinated against coronavirus. Similar anti-vax protests, using the same tactics, have happened in the streets of Belgium, France, Finland, and New Zealand.

How do we make sense of these contradictions in – and, in several cases, outright assaults on – the very concept of liberalism and liberal democracy?

Since the second decade of the twenty-first century the hopes and expectations promised by liberalism have lost all aspiration and hope. The linear understanding of history as a march towards progress is no longer a sociological reality as envisaged by the French philosopher and founder of modern sociology, Auguste Comte (d. 1842). This idea was later developed by political thinkers, such as Francis Fukuyama in his much-cited text, *The End of History and the Last Man,* published after the fall of the Berlin Wall, to signify a critical moment in liberal triumphalism in world history.

In fact, as early as the fourteenth century, the historian Ibn Khaldun (d. 1406) questioned the linear understanding of historical development. Ibn Khaldun's detailed reading of history and observations on political life enabled him to reject a linear understanding of history in favour of a cyclical view, based upon the comparative idea of human nature. Political power, he argued, can be compared with all living organisms – they are born, mature, decline, and perish. For Ibn Khaldun, the secret was to think historically, by looking at the bigger picture especially when it came to understanding, explaining, and thinking through problems of the present. 'History' is not simply the study of the past, but rather lessons and principles inherited from the past that are crucial in making sense of the present.

We are witnessing the reconfiguration of the global world order from a unipolar world controlled by the liberal values of the West to a multi-polar world between China, Russia, the EU, and the US. What is most striking is the speed with which this change is moving – from simply rapid to accelerating and chaotic. Liberalism, it appears, is no longer capable of protecting individual rights, religious freedom, and lifestyle against popular opinion and government power.

The Black Lives Matter movement has further exposed the paradoxes associated with liberal political governance. For example, the dominant liberal thinkers that are often cited range from John Locke, Edmund Burke, Benjamin Constant, and Jeremy Bentham, but a closer reading of their canonical texts displays deeper contradictions of intellectual positions which are taken as received wisdom. A counter-reading of these texts demonstrates how, when it comes to issues of race, liberal thinkers do not appear to be very enlightened. Take the following question: is there an inherent contradiction in being a liberal slave-owner? This premise goes against the very nature of liberty and the fundamental rights of individuals. Yet, Locke (d. 1704), considered by many as the father of liberalism, was one of the last major philosophers to seek justification for absolute and perpetual slavery. This is a paradox, especially given that Locke's condemnation of absolute power which seeks to reduce European men to slavery is written next to dark passages which can be read as justification of the enslavement of Africans in the colonies. His principle of equality, in other words, is predicated upon the humans of the same 'rank', or 'species'. Thus, Locke's ideas of the social contract, whereby the state takes on the responsibility to protect the natural right of life, liberty, and property, only applies for some and not for others. Perhaps the biggest irony is that the institution of slavery continued not despite the success of liberalism in the West, but *following* it.

The rise of liberalism and the birth of nation-states is an idea that has been picked up by several writers, including David Theo Golberg in *The Racial State*. The politics of 'race', Goldberg argues, is critical and essential to the emergence, development, and transformations of modern European nation-states. In many respects the construct of racial superiority of Europeans vis-à-vis the 'other' is baked within the ontological fabric of nation-states. Furthermore, the defining, regulating, overseeing, and, most critically, managing of racial matters are at the essence or the core of governance – a practice that can be called racial governmentality. In short, given the history and the politics of European states, it is not surprising to note that some European states act as racial states, in that they actively 'govern' populations via 'defining populations into racial identified groups, and they do so more or less through census taking, law and policy in and through bureaucratic forms and administrating practice'.

'Tyranny is the inevitable outcome of liberalism,' argues Sohrab Ahmari in a recent article for the politically conservative weekly magazine, *The Spectator*. In defence of his arguments, Ahmari, a much-admired political commentator of the political right, draws upon recent examples of liberal paradoxes associated with the promotion of 'free speech' for some and its refusal or denial to grant 'free speech' to those who want to question liberal orthodoxies, especially relating to gender fluidity and trans-rights. Ahmar is a convert to Christianity from Islam and, like many converts, he is rather evangelical in his criticism of liberalism through normative

Judaeo-Christian ideas of orthodox values, as argued in his recent book, *The Unbroken Thread: Discovering the Wisdom of Tradition in an Age of Chaos*. This sort of critique of liberalism from the perspective of the political right is taking a resurgence across the globe, as seen in the mass appeal of the works of the Canadian clinical psychologist and YouTube personality Jordan Peterson, on identity politics and political correctness. Peterson, who is the author of the highly influential *12 Rules of Life*, rose to prominence following his public criticism of the Act to Amend the Canadian Human Rights Act and the Criminal Code (2016), which gave gender expression and gender identity protected status. More recently, the merger between Peterson and sections of the conservative Muslim community was further consolidated following an interview between Peterson and the popular Muslim YouTuber, Muhammad Hijab, which has over 2.5 million views at the time of writing.

Liberalism is also being critiqued through the lens of liberal hypocrisy – an approach that is also gaining steady momentum worldwide. In Russia, there has been a growing interest in the writings of the philosopher and public intellectual Aleksandr Dugin, who was born in 1962. Dugin's politically conservative ideas of religion, family values, and the Orthodox church, with an emphasis on religious mysticism and obedience to patriarchal authority, have had deep and lasting impact on the political views of Vladimir Putin. Dugin was once a philosopher only known to specialist readers on mysticism, Traditionalism, and Muslim perennialism, exemplified in the works of René Guénon (d. 1951) and other thinkers, such as the Italian philosopher Julius Evola (d. 1974). But Dugin has now taken centre ground in Western and Eurasian political discourse. Dugin's critique of liberalism in general and his views on geopolitics in particular continue to influence Europe's 'new right' and America's 'alt-right'. Along with others writers of his ilk, Dugin belongs to a long tradition of philosophers, theologians, and political thinkers who view the present and the future through romantic notions of the past.

It seems, then, that mainstream defences of liberalism and attacks on liberal tyranny from the political right are motivated by the desire to forge 'exciting times' that are based on a romanticised and highly selective memory of yesterday. But in postnormal times, exciting and interesting times tend to be contradictory and chaotic.

TEN LIBERAL CONTRADICTIONS

How might one define a liberal? A simple answer could be someone who believes in individual rights, civil liberties, democracy and (arguably) a 'free' market. But then how might one explain the ways that 'liberal' is placed on the political spectrum in different contexts? In the US, for instance, it appears to be synonymous with 'left-wing', but in Australia the Liberal Party is politically right-wing. It seems that contradictions are part and parcel of the term 'liberal'.

Here's another conundrum – is it possible to be a liberal and a dictator? According to some admirers of the founding father of independent Singapore, Lee Kuan Yew (1923-2015), the answer would be yes. The island city-state has apparently shown the world that it is perfectly possible to sacrifice democratic politics, civil liberties and human rights to achieve capitalist prosperity, consumerist power, and cultural prowess. A nation that can shop and eat well is a happy nation – the jailing, harassment, and torture of political dissidents and activists notwithstanding. In pursuing his political ambitions for Singapore, Lee famously championed 'Asian values' – the idea that Asians are inherently more collectivist and deferential to authority than their individualistic European counterparts. According to this ideological framework, human rights are simply not part of Asian values.

The love-hate relationship that Lee had with Western observers points to another paradox – can liberalism have universal application, or is it and will it always be Western and Eurocentric? 'Liberalism', as a concept, seems to be part of a family of concepts that are predominantly associated with the 'West' – democracy, human rights, freedom, civilisation, and equality, to name a few. But, surely, these aspirations and achievements can and do exist in non-Western societies. Or do they? And, if they did, would they or do they go by other names?

Taking these considerations into account, this list probes ten contradictions associated with what we commonly think of as liberalism – in no particular order. We've applied analysis, speculation and eye-rolling in liberal doses.

1. Sanctions

On 6 April 2022, the UK government sanctioned Moshe Kantor, the president of the European Jewish Congress (EJC) and vice president of the Jewish Leadership Council (JLC), over his ties to Russian President Vladimir Putin. This was part of the UK's larger package of sanctions in response to Russia's invasion of Ukraine on 24 February. Earlier sanctions imposed on the Russian oligarch Roman Abramovich, owner of Chelsea football club, also hogged the headlines.

Sanctions in times of war are not unusual. But some of the targets of these sanctions seemed questionable, at least according to some interest groups. After all, Abramovich and Kantor are high-profile Jewish philanthropists whose CVs include efforts to combat antisemitism, racism and xenophobia in the UK and Israel – impeccable liberal credentials.

Jewish umbrella bodies have had mixed reactions. The EJC said it was 'deeply shocked and appalled' at the 'misguided' sanctions against Kantor. According to the *Jewish Chronicle*, president of the Board of Deputies of British Jews, Marie van der Zyl – who also chairs the EJC – said very little, apart from claiming that she had not seen the EJC's statement before it was released. The JLC merely announced that Kantor's term of office came to an end in May and would not be renewed.

Perhaps this ambivalence about sanctions is tied to the Board of Deputies' vehement opposition to *specific* organised responses against what Amnesty International has labelled Israel's 'apartheid' in the Occupied Palestinian Territories. When Amnesty's report was released in January, before the invasion of Ukraine, the Board of Deputies wasted no time in calling it 'preposterous' and retorted that 'Israel is a vibrant democracy and a state for all its citizens'. These sentiments carry great political weight, especially in the UK and US where they form the basis of intensifying moves to ban calls for boycotts, divestments and sanctions against Israel.

Perchance the rightfulness of sanctioning a regime is in the eye of its liberal military allies?

2. Dictators

Speaking of rogue regimes, it is undeniable that Putin is a megalomaniacal dictator who has not hesitated to poison, jail, torture and murder his political opponents. He has bombed hospitals and maternity clinics and used chemical weapons in Syria, and now Ukraine. But how *exactly* is Putin different from, say, the Egyptian military dictator Abdel Fattah al-Sisi who, barely a month after seizing his country in a *coup d'état* in 2013, massacred more than 800 civilians in a single day? Or from Saudi Arabian crown prince Muhammad bin Salman, who was personally linked to the assassination – through decapitation – of the *Washington Post* columnist Jamal Khashoggi in 2018 and has orchestrated the Saudi bombing campaign in Yemen since 2015?

Perchance the definition of a dangerous dictator is in the eye of its liberal oil-and-gas-guzzling benefactors and beneficiaries?

3. Democracy

Ah, the Enlightenment. Did it not gift us *liberté*, *égalité*, and *fraternité* in France as well as the American Declaration of Independence? Did it not enable the passage of the great nineteenth-century reform acts in Britain, the mother of parliaments? Did it not enshrine fundamental liberties, the rule of law and democratic governance as the ideals of statecraft and citizenship?

If he were still alive, perhaps we could refer this question to Mohammed Mossadegh, the democratically elected Prime Minister of Iran who was deposed in a 1953 *coup d'état* – there's that phrase again – orchestrated by the intelligence services of the UK (MI6) and the US (CIA). Or with Salvador Allende, the democratically elected president of Chile who was ousted in a CIA-engineered – you guessed it – *coup d'état* on 11 September 1973, which perhaps should be known as The Other 9/11.

Could it be that it's only the Brits and the Americans who have diverged from the supposed Enlightenment ideals of democracy? What about the French? After all, it was the Algerian military, not former colonial master

France, that cancelled Algeria's 1991 elections when it appeared that the Islamic Salvation Front was on the brink of victory. France stayed aloof and merely remarked that the cancellation was 'somewhat abnormal', angering the army *and* the Islamists. The military coup that followed sparked off a bloody civil war that had complex repercussions in both countries. All the while and to the present day, however, France has continued to meddle in the affairs of its former African colonies. This is in contradiction to President Emmanuel Macron's declaration, during his 2017 campaign, that the country's colonial history in Algeria was a 'crime against humanity'.

Perchance democracy is in the eye of liberal ex-colonial overlords?

4. Diversity

Sajid Javid. Priti Patel. Alok Sharma. Rishi Sunak. A few years ago, one would be forgiven for wondering if this was the new cast of the latest Bollywood blockbuster. When Boris Johnson became the UK's Prime Minister in 2019, he appointed them to his cabinet as Chancellor of the Exchequer, Home Secretary, International Development Secretary, and Chief Secretary to the Treasury, respectively. They have since become heavyweights in the British political landscape. (Sunak is now Chancellor of the Exchequer.) Alongside Johnson's other appointments – James Cleverley as Minister Without Portfolio and Kwasi Kwarteng as Minister (now Secretary) of State for Business, Energy and Industrial Strategy – this was hailed as one of the country's most diverse cabinets.

How have they been good for liberty, equality, diversity, inclusion and all that jazz? Let us count the ways.

Demonising and deporting refugees and asylum seekers. Blocking demonstrations against the murder of women, racism, and climate breakdown. Economic policies that have worsened inequality during a crippling pandemic. Paying lip service to environmental legislation whilst the extraction and burning of oil and gas continues apace. You decide.

5. Converts

Tina Turner adopts Buddhism and it becomes an iconic part of her legacy as the Queen of Rock 'n' Roll. Madonna dabbles in Kabbalah and it becomes trendy. Bob Dylan converts from Judaism to Evangelical

Christianity and it's now seen – alongside his deconversion a few years later – as an understandable part of his biography. But Sinead O'Connor becomes a Muslim and she is labelled a 'civilisational traitress'. Actually, the full quote, from the English Anglican theologian John Milbank, reads: 'Sinead O'Connor's conversion suggest that [French author and *enfant terrible* Michel] Houllebecq has it right. Liberals will embrace an authoritarianism to escape their own contradictions if it is respectably other and non-Western. She is a civilisational traitress. And has no taste.'

Burn! Bam! Mic drop! These may or may not have been the thoughts that went through the head of Milbank, the self-styled arch-defender of Western Christendom, with his takedown of sister Shuhada Sadaqat. It's hard to tell and, unfortunately, Milbank's original Tweet has been removed. But it has been captured for posterity in the British analyst Hisham Hellyer's response – a link can be found in the Citations at the back of this issue.

6. *Refugees and asylum seekers*

'They seem so like us. That is what makes it so shocking. Ukraine is a European country. Its people watch Netflix and have Instagram accounts, vote in free elections and read uncensored newspapers. War is no longer something visited upon impoverished and remote populations.'

So wrote Daniel Hannan in *The Telegraph* regarding the suffering of the people of Ukraine under the Russian invasion. By now, this and other similar reactions in Western media outlets have been recognised for what they are – 'racist exceptionalism' (according to Kenyan political cartoonist Patrick Gathara) and 'racist coverage' (according to Egyptian-American academic Moustafa Bayoumi).

In case you were wondering if Hannan's framing was merely an isolated incident, how about Phillipe Corbé's take on behalf of France's BFM TV: 'We're not talking here about Syrians fleeing the bombing of the Syrian regime backed by Putin. We're talking about Europeans leaving in cars that look like ours to save their lives.' Or Charlie D'Agata, from the US's CBS News, who quipped that Ukraine 'isn't a place, with all due respect, like Iraq or Afghanistan, that has seen conflict raging for decades … This is a relatively civilised, relatively European – I have to choose those words carefully, too – city, where you wouldn't expect that or hope that it's going to happen.'

Many European countries have since flung their borders open to Ukrainians fleeing the country. Those same doors remain barely semi-open for African and Indian students and workers trying to escape the carnage in Ukraine. Meanwhile, at the time of writing, the UK government is considering deporting all asylum seekers to Rwanda.

7. Feminism

An American president who opposes women's sexual and reproductive rights insists on bombing a Muslim country to liberate its women. You're probably hard pressed to guess which one, because doesn't this describe more than one US Commander-in-Chief? But just to jog our memories a wee bit – before the menace of Donald Trump, there was George W. Bush. This is why you can't remember the good old days – there weren't any.

After the 9/11 terrorist attacks, the liberation of Afghan women from the Taliban and the *burqa* really was one of the justifications for the War on Terror and the US-led invasion of Afghanistan. Spearheaded by an anti-abortion, homophobic president who could hardly be described even by the most generous commentators as a feminist.

Dubya is not the first to betray this 'liberal' contradiction. Lord Cromer, the British controller-general of Egypt in the nineteenth century, believed that Christianity gave women respect, while Islam only degraded them through the practices of veiling and segregation. Cromer, too, wanted to 'liberate' Muslim women from the veil. But back home in Britain, he founded and was for a time president of the Men's League for Opposing Women's Suffrage.

There's a name for this double standard. Egyptian-American scholar of Islam Leila Ahmed calls it 'colonial feminism', while Indian postcolonial feminist scholar Gayatri Chakravorty Spivak describes it as 'white men saving brown women from brown men'. We'd like to think the liberal democratic West has moved on, especially in the wake of #MeToo and #BlackLivesMatter, but we're not holding our breath.

8. Censorship and free speech

If the UK government has its way, the controversial Policing, Crime, Sentencing and Courts (PCSC) Bill will make it a crime to 'damage memorials'. This particular provision in the Bill – in the ping-pong stages in Parliament at the time of writing – is in response to 'widespread upset about the damage and desecration of memorials with a recent spate over the summer of 2020'. This, of course, includes the spectacular toppling of the statue of the slaver Edward Colston in Bristol at the peak of the British Black Lives Matter protests. The Colston Four – anti-racism campaigners Jake Skuse, 33, Rhian Graham, 30, Milo Ponsford, 26 and Sage Willoughby, 22 – were found not guilty by a Bristol crown court. But at the time of writing, the attorney general has referred the case to the Court of Appeal.

Were we to take the government's argument to its logical conclusion, we might conclude that even in liberal societies, there is a limit to free speech and protest. Even though statues are symbolic and are not living entities – and are possibly offensive to some people – causing 'damage and desecration' to them is off limits because it could cause 'widespread upset'.

Enter the Labour Member of Parliament Naz Shah, who drew parallels between the proposed law and how it could also apply to the 'emotional harm' that offensive caricatures of Muhammad could cause Muslims. Shah was immediately vilified and pilloried by the who's who of the British secularist, libertarian *and* conservative Christian establishment for allegedly calling for an anti-blasphemy law. Was she? Or was she just asking whether it was one rule for colonial relics and one rule for living, breathing members of religious minority communities?

9. Surveillance and restrictions

The majority of Australians seemed to rejoice when tennis star Novak Djokovic was deported and prevented from defending his Australian Open title in January 2022 for not complying with the country's Covid vaccination protocols. But wait, said his supporters and anti-vaxxers – was this not a contradiction in a liberal society? Did Nole not have the freedom of choice to oppose 'someone…forcing me to put something in my body'? Barely a month later, Canadian Prime Minister Justin Trudeau invoked the Emergencies Act to quash protests and blockades against Covid-19 vaccine mandates in Ottawa.

These are merely two of the many Covid-related government interventions – including lockdowns and mask-wearing – that have provoked the ire of those who oppose them purportedly on the grounds of defending their individual liberty. Government restrictions on our lifestyle choices are unacceptable, the argument goes. They amount to a violation of our right to privacy and choice. They are a chilling example of state surveillance, thought policing, and violence towards our bodies and lives.

What salutary liberal principles to defend!

But where were many of these protesters when innocent Muslims were being watched, interrogated, arrested, shot, or jailed under existing counter-terrorism provisions in many Western liberal democracies? Where were they when the many Black men and women were violently stopped and searched – and killed, in the US – by the police?

10. Rationality

Perhaps there is a rational, logical way to think about all these issues. This is also an eminently liberal approach to take, since one of modern liberal thought's main assumptions is the centrality of the human individual as a rational actor in social interactions. As rational actors, individuals will always act in their own self-interest to achieve specific, reasonable goals. A liberal society is therefore one in which rational individuals can come together to negotiate, deliberate and decide on the ways that they are to be governed collectively – the democratic ideal.

This narrative of political liberalism often traces its origins to Classical Athens through the birth of the very concept of 'democracy' – from *dēmos* (people) and *kratos* (rule) – primarily in the thought of Aristotle (384-322 BC). But Aristotle is not the only Greek philosopher whose legacy continues to shape current liberal thought in the West.

It would be messy and beyond the scope of this List to spend too much time complicating the assumed connection between 'rationality', 'liberalism' and Greek civilisation. For brevity, let's just look at Pythagoras (c.570-c.495 BCE). We can all probably recite Pythagoras's theorem by heart – the square of a triangle's hypotenuse is the sum of the squares of its other two sides. Foundationally mathematical and eminently rational, right?

But Pythagoras also believed in reincarnation, which is why he and his followers were religiously vegetarian. You would not want to eat a cow because it could have been someone's uncle in a previous life. It is also said that Pythagoras died at the hands of his enemies when he and his followers were pursued to the end of a bean field but refused to cross it. Why did they refuse to cross the bean field? We'll never know, because Pythagoreans were also known for keeping to a strict code of secrecy and silence. Entry into the Pythagorean community involved arduous initiation, including undertaking a five-year vow of silence. We do know, however, that Pythagoras and his followers had an intensely esoteric and spiritual understanding of the very concept of numbers.

Such mystical and religiously saturated worldviews are hardly prominent in current discussions about concepts such as liberalism, democracy or rationality. But we might have now strayed from what was meant to be our list of 'liberal contradictions', so perhaps we should make like Pythagoras and stop spilling the beans.

CITATIONS

Introduction: Retaking Liberties by Shanon Shah

The scene from *Monty Python's Life of Brian* that I refer to can be viewed at https://www.youtube.com/watch?v=QereR0CViMY.

Some background on the accusations of blasphemy against the film can be found at https://www.bbc.com/culture/article/20190822-life-of-brian-the-most -blasphemous-film-ever.

Excerpts from Sojourner Truth's 'Ain't I a Woman?' speech can be found at https://www.nps.gov/articles/sojourner-truth.htm, while the context for Harriet Tubman's 'you will be free or you will die' quote is given briefly at https://quote.org/quote/youll-be-free-or-you-will-die-6290 58.

Islam and Freedom by Mustafa Akyol

This article is adopted from my book, *Reopening Muslim Minds: A Return to Reason, Freedom, and Tolerance* (St. Martin's Press, 2021); to be published in the UK in June 2022 by Swift Press.

The quotes, in order of appearance, are from:

Roger Olson, 'The Bonds of Freedom', *Christianity Today* 5 October, 2012. F.A. Hayek, *The Constitution of Liberty*, University of Chicago Press, 1978, p12. Bernard Lewis, *What Went Wrong: Western Impact and Middle Eastern Response*, Oxford University Pres, 2002, p156. Al-Mawardi, *Al-Ahkam as Sultaniyyah: The Laws of Islamic Governance*, Taha, London, 1996, p313. Al-Ghazali, *Revival of Religious Sciences*, translated by M M al-Sharif, Bar al-Kotob al-Illmiyah, Bairut, 2011, 2:539, 465-66. Yassine Essid, *Critique of the Origins of Islamic Economic Thought*, Brill, Leiden, 1995, p115. Al-Tabari quote is from Michael Cook, *Commanding Right and Forbidding Wrong in Islamic Thought*, Cambridge University Press, 2000, p24.

Ayatollah H Montazeri, *Religious State and Human Rights*, Saraei, Tehran, 2008, p142-143.

The al-Qaradawi interview can be found on YouTube. The later quote is from the article 'Apostasy: Major and Minor', *Islamonline.net* 13 April 2006.

The two hadith are from *Sahih al-Bukhari*: vol 4 book 52, no 260 and vol 9, book 83, no 17. Procopious, *Anecdota*, XI. 26, quoted in Demetrious J Constantelos, 'Paganism and the State in the Age of Justinian', *Catholic Historical Review* 50 3 372-80, October 1964. Mohammad Hanif, 'Blasphemy, Pakistan's New Religion' *New York Times* 2 November 2018. Fakhruddin ar-Razi, *at-Tafsir al-Kabir,* commentary on 3:186. The quote from Badr al-Din al-Ayni is cited in Ismail Royer, *Pakistan's Blasphemy Law and Non-Muslims*, Lamppost Education Initiative, 2018, p17.

Liberty and Freedom by Jeremy Henzell-Thomas

In *Keywords* (Fontana, London, 1976) Raymond Williams has entries for *liberal* and *liberation* but not for *freedom*. On the connection between *liberal* and *generous*, see *Word Histories and Mysteries: From Abracadabra to Zeus,* from the Editors of the American Heritage Dictionaries (Houghton Mifflin, Boston, 2004), 163.

The different connotations of *freedom* and *liberty* were brought to light in a letter to *The Independent* newspaper on 10 August 2004 by Professor Bert Hornback, who rightly perceived some confusion in the use of the terms by a columnist, and whose explanations are consistent with the corresponding entries in John Ayto, *Dictionary of Word Origins* (London: Bloomsbury Publishing, London, 1990), 240, 322, and Joseph T. Shipley, *The Origins of English Words: A Discursive Dictionary of Indo-European Roots* (John Hopkins University Press, 1984), 327-328.

On Hegel's rejection of John Stuart Mills' licentious conception of liberty, see M. Perry, *On Awakening and Remembering* (Fons Vitae, Louisville, 2000), 285, note 109. The pejorative use of the term 'liberal' to refer to 'do-gooders' who are sometimes considered to get in the way of real progress is referred to in the entries for *Liberal* and *Liberal-minded* in Kenneth Hudson, *The Dictionary of Diseased English* (Macmillan, London, 1977), 136-137. Ibn Khaldun's views on *'asabiyyah* are examined in

'Asyiqin Abdul Halim et el., 'Ibn Khaldun's Theory of 'Asabiyyah and its Application in Modern Muslim Society', *Middle-East Journal of Scientific Research* 11:9 (2012), 1232-1237. The appeal for the revitalization of multilateralism by the World Policy Forum (Global Solutions) in the run-up to the G20 summit in Rome at the end of October 2021 can be accessed at https://www.global-solutions-initiative.org/press-news/g20-appeal-revitalizing-multilateralism/.

On procedural secularism, see Rowan Williams, *Islam, Christianity and Pluralism*, first Zaki Badawi Memorial Lecture, Joint publication by Lambeth Palace and the Association of Muslim Social Scientists, Richmond, 2007. See also two reports published by the Centre of Islamic Studies, University of Cambridge: *Contextualising Islam in Britain: Exploratory Perspectives*, 2009, 33-35, and *Contextualising Islam in Britain II*, 2012, 107-108. On liberty of conscience, see Martin Luther, *On Secular Authority: To What Extent It Should be Obeyed*, 1523. On *adab al-ikhtilaf,* see Taha Jabir Fayyad 'Alwani, *The Ethics of Disagreement in Islam,* English translation of *Adab al Ikhtilaf Fil Al Islam* by Abdul Wahid Hamid (IIIT, Herndon, 1993). For Tariq Ramadan's views on the balance needed between freedom of speech and civic responsibility, see the interview with Nathan Gardels in *New Perspectives* posted on 2/2/2006 at http://www.digitalnpq.org/articles/global/56/02-02-2006/tariq_ramadan. See also Jeremy Henzell-Thomas, 'Cartoon Wars: The Challenge for Muslims in the West', *Emel Magazine*, February 2006. On the reaction of the Insted Consultancy to the *Charlie Hebdo* shooting in Paris, and their list of 28 articles which question the dominant narrative, see the *Insted Consultancy News* at https://instedconsultancy.wordpress.com/2015/01/15/charlie-hebdo-free-speech-us-and-them-thinking/#comments. On the fact that freedom of speech is not an absolute value, see Simon Dawes, '*Charlie Hebdo*: Free speech, but not as an absolute value' at https://www.opendemocracy.net/can-europe-make-it/simon-dawes/charlie-hebdo-free-speech-but-not-as-absolute-value, and Rey Barry, 'United States Myths and their Realities: Americans have Free Speech' at http://www.freewarehof.org/speech.html. US myths about freedom are also highlighted by Glenn Greenwald, 'Julian Assange's Imprisonment Exposes US Myths about Freedom', *Scheerpost,* 2/1/2021 at https://scheerpost.com/2021/01/02/

julian-assanges-imprisonment-exposes-u-s-myths-about-freedom/. In discussing the case of Julian Assange, I have also referred to Matthias von Hein, 20/4/2021, at https://www.dw.com/en/the-case-of-julian-assange-rule-of-law-undermined/a-57260909. Pankaj Mishra's plea for a 'new enlightenment' can be accessed at http://www.theguardian.com/news/2015/jan/20/-sp-after-paris-its-time-for-new-enlightenment.

For the Human Freedom Index, see https://www.cato.org/human-freedom-index/2021, and for theocratic countries, see https://worldpopulationreview.com/country-rankings/theocracy-countries. Kenan Malik's article 'Strange beasts, these "libertarians" who love to curb the freedom of others' (*Observer* 19/12/21) can be accessed at https://www.theguardian.com/commentisfree/2021/dec/19/libertarian-tories-still-ask-to-see-papers-of-those-they-deem-not-worthy-of-freedom. On the rolling back of individual rights in recent years, I have referred to https://www.positive.news/society/the-best-countries-for-social-progress/?fbclid=IwAR1KRx7ZwKqfYCD CvZ_NvnVux2fU__wcx952uGL8Nl6Jv4mQo6R8Gj2YuiQ

A Very Short History of Liberty by Vinay Lal

Classical texts, whether Greek, Indian, or Chinese, are usually referenced not by page number but by book number, followed by paragraph or verse, or simply by line number. For Aristotle, Keith Barker's ed. and trans. of *The Politics* has been used (New York: Oxford University Press, Galaxy Books, 1964), 1310, 1317b; for Herodotus, see *The Histories*, trans. Aubrey de Selincourt (Harmondsworth: Penguin Books, 1955), 7:133. I have used the translation in *The Landmark Thucydides*, ed. Robert B. Strassler (New York: The Free Press, 1996), 6:56-59, 3:62, and 1:122-24. The quotation in the last paragraph is from Confucius's *Analects*, trans. Burton Watson (Columbia University Press, 2007), II.12. The quotation from Ludwig von Mises is drawn from chapter 21 of a collection of his essays, *Money, Method, and the Market Process* (Dordrecht, The Netherlands: Kluwer Academic Publishing, 1990), while Moses Finley's assessment is taken from his article, 'Between Slavery and Freedom', *Comparative Studies in Society and History* 6, no. 3 (April 1964), 233-49; the quotation is from pp236-37.

There are many editions of Francois Bernier, *Travels in the Mogul Empire: AD 1656-1668*. The 1891 edition revised and published by Archibald Constable, based on Irving Brock's translation, is readable; quotations are from pages 5, 204, and 225. John Logan's *A Dissertation on the Governments, Manner and Spirits of Asia* (London, 1787) and William Robertson's *The Progress of Society in Europe* (1769) are discussed in Peter J. Marshall and Glyndwr Williams, *The Great Map of Humankind: British Perceptions of the World in the Age of Enlightenment* (London: J. M. Dent & Sons Ltd., 1982). Robert Orme's essay on the effeminacy of Indians (1761) is in *Some Historical Fragments of the Mogul Empire* (reprint ed., New Delhi: Associated Publishing House, 1974) while the passage from Alexander Dow is from Volume 3 of *The History of Hindostan* (1770, reprint ed., Delhi: Today & Tomorrow's Printers & Publishers, 1973), vii-xxxv. Thomas Munro's 'Minute' of 31 December 1824 is in Vol 28. of *Parliamentary Papers* (1830), while John Malcolm's Notes of Instruction to Assistants and Officers acting under the order of Major-General Sir John Malcolm' [1821] is reprinted in the author's *A Memoir of Central India*, 2 vols. (New Delhi: Sagar Publications, 1970), 433-475 of Vol. 2; the quotation is at p436.

The passages cited from Madison Smartt Bell's biography, *Toussaint Louverture* (New York: Pantheon Books, 2007) appear on p3 and p284. See also Michel-Rolph Trouillot, *Silencing the Past: Power and the Production of History* (Boston: Beacon Press, 1995), p72-88, and C. L. R. James, *The Black Jacobins: Toussaint L'Ouverture and the San Domingo Revolution*, 2nd rev. ed. (New York: Random House, 1963; Vintage Books, 1989), p88-95. The passing reference to Toussaint in C. A. Bayly, *The Birth of the Modern World 1780-1914* (Oxford: Blackwell Publishing, 2004), is at p99. The testimony of the slave is cited by Jon Henley, 'Haiti: A Long Descent to Hell', *The Guardian* (14 January 2010), online: https://www.theguardian.com/world/2010/jan/14/haiti-history-earthquake-disaster

For the first of the two quotes from Immanuel Kant, see *Toward Perpetual Peace and Other Writings on Politics, Peace, and History* (New Haven: Yale University Press, 2006), p76; the quote in the last paragraph is from the *Groundwork of the Metaphysics of Morals*, of which there are many editions.

Quotes from John Stuart Mill are taken from *Considerations on Representative Government* [1861], introduction by F. A. Hayek (Chicago: Henry Regnery Co., 1962), p38; *Autobiography*, in *EssentialWorks of John Stuart Mill*, ed. Max Lerner (NewYork: Bantam Books, 1961), p12; and the edition *Of Liberty* I have used is edited by Elizabeth Rapaport (Hackett Publishing Company, 1978). Isaiah Berlin's 'Two Concepts of Liberty' is anthologized in his *The Proper Study of Mankind: An Anthology of Essays* (New York: Farrar Straus Giroux, 1998), 191-242. John Locke's description of slavery as 'so vile and miserable an estate' is the opening line of *The Two Treatises of Civil Government* (1689) and his own involvement in the Carolinas is discussed in James Farr, "'So Vile and Miserable an Estate": The Problem of Slavery in Locke's Political Thought', *Political Theory* 14, no. 2 (May 1986), the quote being from p265. Britain's role in the slave trade is reviewed by Howard W. French, 'Slavery, Memory, Empire', *The New York Review of Books* (7 April 2022), 22-24. For Walter Benjamin's famous aphorism, see *Illuminations*, trans. Harry Zohn and ed. Hannah Arendt (New York: Schocken Books, 1969), p256.

On 'frightfulness', see Great Britain, *Parliamentary Papers*, 'Report of the [Bryce] Committee on Alleged German Outrages', Cd 7894, in *Parliamentary Papers*, 1914-1916 [1915] Vol. 23; Churchill's and Montagu's remarks are from the debate in the House of Commons on 8 July 1920, 5 Hansard 131, columns 1707-28. David Cameron's refusal to apologize for the Amritsar Massacre was reported in *The Guardian* on 20 February 2013, and Gordon Brown's remarks are taken as reported in *The Daily Mail* on 15 January 2005.

Gandhi's relationship to the Western intellectual tradition is explored by Vinay Lal, 'Gandhi's West, the West's Gandhi', *New Literary History* 40 (Spring 2009), 281-313, and from the same author there is an article on Gandhi's position on rights: 'Gandhi, citizenship and the idea of a good civil society, Mohan Singh Mehta Memorial Lecture April 2008 (Udaipur: Seva Mandir, 2008). Nearly everything that Gandhi wrote has been assembled in *The Collected Works of Mahatma Gandhi*, 100 vols. (New Delhi: Publications Division, Ministry of Information & Broadcasting, Government of India). But there are two different editions of this series with not merely different pagination but different content owing to the attempt by a previous Hindu nationalist government to tamper with the text. The pieces are best cited by date and title, where available. Some of the quotations are drawn from his essay on 'Liberty', *Indian Opinion* (8 January 1910); 'Limits to Freedom', *Navajivan* (31 May 1931); 'Freedom to the Free', *Young India* (1 November 1928); and 'Congress Position' (27 January 1948). The letter from Gandhi to Du Bois of 1 May 1929 can also be accessed online at http://credo.library.umass.edu/view/full/mums312-b181-i615

For the polemic against Thoreau, see Kathryn Schulz, 'The Moral Judgments of Henry David Thoreau', *The New Yorker* (19 October 2015). Orwell's essay on 'England Your England' from 1941 is widely reprinted. Beethoven's attitude towards Napoleon is discussed by Romain Rolland, *Beethoven the Creator*, trans. Ernest Newman (New York: Harper & Brothers, 1929), p62-63.

Liberty, Hypocrisy, Neutrality by Naomi Foyle

Liberty and Rhetoric
Environmentalist Bill McKibben explains the umbilical link between autocracy and the fossil fuel industry: https://www.theguardian.com/environment/2022/apr/11/putin-autocracies-fossil-fuels-climate-action. For fact checks on Putin's claims about Ukraine, see: https://www.politifact.com/factchecks/2022/feb/25/vladimir-putin/putin-repeats-long-running-claim-genocide-ukraine/, https://www.factcheck.org/2022/03/the-facts-on-de-nazifying-ukraine/ and https://en.wikipedia.org/wiki/Far-right_politics_in_Ukrain.
Alisher Ilkhamov's article 'Is Putin's Regime Nazi' (academia.edu, 2022), can be downloaded at https://www.academia.edu/s/f780fcd688?source=ai_email. Putin's biographer, scholar Mark Galeotti, gives his opinion of Putin's current state of mind here: https://www.ucl.ac.uk/news/2022/feb/opinion-isolated-paranoid-deluded-vladimir-putin-isnt-mad-despot-hes-evil. Andrey Kurkov's conversation with Kelly Falconer at the Conduit Club in London on 12

April 2022 can be accessed here: https://www.theconduit.com/conduit-conversations-podcast/conduit-conversations-live-with-andrey-kurkov/. https://www.theguardian.com/world/2022/mar/11/a-necessary-war-reporting-on-the-ukraine-disagreement-outside-the-west.

Liberty and Hypocrisy
To join Mazin Qumsiyeh's mailing list, find him on Facebook, or contact him via his website: http://qumsiyeh.org/aboutqumsiyeh/.
https://www.theguardian.com/commentisfree/2022/mar/10/russia-ukraine-west-global-south-sanctions-war. Emma Harrison and Joe Dyke summarise the 'Russian Playbook' here: https://www.theguardian.com/world/2022/mar/24/how-russia-is-using-tactics-from-the-syrian-playbook-in-ukraine. Claire Berlinski and Adnan Hadad's conversation can be read here: https://www.cosmopolitanglobalist.com/a-syrians-advice-to-ukrainians/. In *Ukraine Diaries: Despatches from Kiev* (Harvill Secker, 2014), Andrey Kurkov discusses, among much else, the situation of the Crimean Tatars at the time of the Russian annexation of the peninsula. That Crimean Tatars are being persecuted by their Russian occupiers, and the Roma people face discrimination in Ukraine, is not in doubt: https://www.rferl.org/a/crimean-tatar-activist-detained-searched/31788653.html; https://fra.europa.eu/sk/news/2022/ensure-equal-treatment-roma-fleeing-ukraine. Shaun King's reflections on Ukrainian racism, Western hypocrisy, and the need for solidarity, can be read here:
https://www.newsweek.com/hypocrisy-support-ukraine-must-not-harden-black-americas-hearts-1687360. Robin Yassin-Kassab can be found on Facebook, where he hosts open discussions on the political situation in the Middle East, Europe and beyond.

Liberty and Peace
Peter Ryley's article 'The Manifesto of the Sixteen: Kropotkin's rejection of anti-war anarchism and his critique of the politics of peace' appears in *Anarchism, 1914-18: Internationalism, Anti-Militarism and War*, edited by Ruth Kinna, and Matthew S. Adams, Manchester University Press, 2017. [ProQuest Ebook Central, http://ebookcentral.proquest.com/lib/

chiuni-ebooks/detail.action?docID=4865640. Created from chiuni-ebooks on 2022-04-12 12:42:27.]

Volodymyr Zelenskiy addressed the UN on 5 April 2022: https://www.theguardian.com/us-news/2022/apr/05/volodymyr-zelenskiy-un-security-council-sketch. Lyudmyla Pavlyuk is quoted with permission from private correspondence. Despite being an active campaigner for an arms blockade on Israel, my MP Lloyd Russell-Moyle has argued to me in the past (on a bus) that the Israeli regime can't be called apartheid because the Palestinians have their own governments. Such a weak argument, riddled with holes, misinformation about the definition of apartheid, and complete disregard for the Arab citizens of Israel – but it proved to be impossible, on a bus at least, to get him to listen to reason. Yevhen Nyshchuk's interview in the *Scotsman* can be read here: https://www.scotsman.com/arts-and-culture/theatre-and-stage/ukraine-will-survive-actor-yevhen-nyshchuk-looks-to-the-future-3616488.

Liberty and Neutrality

Pierre Sané is quoted in David Adler's 28 March 2022 article for the *Guardian*, 'The west v Russia: why the Global South isn't taking sides': https://www.theguardian.com/commentisfree/2022/mar/10/russia-ukraine-west-global-south-sanctions-war. More information on the Non-Aligned Movement can be found at various places on the internet, including the Nuclear Threat Initiative, https://www.nti.org/education-center/treaties-and-regimes/non-aligned-movement-nam/, and the International Institute for Non-Aligned Studies, a 'Think Tank for the Non-Aligned Movement': https://iins.org/.

Epigraph and Conclusion

'The Sunlight' by Ihor Pavlyuk, translated by Steve Komarnyckyj, is published in *A Flight Over the Black Sea* (Waterloo Press, 2014). *The Children of Grad* by Maria Miniailo (Waterloo Press, 2022) was translated by Michael Pursglove and Natalia Pniushkova from the original Russian-language edition (Summit-Book, Ukraine, 2019).

A Passage to Liberty by Giles Goddard

The E.M. Forster novels cited in this essay are *A Room with a View* (1908, Edward Arnold, London), *Howards End* (1910, Edward Arnold, London), *A Passage to India* (1924, Edward Arnold, London) and *Maurice* (1972, Edward Arnold, London). Other Forster quotes are taken from *Abinger Harvest* (1936, Edward Arnold, London), *Two Cheers for Democracy* (1951, Edward Arnold, London), and *The Hill of Devi* (1953, Edward Arnold, London).

Bethan Roberts wrote about the relationship between Forster and Bob Buckingham in *The Guardian*, 2012: https://www.theguardian.com/books/2012/feb/17/e-m-forster-my-policeman

Other books cited are Edward Said, *Orientalism* (1978, Pantheon, New York), Lionel Trilling, *E.M. Forster*, (1943, New Directions Publishing, Norfolk, Conn).

The articles referred to were Quentin Bailey, 2002, 'Heroes and Homosexuals: Education and Empire in E. M. Forster', *Twentieth-Century Literature* 48(3), pp. 324-47, Stefan Collini, 2021, 'The Higher Feebleness: E.M. Forster as a Public Intellectual', *The Cambridge Quarterly* 50(2), pp. 185–93, and Todd Kuchta, 2003, 'Suburbia, Ressentiment and the end of Empire in *A Passage to India*', in *Modernisms* 36(3), pp. 307-29.

My Quest by Ole Jørgen Anfindsen

I have relied upon, or am implicitly referencing, the following works in my essay:

100+ Muslim scholars, 'A Common Word between Us and You' (acommonword.com). Ole Jørgen Anfindsen, 'The Beautiful Message of The Qur'an' (honestthinking.org/en/Islam). Reza Aslan, *No god but God: The Origins, Evolution, and Future of Islam* (Arrow Books, New York, 2011). Charles Hasan Le Gai Eaton, *Islam and the Destiny of Man* (The Islamic Texts Society, London, 1994); and *Remembering God: Reflections on Islam* (The

Islamic Texts Society, London, 2000). Khaled Abou El Fadl, *The Great Theft: Wrestling Islam from the Extremists* (HarperOne, New York, 2007). Jonathan Haidt, *The Righteous Mind:Why Good People Are Divided by Politics and Religion* (Allen Lane, London, 2012). Muhammad Abdel Haleem, *Understanding the Qur'an: themes and style* (I.B. Tauris, London, 1999, 2011). Kabir Helminski, *Holistic Islam: Sufism, Transformation, and the Needs of Our Time* (White Cloud Press, Ashland, 2017). Jeremy Henzell-Thomas, 'The Windows Opened by Music' in *Critical Muslim 32: Music,* (Hurst, London, October 2019). Joram van Klaveren, *Apostate: From Christianity to Islam in times of secularisation and terror* (Kennishuys & Sunni Publications, Den Haag, 2019). Alister McGrath, *The Great Mystery: Science, God and the Human Quest for Meaning* (Hodder & Stoughton, London, 2017). Abdal Hakim Murad, *Commentary on the Eleventh Contentions* (The Quilliam Press, Cambridge, 2012). Seyyed Hossein Nasr, Caner K Dagli, and others, *The Study Qur'an,* (HarperOne, New York, 2017). Mark A. Noll, *The Scandal of the Evangelical Mind* (Eerdmans, Grand Rapids, 994). Ziauddin Sardar, *Desperately Seeking Paradise: Journeys of a Sceptical Muslim* (Granta, London, 2004), *Reading the Qur'an:The Contemporary Relevance of the Sacred Text of Islam* (Hurst, London, 2011); and Ziauddin Sardar and Merryl Wyn Davies, 'Sectarianism unbound', in *Critical Muslim 10: Sects* (Hurst, London, April–June 2014). Kenton L. Sparks, Sacred Word, *Broken Word – Biblical authority and the dark side of Scripture* (Eerdmans, Grand Rapids, 2012). Thom Stark, *The Human Faces of God:What Scripture RevealsWhen It Gets GodWrong (AndWhy Inerrancy Tries to Hide It)* (Wipf and Stock Publishers 2011). Hamza Yusuf, 'Letter from the Editor: Why "Renovatio?"', *Renovatio – journal of Zaytuna College*, No 1, 2017 (renovatio.zaytuna.edu/article/letter-from-the-editor).

Postnormal Ukraine by Petro Sukhorolskyi

On postnormal times, see Ziauddin Sardar, editor, *The Postnormal Times Reader* (IIIT, London, 2017). On Ukrainian history, see Serhii Plokhy, *The Gates of Europe: A History of Ukraine* (Penguin, London, 2016); Matthew Rojansky et ell, editors, *From the Ukraine to Ukraine:A Contemporary History, 1991 - 2021* (Ibidrem-Verlag, Stuttgart, 2021); and Mykhailo Hrushevsky, *History of Ukraine-Rus* (Canadian Institute of Ukrainian Studies Press, Edmonton, Toronto, 1997–, ten volumes in twelve books). See also:

Gideon Rachman, *The Age of the Strongman: How the Cult of Leader Threatens Democracy and the World* (Bodley Head, London, 2022).

Adam Curtis's 2016 BBC documentary, 'HyperNormalisation' has an interesting section on how Putin uses political technologis to create mass confusion. Putin's theology is best explored in the novels of Vladimir Sharov, particularly *Tsarstvo Agamemnona* (*The Kingdom of Agamemnon*) (Moscow, 2018). See also: Mark Lipovetsky and Anastasia de La Fortelle, editors, 'Vladimir Sharov: On the Far Side of History' (Moscow, 2020); Carly Emerson, 'Vladimir Sharov on History, Memoir, and a Metaphysics of Ends' *Slavic and East European Journal* 63.4 2018; and Mikhail Epstein, 'Stalin and Satan', *TLS* 8 April 2022, p10.

Living in Freedom by Katharina Schmoll

The insights from Zygmunt Bauman are taken from *Liquid Love: On the Frailty of Human Bonds* (2003, Cambridge, Polity Press). The quote by Manuel Castells is from *The Rise of the Network Society. The Information Age: Economy, Society, Culture (Vol 1)* (1996, Oxford, Blackwell Publishers). The poem by Abu Firas al-Hamdani can be found at https://blogs.harvard.edu/sulaymanibnqiddees/2014/03/13/if-you-are-sweet/.

How *Distorted Imagination* Changed me by Jack Wager

Salman Rushdie's *The Satanic Verses* was published by Vintage, London, 1998. *Distorted Imagination: Lessons from the Rushdie Affairs* was published by Grey Seal, London, 1990. The background to how *Distorted Imagination* was written can be found in Ziauddin Sardar's *Desperately Seeking Paradise* (Granta, London, 2004), chapter 13. Bhikhu Parekhs' review, 'How shall we talk about Rushdie' appeared in *Futures* April 1991 pp.322-327.

On Liberty Unthought by C Scott Jordan

Much of the understanding of the American conception of liberty comes from a youth filled with listening carefully to the lyrics of patriotic (propaganda) American songs and being bushwhacked by the overabundance of star-spangled banners that fly on any given day within the borders of the United States of America. For a more intellectual understanding of the roots of liberty that has become all the rage in the US and across the West, see John Stuart Mill's *On Liberty,* (Penguin, London, 1985) and John Locke's *Second Treatise on Government,* (Hackett, London, 2005); The Islamic discourse on liberty is rich and storied, but for a nice contemporary survey of the conception and its application in law and governance, see Mohammad Hashim Kamali's *Freedom, Equality and Justice in Islam,* (Islamic Texts Society, Kuala Lumpur, 2002);

To learn more about the origins of the 'unthought' see Mohammed Arkoun, *The Unthought in Contemporary Islamic Thought*, (Saqi Books, London, 2002); For the application of the unthought to postnormal times see Ziauddin Sardar and John A. Sweeney's 'The Three Tomorrows of Postnormal Times,' *Futures* 75 (January 2016): 1–13. doi:10.1016/j. futures.2015.10.004.

For more insight on the unthought and unthought futures, readers are encouraged to explore further the writings and contributions made by members of the CPPFS that can be found at the website: postnormaltim.es.

The Nature of the Game by Marjorie Allthorpe-Guyton

To read more on Cecilia Alemani's *The Milk of Dreams Biennale Arte 2022*, see https://universes.art/en/venice-biennale/2022/the-milk-of-dreams; to read more of Adrian Searle's impressions on the Venice Biennale, see 'A glorious cacophony of Black female voices' – Sonia Boyce's soul train hits Venice,' *The Guardian*, 19 April 2022, https://www.theguardian.com/artanddesign/2022/apr/19/sonia-boyce-soul-train-venice-biennale-british-pavilion-glorious-cacophany-black-female-voices; To hear more from Francis Alys see his 2020 interview with Judith Benhamou Huet on Youtube, https://www.youtube.com/watch?v=uv469amkCCo; To read more on art, war, and Iraq see Azadeh Sarjoughian, 'Boring, Everyday Life in War Zones'. A conversation with Jonathan Watkins', *Third Text Online*, 21 April 2020, http://www.thirdtext.org/sarjoughian-watkins; and for more on the European Avant-Gardes across Europe from east to west, see Tomáš

Strauss's *Beyond the Great Divide, Essays on European Avant-Gardes from East and West*, ed. Daniel Grún, Henry Meyric Hughes, Jean Marc Poinsot, AICA Series Art Critics of the World, Series editor Jean-Marc Poinsot, Les Presses du Reel, Paris, 2020.

Chinese 'Re-education' by Maha Sardar

The Amnesty International report, '"Like we were enemies in a war", China's Mass Internment, Torture and Persecution of Muslims in Xinjiang', published on 10 June 202, can be downloaded from: https://www.amnesty.org/en/documents/asa17/4137/2021/en/ And the Human Rights Watch report, '"Break their lineage, break their roots"', China's crimes against humanity targeting Uyghurs and other Turkic Muslims', published on 19 April 2021, can be accessed at: https://www.amnesty.org/en/documents/asa17/4137/2021/en/
Weekly briefs and tribunals of The Uyghur World Congress can be found on its website: www.uyghurcongress.org

Ways of Being Feminist by Samia Rahman

Nicholas Masterton's article, 'Building Chronicles' was published in *CM28: Narratives* (Hurst, London, 2018). Rafia Zakaria's *Dawn* column, 'Demons of British Ghetto', can be accessed at: https://www.dawn.com/news/1128557. The National Coalition Against Domestic Violence's 2022 report can be accessed at: ncadv.org

Last Word: On Liberal Tyranny by Shamim Miah

Books and scholars mention include: Ziauddin Sardar, *The Postnormal Times Reader* (IIIT, London, 2017); Judith Butler, *Precarious Life: The Powers of Mourning and Violence* (Verso, London, 2004); Francis Fukuyama, *The End of History and the Last Man* (Penguin, 1992). See also his recent book which responds to some of the challenges to liberalism: *Liberalism and its Discontents* (Profile Books, London, 2022).

Ibn Khaldun, (1952) *The Muqaddima* (London: Routledge) Translated by

Rosenthal, F. in 3 volumes. See also, Miah, S. (forthcoming, 2022) *Ibn Khaldun: History, Education and Society* (Beacon Books, Manchester).

A. Dugin, *The Fourth Political Theory* (Arktos Media, Budapest, 2012) and *The Great Awakening vs the Great Reset* (Arktos Media, Budapest, 2021).
Ahmari, S. (2021) *The Unbroken Thread: Discovering the Wisdom of Tradition in an Age of Chaos* (Hodder and Stoughton, London, 2021); his *Spectator* article is available at: Tyranny is the inevitable consequence of liberalism – *The Spectator World*

J. Peterson, *12 Rules of Life* (Penguin, 2018); his interview Muhammad Hijab can be accessed via: Islam and the Possibility of Peace | Mohammed Hijab | The Jordan B. Peterson Podcast – S4: E66 – YouTube.

See also: M. Sedgwick, *Against the Modern World: Traditionalism and the Secret Intellectual History of the Twentieth Century* (Oxford University Press, 2009); D. Lasurdo, *Liberalism: A Counter History* (Verso Books, London, 2014); and D.T. Golberg, *The Racial State* (Blackwell, Oxford, 2001).

The List: Ten Liberal Contradictions

On the British government's sanctioning of Moshe Kantor, see Josh Kaplan (6 April 2022), 'UK Government Sanctions Moshe Kantor, President of European Jewish Congress, for Ties to Putin', *The Jewish Chronicle*, https:// www.thejc.com/news/news/uk-government -sanctions-moshe-kantor-president-of-european-jewish-congress-for-ties-to-putin-7HV4kE5jEvrf6vmwOTtJlz

The rebuttal by the Board of Deputies of British Jews to Amnesty International's report can be found at https://bod.org.uk/bod-news/ jewish-community-condemns-biased-amnesty-apartheid-slur-against-israel/

On General Sisi's massacre at Rabaa, see Max Fisher (14 August 2015), 'Egypt's Dictator Murdered 800 People Today in 2013. He's Now a US

Ally and GOP Folk Hero', *Vox*, https://www.vox.com/2015/8/14/9153967/rabaa-sisi

The following pieces give useful background on France's (neo)colonial history: Jonathan Laurence (2015), 'The Algerian Legacy: How France Should Confront Its Past', *Brookings*, https://www.brookings.edu/opinions/the-algerian-legacy-how-france-should-confront-its-past/, and Adam Ramsay (6 April 2022), 'The French Election Is All about Imperialism. Here's Why', *openDemocracy*, https://www.opendemocracy.net/en/french-election-macron-le-pen-far-right-zemmour-imperialism/?source=in-article-related-story. Read Kenan Malik's evaluation of Boris Johnson's 'diverse' cabinet at https://www.theguardian.com/commentisfree/2019/jul/28/johnsons-cabinet-may-be-diverse-but-it-doesnt-reflect-modern-britain

John Milbank's Twitter outburst about Sinead O'Connor / Shuhada Sadaqat is addressed by Hisham Hellyer, 29 October 2018, 'Are Western Muslims Civilisational Traitors?', *ABC Religion & Ethics*, https://www.abc.net.au/religion/muslims-of-the-west-civilisational-traitors/10443052

On the double standards in Western media reporting on the Ukraine crisis, see Moustafa Bayoumi (2 March 2022), 'They Are "Civilised" and "Look like Us": The Racist Coverage of Ukraine', *The Guardian*, https://www.theguardian.com/commentisfree/2022/mar/02/civilised-european-look-like-us-racist-coverage-ukraine, and Patrick Gathara (1 March 2022), 'Covering Ukraine: A Mean Streak of Racist Exceptionalism', *Al Jazeera*, https://www.aljazeera.com/opinions/2022/3/1/covering-ukraine-a-mean-streak-of-racist-exceptionalism

Lord Cromer's colonial feminism is discussed in Leila Ahmed's *Women and Gender in Islam* (1992, New Haven, Yale University Press).

The UK government's rationale for its proposed legislation on 'criminal damages to memorials' can be found at https://www.gov.uk/government/publications/police-crime-sentencing-and-courts-bill-2021-factsheets/police-crime-sentencing-and-courts-bill-2021-criminal-damage-to-memorials-factsheet and Naz Shah's tweet is at https://twitter.com/NazShahBfd/status/1412156993679376387

Novak Djokovic's stance on Covid-19 vaccines can be found in Lara Keay (10 January 2022), 'Novak Djokovic: Why Is Tennis Star Being Denied Entry to Australia - and What Are Their Travel Rules?', *Sky News*, https://news.sky.com/story/novak-djokovic-why-is-tennis-star-being-denied-entry-to-australia-and-what-are-their-travel-rules-12510008

On the secret teachings of Pythagoras, see Will Buckingham's website, *Looking for Wisdom*, https://www.lookingforwisdom.com/philosopher-file/pythagoras/

CONTRIBUTORS

Mustafa Akyol is a senior fellow at the Cato Institute, Washington D.C., focusing on the intersection of Islam and modernity ● **Marjorie Allthorpe-Guyton** is former President of the International Association of Art Critics (AICA), British Section ● **Ole Jørgen Anfindsen**, a Norwegian author and social commentator, as well as a former anti-Islam and anti-immigration activist, converted to Islam in 2020 ● **Naomi Foyle** is a celebrated science fiction writer ● **Giles Goddard** is Vicar of St John's Church, Waterloo, London ● **Sulaiman Haqpana**, a British Afghan musician, is pursuing his doctorate at Brunel University ● **Jeremy Henzell-Thomas** is a Research Associate and former Visiting Fellow at the Centre of Islamic Studies, University of Cambridge ● **C Scott Jordan** is Executive Assistant Director of the Centre for Postnormal Policy and Futures Studies ● **Olexander Korotko**, Ukrainian poet and writer, represents the modern avant-garde trend in philosophical poetry ● **Vinay Lal**, Professor of History and UCLA, is the author of *The Fury of Covid-19* ● **Shamim Miah** is Senior Lecturer in Sociology at University of Huddersfield and Senior Fellow of the Centre for Postnormal Policy and Futures Studies ● **Ihor Pavlyuk** is a well-known Ukrainian poet ● **Samia Rahman** is Director of the Muslim Institute ● **Maha Sardar** is a human rights barrister ● **Katharina Schmoll** is Lecturer in Media and Communications at the University of Leeds ● **Shanon Shah** is Senior Deputy Editor of *Critical Muslim* ● **Nur Sobers-Khan** is the former Director of the Aga Khan Documentation Center at MIT ● **Petro Sukhorolskyi**, an associate professor at Lviv Polytechnic National University, Ukraine, is a futurist who studies the influence of information technologies on human rights, democracy, and international law ● **Jack Wager**, editor-in-chief at Vellum Publishing in Manchester, is founder of The Custard Practice, which aims to break down social class barriers in education and creative industries ● **Robin Yassin-Kassab** is the author of *The Road from Damascus* and other books.